Praise for

THE POLITICAL VISE

"As governor and now working with students, I've seen how the Radical Left has co-opted power from the American people. In *The Political Vise*, John Tillman exposes their strategy and then presents a plan to restore power where our founders intended—with We the People. Conservatives young and old should read this book."

SCOTT WALKER, former governor, Wisconsin

"In *The Political Vise*, John Tillman reveals why so many politicians regularly vote for policies that are counter to the views of their constituents. Politicians respond to pressure. Too often the greatest pressure is not coming from the voters but rather from the insiders, dealmakers, and special interests. Tillman explains how and why this happens and provides a road map for the American people to fix it."

SCOTT RASMUSSEN, founder, Napolitan Institute; president, RMG Research

"*The Political Vise* tells the truth so many don't want to hear: government unions, the trial bar, corporate interests seeking tax and regulatory favors, and do-gooder progressive ideologues mount continuous pressure campaigns to move politicians to vote against America's best interest. I learned long ago that the best antidote is a robust grassroots movement. Tillman shows how the American people, starting with the grassroots activists, can retake control of our republic."

NED RYUN, founder and CEO, American Majority

"*The Political Vise* is a battle plan for conservatives and free marketeers to take back our country from the Radical Left and win the twenty-first-century war of ideas. Losing is not an option."

STEPHEN MOORE, author of *Trumponomics* and cofounder, Club for Growth

"Ours is indeed a system of We the People, but it is often really 'We the People ... who show up.' In *The Political Vise*, John not only lays out what happens when showing up is left to the Radical Left—he offers a clear, empirical, and important blueprint for how the right can start winning again."

JASE BOLGER, former speaker, Michigan House of Representatives

"John Tillman's *The Political Vise* is a must-read for conservative warriors. Tillman offers his unique insights into how the Radical Left has altered the political landscape. He outlines how a ruling class of influencers has captured large swaths of the voter, using tactics like fear mongering to sway impressionable voters and prop up unprincipled politicians to enact their agenda. We must continue our fight at the grassroots level and ensure freedom reigns over the United States for generations to come."

DAVID MCINTOSH, president, Club for Growth; former congressman from Indiana

"The left has waged a war on truth in hopes of one day eviscerating the ultimate truth that we have been endowed by our creator with inalienable rights and liberties. John Tillman brilliantly defines that war, its tactics, its perpetrators, and its antidote. *The Political Vise* is a must-read for anyone hoping to restore sanity and freedom to this great country."

JOHN SOLOMON, award-winning investigative journalist and founder of Just the News

"John Tillman doesn't merely diagnose problems in *The Political Vise*, though he does that quite well. He also offers proactive solutions to these thorny and persistent challenges, forged from decades of fighting on the front lines in one of the least hospitable political climates for conservatives in the country. Elected officials and Americans broadly must read this book and consider his advice."

GUY BENSON, conservative commentator and writer

JOHN TILLMAN

THE
POLITICAL
VISE

How THE RADICAL LEFT Controls America
and the Path to Regaining Our Liberty

RealClear
Publishing

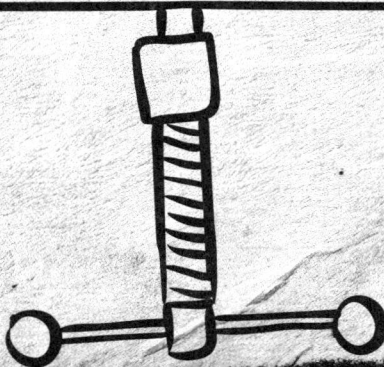

RealClear
Publishing

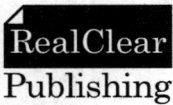

www.amplifypublishinggroup.com

The Political Vise: How the Radical Left Controls America
and the Path to Regaining Our Liberty

For more information, please contact:
RealClear Publishing, an imprint of Amplify Publishing Group
620 Herndon Parkway, Suite 220
Herndon, VA 20170
info@amplifypublishing.com

Library of Congress Control Number: 2025917029

CPSIA Code: PRV1025A

ISBN-13: 979-8-89138-832-1

Printed in the United States

This book is dedicated to Richard Uihlein,
a great American patriot
and a visionary political and charitable philanthropist.

Mr. U has changed America for the better.
Because of his commitment to our liberty,
we live freer today than we otherwise would.

Mr. U is a twenty-first-century founder of what
will be America's next great century.

Thank you, Dick, for all you have done for me,
personally and professionally, and most importantly,
for America.

"The Party seeks power entirely for its own sake.
We are not interested in the good of others;
we are interested solely in power, pure power."

—George Orwell, *1984*

CONTENTS

FOREWORD

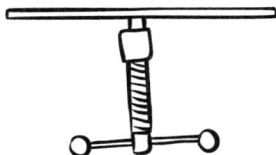

The Trump era laid bare a lot of realities about politics that many on the right still refuse to acknowledge. While politics need not be a winner-take-all, zero-sum game—in fact, in its idealized form, politics should be the exact opposite—the American left's singular focus on obtaining and wielding power aims to make it that way.

Far too often, many on the right see the left engaging in lawfare, mass censorship, and the undermining of the democratic process as an excuse to do little besides issuing moralizing condemnations of how unjust and wrong this is. They can't be bothered to do anything to actually fight the forces that want to shred the Constitution and persecute innocent Americans advocating for their basic rights. This was the story of the Republican Party for decades.

Then along came Donald Trump, who had the temerity to bluntly state that the unholy union of hard-left ideology and unaccountable federal bureaucracy was destroying the country. The problem wasn't necessarily that Trump was wrong. The trouble was that many on the so-called right thought that the impolitic way that Trump was expressing himself was a bigger problem than the problems he had identified.

Donald Trump had the gall to actually get elected, and the validity of what he was saying about the destructive intentions of the left could not be denied. Half the country was gaslit for years by a destructive deep state, aided and abetted by an equally malicious media, into believing a complete conspiratorial fiction that Trump treasonously colluded with Russia to steal an election. After that lie was exposed, these same dark forces sabotaged President Trump's re-election by burning dozens of American cities to the ground and lying about a global pandemic to rewrite America's election rules.

Trump's shockingly narrow loss was followed by one of the most destructive presidencies in history. More than ten million illegal immigrants have been encouraged and aided to cross the border in defiance of the law and the will of the American people. Americans saw record inflation that the country still hasn't recovered from, the Middle East is mired in a brutal war that was set off by the kidnapping and torturing of complete innocents, and we are in the middle of the worst conflict in Europe since the end of World War II, a war that has seen over a million casualties to date.

And *still,* many leaders on the right insist on playing into the left's hands by acting as if they are somehow above the confrontations that are necessary to save America. Above all, they believe they must act in good faith, even when their opponent sees decency as a weakness to be exploited. As my friend John Tillman aptly observes, "conservatives respond to ignorance with efforts to educate. Increasingly, progressives respond to perceived 'ignorance' with efforts to eradicate."

John Tillman's *The Political Vise* is not a call for conservatives to abandon their morals and sink to the level of the left. However, the first step toward an effective response is to understand the tactics of the left, and specifically how they are so effective at applying pressure to move politics steadily in the direction of consolidation of power—even when they pursue radical goals that are antithetical to what voters want.

The Political Vise is an exceptionally smart examination of the forces that shape debate in America to produce the outcomes the left desires. Though Tillman helpfully categorizes dominant forces applying political pressure into basic groups—the media, the people, and influencers—ultimately this is a beast that has many heads. But whether Tillman is examining the specifics of how public-sector unions work or the pernicious beliefs of social engineers in academia, he has much to offer.

So many books of this nature do a good job of identifying problems only to hastily attempt to come up with some solutions tacked on to the end of the book. Here, the second chapter is titled "Learning to Win"—and in it he relates the lessons of his own involvement in winning one of the most important legal victories of the last few decades. Tillman isn't just interested in examining how the political process produces outcomes—he wants to harness that understanding to produce victories for the underfunded and outgunned forces that still believe in fairness and constitutional order.

Make no mistake, our success in restoring America to align with its founding principles will ultimately depend heavily upon how we understand the forces that are corrupting it. While figures on the resurgent right have spoken with courage about the nature of the problems facing America, we now look to people such as John Tillman who can bring real clarity to the hard work of finding solutions. Tillman has responded to ignorance with not just a desire to educate, but also to *win*.

Mollie Hemingway,

New York Times bestselling author of *Rigged: How the Media, Big Tech, and the Democrats Seized Our Elections*

Introduction

WHAT IS
THE POLITICAL VISE?

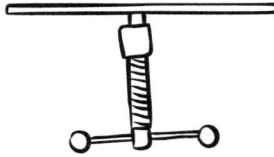

The natural state of politics is for politicians to move left once in office. The Political Vise is my theory of why that happens and how political power is created and deployed.

There are many different types of vises. The most basic—a two-sided vise—functions simply as a clamp to hold things together. A slightly more complex vise may have three sides. It does more than hold things together: it exerts intense pressure from three sides to force something out of the fourth side.

The traditional version of the Political Vise is three-sided. On the left is the media, on the right is the people, and on the bottom are influencers, or elites. In the middle of the Vise, feeling the pressure from all three sides, are politicians. Responding to pressure from the other elements, politicians make policy decisions (influencing laws, culture, and norms), which are squeezed out of the top of the Vise. Those at the bottom of the Vise, in this case the influencers, have the most power because they not only apply pressure directly to the politicians, but they also influence (as represented by the arrows to the left and right of the influencers in the graphic that follows) the other two sides of the Vise. The key motivators for the politicians are politically based expediency, fear, and principle.

THE TRADITIONAL POLITICAL VISE

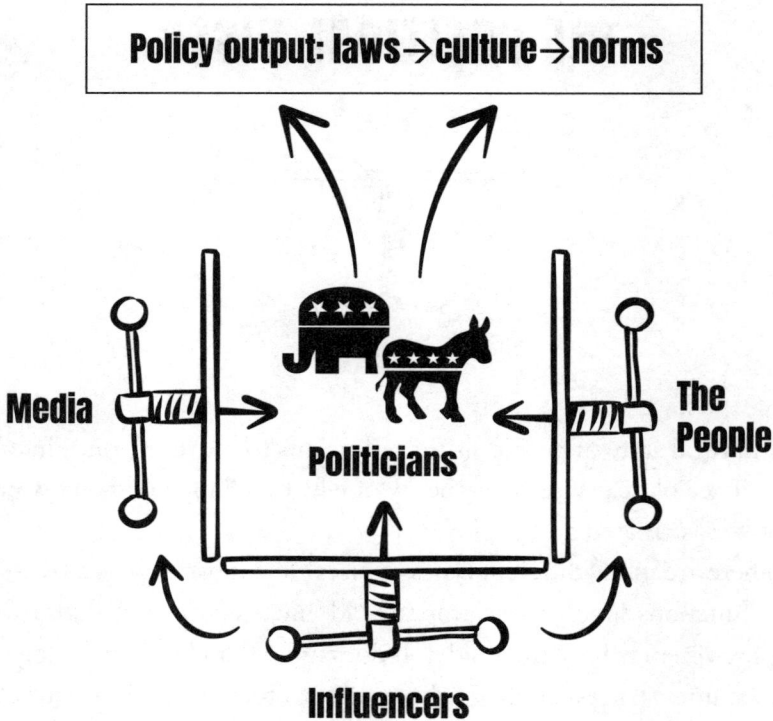

Politicians are compelled to make decisions based upon three criteria:
1. Political Expediency
2. Political Fear
3. Political Principle

Perhaps the best contemporary illustration of the Political Vise at work has been the vicious attacks on the Department of Government Efficiency (DOGE). As President Trump launched his second term, he appointed Elon

Musk and Vivek Ramaswamy to head up an unprecedented effort to root out waste, fraud, and abuse within all areas of the executive branch. Who could be against that? Well, practically everyone, or so it seemed!

In what was and remains a clearly coordinated effort, the media, partnering with the left's vast network of influencers, progressive Democrat politicians, and embedded deep-state employees themselves, launched a whole-of-system counterstrike. This effort used every tool in the toolbox, leveraging all three sides of the Vise.

Ramaswamy left to run for governor of Ohio. Musk carried on months longer, soon to be labeled a Nazi and to see his Tesla dealers firebombed and Tesla cars vandalized nationwide. The courts issued nationwide injunctions, and sympathetic stories of displaced government workers permeated the news.

What was a very popular undertaking that Trump ran on became less popular and ever more controversial, all orchestrated by the coordinated wielding of the power of the Political Vise.

The attacks on DOGE are just the latest illustration of how the Vise is the most powerful force in our American political system. Its powers are presently dominated by the radicalized left that aims to destroy America's founding principles. My goal is simple: to explain the history of the Vise and how we who are champions of freedom can reclaim its use. The stakes are high. If we fail, our bold American experiment will come to a shattering end.

■ ■ ■

The fundamental question that started me on the journey to understanding the principle of the Political Vise was a simple one: Why do so many people of good intent, who ran as conservatives, move left once in office—while virtually no one moves to the right?

To better understand how I developed the theory of the Political Vise, it might be helpful to understand how I got involved in the first place.

I have been a political junkie my entire life. That question, why does everyone move left once in office, had long haunted me. I am sure I was the only nine-year-old to watch both political conventions in 1968 gavel to gavel and thought it was as good as baseball and football. In high school I worked in the library and loved when the papers from around the country arrived. I read them all cover to cover. Sure, I read the sports, but I also read all the articles on politics. This was the Vietnam, Watergate, protest era, and I was hooked.

By the time I entered college I knew what I wanted to be: a journalist writing about politics. I started out as a journalism major and a political science minor. I fulfilled all the minor requirements in about three semesters—I could not get enough.

Eventually I changed schools and switched to business, but I never lost my passion for politics and policy. I came to understand that my skills revolved around sales and marketing. I began to more closely observe how conservatives and liberals sold their ideas to the public. It always seemed to me that conservatives were perpetually on defense while liberals, later progressives, were always on offense. This perplexed me.

As the years passed I consumed information voraciously. I was that person at the cocktail party who knew every Supreme Court justice, who the legislative leaders were, who was on the world stage in international affairs, and more.

By the time I sold part of my business in 2004 I was debating between starting another business, going into the corporate world or, as crazy as it sounded, finding a way to get involved in politics and public policy. A friend of mine, Regina Hart, pushed me. "Your passion is politics and free markets. You should find a way to get involved in that."

I started calling every organization I could identify—the Cato Institute, the Club for Growth, the Heartland Institute, the Heritage Foundation, the American Enterprise Institute, and many more. I made hundreds of calls with a terrible pitch for someone who thought of himself as a salesman: "I just sold my business and would like to get involved in public policy." Weak, to say the least. It turned out that academic, policy-focused organizations had little use for a marketer in his midforties with no particular qualifications.

But I did not give up. I kept calling until one day I spoke to a woman named Lynn Bradshaw. She worked with Steve Moore, who was then president of the Club for Growth. (Steve has gone on to become one of the most prominent economists of the conservative movement and a great friend as well.) By this time, I had refined my pitch. I suggested that the Club for Growth (CFG) should set up state chapters to pursue their mission to elect more fiscally conservative, pro-free-market candidates at the state level. Voila! They were thinking of doing exactly that. She gave me the phone number for a CFG board member, Howie Rich.

I called Howie, and he spelled out how they envisioned setting up state chapters of the Club for Growth. Howie suggested we meet when he would be in town for Resource Bank. "You are going to Resource Bank, I assume?" he asked.

"Of course," I replied. Then I began my desperate attempt to learn what Resource Bank was (a meeting of people from around the country dedicated to conservative policies organized by the Heritage Foundation) and find out how to attend.

I met Howie there as well as Eric O'Keefe. In those years Howie and Eric worked closely on school choice, term limits, spending limits, Social Security reform, and more. Over two days of conversations, they drilled me on all things politics—my foundational beliefs, my governing philosophy, my attitude about the two major parties, my organizational and leadership experiences, and much more.

All that reading and learning paid off. Within a couple of weeks Howie offered me the position of president of a then dormant organization, Americans for Limited Government. On May 24, 2004, my journey in public policy, politics, and advocacy began. I was as naïve as one could be, but I learned quickly.

My job would be to build a team to pursue a variety of constitutional ballot initiatives in the 2006 election cycle. Eventually, with the help of many people, Howie, Eric, I, and many others collected millions of signatures in thirteen states. We focused primarily on measures that would impose constitutional spending limits on state government spending as well as protect property rights from abuses of eminent domain made possible by the US Supreme Court decision in *Kelo v. City of New London.*

We mostly got our butts kicked in 2006. It was a down year for conservative ideas as the Bush presidency sputtered toward its end. Democrats took control of Congress, and the precursors to the Obama rise to come in 2008 were obvious—and ominous.

After that election, Eric O'Keefe and I launched a new organization, the Sam Adams Alliance, dedicated to providing support to grassroots activists around the country. In the spring of 2007, we parted ways and I began my journey to relaunch the Illinois Policy Institute and all that has come since.

This book shares all the lessons from these years. Most of all, I have tried to explain why seemingly good people lose their commitment, lose their principles, and become just another vote for yet another spending bill that ratchets up our debt yet again.

Think about names like Paul Ryan, Mitt Romney, the late Arlen Specter, or Jeff Flake. Each was touted as a genuine conservative. Each became far more liberal once in office. Specter and former Florida Governor Charlie Crist even changed parties and became Democrats!

Flake ran a libertarian think tank, the Goldwater Institute, before running for office. He was an idea man and a policy wonk. He had a backbone and would stand on principle—or so his supporters thought. I was so impressed by Flake's early record and reputation that I hosted a luncheon for him in 2012. I confess I did not see what was coming years later—I thought he was one of the rare ones who could stay true to his principles. I was wrong. It turned out that under pressure, he was a malleable piece of clay to be worked into the shape the far left preferred.

During the 2018 hearings on Brett Kavanaugh's confirmation to the Supreme Court, then-Senator Flake provided a painful and unwitting example of capitulation to the power of the Political Vise. On a break from the hearings, Flake was confronted in a Capitol elevator by left-wing activists screaming in his face, demanding he oppose Kavanaugh (the video is on YouTube—it is amazing). If you look closely, you can see Flake shrink under the pressure right before your eyes. The Arizona senator changed his vote on a procedural matter the next day, forcing a delay in hearings pending a further FBI investigation. He shrank more and more and finally left office. He could not take the Vise's pressure.

That elevator confrontation was part of an orchestrated campaign to target, intimidate, and pressure him. Paid political operatives, professional influencers, were portrayed by the media as grassroots activists anguished about the accusations against Kavanaugh. Instead of pushing back against this astonishing breach of decorum, Flake let himself be crushed. The left lost the Kavanaugh battle, but they took Flake's capitulation as a win.

This incident and so many others you may have observed are the public version of the Vise at work. The more frightening fact for our republic is that the power of the Political Vise is being used by the Radical Left every day, out of sight and behind the scenes. This relentless pressure moves political decision-makers to policy decisions that are more and more out of step with the country as a whole.

You might be tempted to say that all politicians are fundamentally self-serving. Of course, they capitulate to pressure. Surely, you might believe, politicians across the spectrum demonstrate this same absence of courage. Yet the capitulations always happen in one direction.

One reason is the 1971 book, *Rules for Radicals*, written by the legendary left-wing community organizer Saul Alinsky. His book and its rules have fueled generations of activists to refine and perfect the political pressure game. Hillary Clinton and Barack Obama are two of the most famous of Alinsky's disciples. Alinsky's rules (rule no. 8 is "Keep the Pressure On") outline a theory of power that has worked all too well for the left to shape our politics toward the progressive vision for more than five decades.

Of course, politics has evolved since Alinsky's book was first published. It is my hope that the concept of the Political Vise, once understood and then adapted to the needs of our times, will inspire the American people to use its power to build a twenty-first-century liberty movement. Donald Trump is creating a movement right now, and his winning a second term means we have an opportunity to shape that movement for when he leaves the stage to restore our constitutional republic with the people in their proper role as the sovereign.

The left and the media have been obsessed with "protecting our democracy" in recent years. Perhaps it would be good to remind us all that what needs protection is our republican form of government. A republic is a representative form of government, rather than a direct democracy, that places limits on the power of the government itself. In our unique American form, it is the people that are sovereign, not the government. In a monarchy it is the monarch that is sovereign. In most Western democracies, it is the government that is sovereign.

This distinction matters because the source of power and authority comes from sovereignty. Thus, a monarchy assumes rights over the populace's property and persons. Most Western democracies grant rights to the people—but also take them away. In America, our rights are God-given (or natural) and thus inalienable. While we have majority rule on most issues, when it comes to our rights, government is limited and cannot take them away from us . . . in theory.

The point of this book is that bad actors on the ideological left and some misguided allies on the right—*politicians*, the *media, influencers,* and manipulated *people*—have been using the Vise for over 130 years to take away our inalienable rights. It has been a slow, relentless erosion that is peaking in this era. As the disruption caused by the COVID-19 pandemic fades into the background, the forces advocating for government sovereignty grow.

The only antidote resides in the *people*, for they are the sovereign. A people fully engaged will protect their freedom. A people disengaged will let it slip away.

In the pages that follow, I share how I got involved in politics and outline the history and evolution of the Political Vise and the strategic concepts that flow from it. These strategic imperatives will help practitioners and citizens learn how to better allocate resources and harmonize capacities. They will also help conservative elected officials distinguish between actual pressure from an engaged citizenry that should be respected and false pressure from special-interest influencers and the media.

This book is intended to both inform and recruit you to the cause of championing human liberty. Without deeper engagement by you and many of our fellow citizens, our republic will continue to slip away. I am hopeful that sharing the story my colleagues and I have experienced will help you see the pathway to your own story to become a more engaged citizen of America . . . and thus help save our republic.

Over the course of my career, I learned the truth about the way the left was exploiting our political system—and the danger that created to our republic and our freedom. To address that danger, I began to build (with the help of many amazing people) a variety of capacities to engage and compete in the political and policy arenas. The goal was always simple but audacious: a vision to restore America's reverence for the founding principles that created the greatest force ever conceived to improve the human condition.

A perhaps unexpected note—nothing can be accomplished in politics without politicians. As you will read, some are really terrible (Flake, Crist, Romney, etc.). Others, however, are incredible, courageous fighters for human freedom. I admire and respect the many brave elected officials that enter the arena to advance the cause of freedom and preserve liberty. In the end, they take the votes and all too often pay the price.

We will begin with the story of the Traditional Political Vise as outlined earlier in this section. This is how I originally thought of the Vise and its power dynamics. But it's important to understand that the Vise's sides are not fixed in place. They can be rearranged. The radical progressives that have taken over the Democratic Party have reshaped the Vise from its traditional structure to one (the Progressive Political Vise) that puts the American people inside the Vise instead of the politicians. They are working to have the people relinquish their sovereignty and submit to the state and its collective, coercive demands. Finally, we will learn about the Liberty Political Vise that positions the politicians back inside the Vise and moves the people into the bottom position. That bottom position is the most powerful, for it applies pressure to the other two sides as well as the politicians themselves. It's this Vise that we must start to use if our nation is to remain based on the premise of "We the People."

Pressure works in politics. In fact, the singular driving force of our political system is pressure. The left has long mastered creating pressure. The Political Vise explains how this pressure works, what activists and donors on the right can learn from it, and how we can adapt for the twenty-first century and win.

Remember, one person can change the world. Will you?

Chapter 1

HOW DID WE GET HERE?

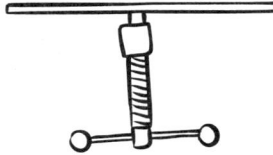

January 27, 2024
New York City

A group of illegal migrants savagely attacks two NYPD officers near Times Square. The unprovoked beating is captured on surveillance cameras. Of the more than a dozen assailants, only five are arrested. Those taken into custody are quickly released without bail. Barely two weeks later, one of the released illegals, Darwin Gomez-Izquiel, is arrested again and charged with shoplifting from a Macy's in Queens in an incident in which a security guard is punched in the face.

May 1, 2023
New York City

A disturbed homeless man, Jordan Neely, threatens passengers on the F Train. A Marine veteran, Daniel Penny, seeking to protect his fellow subway passengers, wrestles Neely to the floor and restrains him in a chokehold. Neely later dies. Penny is charged with second-degree manslaughter

*and criminally negligent homicide. He faces nearly twenty years behind bars
if convicted. Thankfully, he is found not guilty and released.*

These kinds of perversions of justice do not just happen in Gotham. Violent
migrants attack American citizens with impunity all across this country.
Dangerously disturbed petty criminals threaten and harass riders on buses
and subways in almost every major city. A parade of Democratic House
members as well as Maryland Senator Chris Van Hollen traveled to El Sal-
vador to show solidarity with a deported, violent Venezuelan gang member,
Kilmar Abrego Garcia. Meanwhile, American victims are left wondering
why they are standing alone against the violence with a government more
interested in the criminals than the victims.

How did we end up in a world where the Darwin Gomez-Izquiels of
the world flout our laws without consequence and heroes like Daniel Penny
face long legal battles—and the threat of even longer prison sentences? How
did we come to the point where instead of condemning these scandals, a
major political party and its allies in the media defend and promote danger
and decay?

I could share hundreds of other similar anecdotes. I suspect you can
think of many yourself. Separately, these stories of misplaced justice are
bewildering. Taken together, they are a damning indictment, and not just
of the Manhattan District Attorney's office. How did we get here? How
did we end up in this upside-down world where criminality is celebrated
and virtue is condemned? How have we handed over so much of our power
to elite forces that despise our values? As one friend put it to me recently,
"I always knew the left hated us. I just didn't realize they had this much
power to put that hate into action."

Seeing a hero like Daniel Penny in handcuffs makes me furious. Watching millions of illegal, often violent, immigrants flow over the border by
design, and then watching as every roadblock possible is erected when the
Trump administration attempts to return them, is exasperating. I know
many of you share this anger, and some of you have channeled that fierce

emotion into political activism. A healthy anger, though, isn't just one that gets directed toward creating change. A healthy anger seeks to understand the root of the problem in order to ensure that the change we want is the change we get.

This book explains the origins of our contemporary crisis. Far more importantly, I think, it also offers a blueprint for effectively restoring the American system to its sacred and essential origins. My own understanding of "how we got here" began with a question.

May 2006

With the entrees cleared away and the coffee poured, I sensed my opportunity and turned to the distinguished gentleman seated next to me.

"I have one question, if you don't mind. Why is it that when conservatives are elected, they immediately begin moving to the left, and when progressives are elected, they simply move further left? Why is it no one moves to the right once in office?"

The organization I helped run held regular meetings with like-minded state and federal officials, and on this occasion, one of our guests was Senator Tom Coburn, Republican of Oklahoma. A successful businessman and obstetrician, Coburn had delivered some 4,000 babies before entering politics. Elected to the House in the Republican wave of 1994, Coburn ran successfully for Senate in 2004. He was, I sensed, very familiar with challenging questions from frustrated conservatives.

Coburn laughed. "I can explain that. Oklahoma is as conservative a state as it gets. And yet . . . as soon as I arrived in Washington, my calendar began to fill up with all the important people from back home. The oil men, the farmers and ranchers, the car dealers, all sorts of people who had supported my campaign in one way or another. Every last one of them bought into our vision of limited government. But somehow, the conversations were always the same: 'Dr. Tom,' they'd say, 'we sure are proud of you back home. You're doing a great job holding the line on spending and earmarks. Keep up the good work. Now, there is one little thing I need to talk to you about . . .'"

The constituents who lobbied Senator Coburn thought of themselves as conservatives. They would have bristled at the suggestion they weren't. They saw these "favors" as a necessary part of good government. They also thought of themselves as smart businessmen who needed just a little help from the government—a tax incentive here, a new bridge there. The net effect of helping each of these constituents was, invariably, an expanded and more activist government. The folks who lobbied Dr. Tom shared his vision. They didn't think of their requests as hypocritical exceptions to their conservative views, and they certainly didn't think they were damaging the conservative cause.

The left wants to expand the reach of government. Most left-wing policy and advocacy groups focus on emboldening and encouraging ever more substantial government intervention in public (and private) life. Lobbying a typical Democrat for a more activist government is like pleading with a toddler to eat more candy. You are urging them to do something they already very much want to do. Their instincts and philosophies are already oriented toward expanded government—when the left lobbies their own elected officials, it's mostly about quickening an already willing and enthusiastic pace.

When you lobby a liberal politician for "one little thing," they might reply, "Why not ten big ones instead?" When you lobby a conservative for "one little thing," no matter how good or sensible that "thing" is, you are slowing (if not actively derailing) a genuinely conservative policy agenda. Tom Coburn was as staunch a conservative as ever served in the modern US Senate. Even he had difficulty resisting the sum total of all the requests for "one little thing." Less conscientious conservatives (and we can stipulate that phrase characterized most of Coburn's colleagues) found it much easier to give in to the pressure. And as Dr. Coburn implied, at least some of the activists who lament that Republicans "always move to the left when elected" need to look in the mirror. Too many who support conservative ideas in theory lobby hard for pet exceptions to the policy consequences of those ideas.

The end result is disillusionment on the right and a government that never stops expanding.

That conversation with Dr. Coburn crystallized a theory that I had been formulating for years: the notion of the Political Vise. Now let me be clear: the Vise is not inherently good or bad. It is a mechanism that can be used to achieve good outcomes or bad ones. The success of the Vise is not a sign that our system is hopelessly corrupted, or that we need to return to some idealized time—perhaps to the era of the Founders—when the Political Vise did not exist. The Vise has always existed.

The problem is that the right doesn't know it exists. The left, on the other hand, understands the Vise intuitively. The left has invested in and built a complex and highly effective infrastructure around deploying this powerful tool. The right doesn't even understand the tool is there.

Go to any conservative conference or policy gathering, and you'll hear the same laments. *How did we get here? Why are we winning so many battles but losing the larger war? How is it that the left is able to implement so many unconstitutional, immoral, and clearly unpopular policies with so little resistance?* We will hear that we need to fight harder, raise more money, recruit better candidates! We need to take back this school board, that legislature, this governor's mansion! I'm all for raising money, fighting hard, identifying great leaders, and winning elections. I also know that if we don't understand how to use the Political Vise to our advantage, none of that will matter.

A vise, political or otherwise, is a tool for applying pressure to achieve a particular outcome. A toothpaste tube is a kind of vise. You don't get your Colgate or Crest onto your toothbrush by pressing just one side of the tube. You take off the cap, press from both sides—and then later press from the bottom—to get the paste you want. The Political Vise works much the same way.

Once elected, politicians find themselves operating inside the Vise, and they do so under constant pressure from all three sides. That pressure is necessary. If there is no pressure, nothing gets done. The problem isn't that pressure inherently produces bad outcomes. The problem is that too many, especially on the right, do not understand how to apply the correct "squeeze" to produce the desired result. In order to understand how to do that, we first need to understand how politicians generally respond to pressure. For more than twenty years, I have been informally interviewing politicians of all stripes (like Senator Coburn) to discover how they make voting decisions. What I have found is that they have three primary decision-making filters.

The first filter is political expediency. This filter involves the standard currency of Washington (or any state capital): compromise. *I will vote for your bridge in your district if you vote for my new highway in mine.* Dealmaking is a normal part of politics. Sometimes dealmaking is honorable and serves the public's interest. Most of the time, this dealmaking serves a special interest at the expense of the public. That special interest has applied sufficient pressure and has earned their desired result. A back-of-the-envelope estimate, based on years of observation, is that 65% of all votes cast in legislatures are cast through the expedience filter.

The second filter is fear. The one thing incumbents from both parties have in common is a deep fear of losing their seat in the next election. This worry unites them to work collectively against policies that would make incumbents more vulnerable. That is why the push for campaign finance reform, which inevitably restricts the people's ability to hold elected officials accountable, is always a bipartisan project. The fear of offending an important constituency (climate change lobbyists, public-sector unions, or Second Amendment advocates, for example) also drives voting decisions. Bad publicity, unhappy donors, and unhappy allies guarantee unhappy voters, and unhappy voters mean you'll soon be looking for a new job. I estimate that the *fear filter* drives about 30% of all votes cast.

I grew up believing that most political decisions were made based on principle. Yes, I was naïve! As Senator Coburn explained, even the most committed politicians eventually abandon their principles under pressure. Expedience or fear win out almost all the time. Not always—I estimate that perhaps as many as 5% of all votes are cast based on genuine principle. The reality is that while many politicians start out with a political philosophy, for most that philosophy quickly gets crushed by the pressures of the Vise.

What are the different sides of the Vise that apply pressure? As shown in the diagram in the introduction, they are the media, influencers, and the people. When you think of the media, you might think of cable news or legacy newspapers like the *New York Times*. When you think of influencers today, perhaps you think of celebrities selling products on TikTok and Instagram, though for our purposes, we're thinking more of powerful lobbying groups like the trial bar, trade unions, and the Green Lobby. The truth is that all three sides of the Vise were present at the very beginning of our nation, long before the internet and television. Though the nature of both media and influencers has changed enormously over the past two centuries, both media and powerful influencers have applied intense pressure to politicians from the very earliest days of our republic. That pressure has shaped the destiny of our nation.

Let's examine a few short examples of the Traditional Political Vise in action, chosen from three pivotal moments in American history.

When Thomas Jefferson lost the 1796 presidential election to John Adams, he immediately began considering a rematch. As he assessed what he needed to do differently to get a different outcome, Jefferson realized he would need to do something that hadn't been done yet in our country's very brief history: *campaign*. He needed to shape public opinion and create pressure on potential electors. As Jefferson wrote to his close political ally, fellow founder, and future president, James Madison, "The engine is the press. Every man must lay his purse and his pen under contribution."

In other words, he needed to put the electors in a vise. As was so often the case, Jefferson's planning proved prescient. The election of 1800 ended in an electoral college tie, and as the Constitution provided, the House of Representatives was required to choose the president. If you've seen the musical *Hamilton* (or maybe paid attention in history class), you know what happened: the House chose Jefferson over Aaron Burr. The popular musical gives a tuneful explanation, but the real reason Jefferson prevailed was that he was the first—but by no means the last—aspiring American politician to grasp the decisive power of the Political Vise.

Nearly a century later, the United States was divided over the question of whether to intervene in Cuba's fight for independence from Spain. President William McKinley was initially reluctant to involve the country in a foreign conflict. History teachers often emphasize the pivotal role of the media (particularly the newspapers controlled by legendary publisher William Randolph Hearst) in "beating the drum" for war. Others—Assistant Secretary of the Navy Theodore Roosevelt chief among them—saw not only the moral obligation to assist the Cuban people but grasped that a war would serve American interests both in the Caribbean and in the Pacific. The coordinated efforts of the media and influencers (like Roosevelt and the great advocate for naval power Alfred Thayer Mahan) drove public opinion and turned the handle of the Vise. Squeezed from three sides, President McKinley was forced to act. America entered a war that would make us into a global power.

Few things are rarer than a politician voluntarily relinquishing power. In 1968, President Lyndon Johnson's surprise decision not to run for re-election was described as a "political Pearl Harbor." In part, LBJ didn't want to run again because he felt tired and unwell. The far more significant reason was that he had grown deeply unpopular. LBJ was despised by his own Democrat party, which was angry at the president's mishandling of the Vietnam War. Conservatives, meanwhile, were aghast at Johnson's profligate spending, rapidly rising crime and disorder, and spiraling inflation.

Many around the president expected him to defy the pressure and turn a deaf ear to his critics on both the right and the left. Instead, Johnson decided that the media, the influencers, and popular opinion were right: for the good of the country, he should step aside. By letting the Vise work as it was intended, LBJ reminded Americans that the system still functioned as the Framers intended. As historian Matthew Dallek put it:

Much of the public and the news media interpreted Johnson's announcement as a Godsend that made the project of national repair more feasible for 1968; LBJ's withdrawal offered hope, however scant, of national reconciliation, hope that new leaders would step up and somehow unite a fractured Republic. Johnson's decision not to seek re-election was a sign that the political system was still responsive to the people's will.[1]

That last sentence captures one of the most important functions of the Political Vise: when it operates as it was designed, the public is reassured that the system is "still responsive to the people's will." I don't need to tell you that very few Americans have that confidence today.

The fourth side of the Political Vise is the output. In 1800, that "output" was the triumph not only of Thomas Jefferson but of a political philosophy that sought to decentralize authority and maximize freedom. In 1898, the output was not only a popular war but an America ready to accept its destiny as a global power. In 1968, the output was an incumbent bowing to popular will—a reminder to Americans that their president is a servant, not an emperor.

More often, though, the output isn't a single resignation or a declaration of war but the establishment of an enduring policy—and a bureaucracy to implement and entrench it. The Vise worked to compel Johnson's resignation. It also worked to compel that same president's most famous achievement, the establishment of Medicare. Over the last sixty years, bureaucrats have worked hard to entrench Medicare and other entitlement programs, rendering them impervious to pressure to reform. What was created by the Vise often seeks to use the Vise for its own survival, at all costs. Generations of conservatives (like Senator Coburn) have come to Washington and discovered that the moment they seek to cut or reform a bloated government program, the Vise tightens. The opposition by the media and the left to the Department of Government Efficiency proves this point in spectacular fashion.

The "output" is very good at ensuring its own survival. Shortly after his re-election in 2004, President George W. Bush declared that his top domestic priority for his second term would be Social Security reform. In early 2005, he embarked on a national tour to advocate for a reimagined—and much more fiscally sound—Social Security system. President Bush saw that, left unchanged, our nation's most famous entitlement program could not be sustained. He wanted American workers to be able to invest part of their Social Security contributions in private accounts, thus betting both on themselves and on America. Despite the considerable political capital that came with a successful re-election, Bush's reform effort bombed—or rather, it got squeezed in the Vise. The media and the influencers successfully portrayed the Bush plan as destroying, rather than preserving, Social Security. By September 2005, the president had abandoned his reform efforts.

What happened with Social Security reform was disappointing. It was also an example of the Political Vise operating as it has for decades. Since the 1930s and the advent of New Deal social welfare programs, the left has deployed the Vise far more effectively than has the right. This isn't new—it's at the heart of what the late Dr. Coburn lamented to me nearly twenty years ago. What is new is that the Traditional Political Vise (revisit the diagram in the introduction for comparison) has been almost entirely superseded by something far more sinister, and something far from the intent of the Framers and the Founders: the Progressive Political Vise.

In this new vise, it is the American people who are held accountable to the politicians, to the influencers, and to the media. It is ordinary citizens who are nudged, exhorted, cajoled, threatened, and squeezed. The Progressive Political Vise operates on the assumption that the American people are racist, ignorant, selfish, and stupid. It presumes that our deepest convictions are foolish superstitions. It sees government not as an instrument to serve the people but as a machine for transforming them. Resistance to that transformation will be punished.

THE PROGRESSIVE POLITICAL VISE

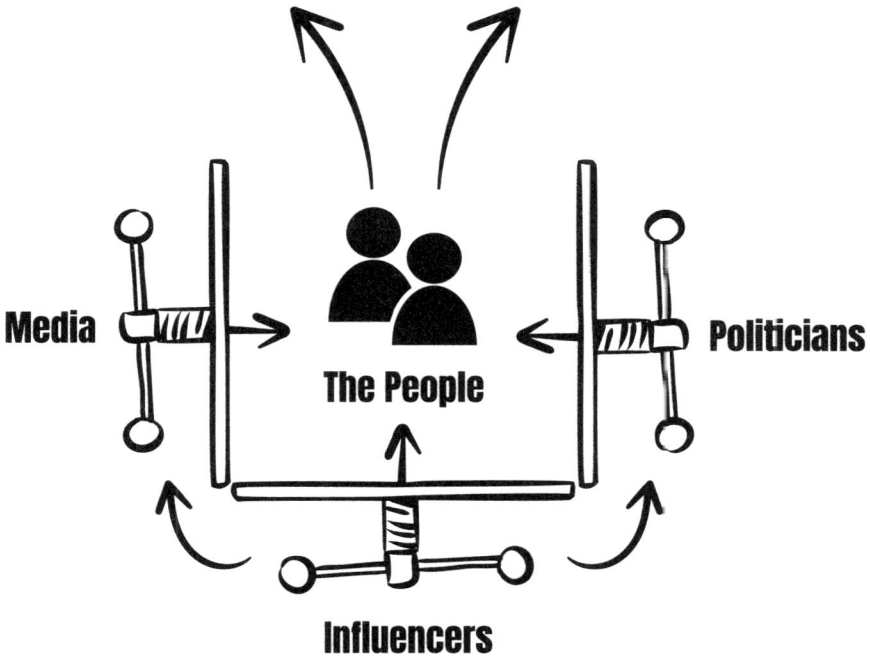

Output: Conform & submit or risk cancellation, prosecution, or incarceration.

Media

The People

Politicians

Influencers

People are compelled to make decisions based upon three criteria:
1. Personal Expediency
2. Personal Fear
3. Personal Principle

"Progressive" shouldn't be a bad word. After all, we all welcome technological, medical, and scientific innovations that help human beings to live longer and more comfortable lives. We all dream of better lives for our children. In that sense, we are all progressives. Of course, that's not how contemporary "progressives" understand the concept. Their goal isn't to encourage innovation and invention. Their goal is to coerce and compel individual Americans to live according to a particular set of collectivist, secular values. For these elites, progress is defined not by human flourishing, but by submission to an all-powerful, all-knowing state. It is not government by the people. It is government for the people as the government believes the people should be. Taken to its natural end, as the former Soviet Union did, tens of millions of lives were sacrificed in the name of progress. When coercion and thus submission are required, there can be no progress or progressivism.

What are they thinking? How could they be so misguided? Who could possibly believe that nonsense? Those words have come out of my mouth many times while watching the news in recent years. I'm fairly sure you've said similar things. No matter where you are on the political spectrum, there will be moments where you find yourself confronted (and confounded) by the reality that other people frequently come to very, very different conclusions about the real meaning of justice, or democracy, or freedom. I'll discuss the reasons for this rising tide of ignorance later in this book. What is striking is that it is the progressive left, not the right, that uses the Political Vise to coerce and to crush anyone who disagrees with its agenda. Put simply, conservatives respond to ignorance with efforts to educate. Increasingly, progressives respond to perceived "ignorance" with efforts to eradicate.

This isn't hyperbole. I wish it were! To name one example (there are many more), think of the way the Progressive Political Vise worked to crush anyone who dared question the outcome of the 2020 presidential election. The left mocks anyone who suggests the election was stolen—and yet, given the chance, the left gleefully admits what really happened that year:

> There was a conspiracy unfolding behind the scenes, one that both curtailed the protests and coordinated the resistance from CEOs. Both surprises were the result of an informal alliance between left-wing activists and business titans . . . Their work touched every aspect of the election. They got states to change

voting systems and laws and helped secure hundreds of millions
in public and private funding.[2]

Those aren't the words of a right-wing crackpot. They're from a February
2021 *TIME* magazine article by progressive journalist Molly Ball, best
known for her worshipful, award-winning biography of Nancy Pelosi. Rather
than deny the allegations that, at least in part, the 2020 elections were rigged,
the left—like a criminal unable to resist boasting of his cleverness—seems to
be gleefully admitting the rigging. They changed the laws. They spent millions on ballot harvesting. They threw out decades of established practice for
counting and securing ballots. (For more on how they did this, I recommend
the work of another Mollie: *Rigged: How the Media, Big Tech, and the
Democrats Seized Our Elections*, by Mollie Hemingway.) Having achieved
the desired outcome—the defeat of President Trump—the left swiftly pivoted
to crushing those who challenged the result.

The persecution of the January 6 "insurrectionists" is one very obvious
example of politicians, the media, and wealthy influencers putting ordinary
Americans in the Vise. It is not just average Americans. There is no living
human being whom the Progressive Political Vise is more desperate to crush
than Donald Trump. You do not have to agree with all of the president's
policies and pronouncements to recognize that the left is frantically eager
to destroy him. The countless criminal and civil suits, the obscenely con-
fiscatory judgments (particularly in New York), and the relentless "lawfare"
against his person, his businesses, and his family offer the best possible
example of the contemporary left's ruthlessness.

Of course, it isn't just President Trump and his supporters crushed in the
Progressive Political Vise. It's girls who just want to play sports—but whose
trophies are stolen and whose bodies are injured by young men masquerading
as women. It's parents who demand to know why pornography is in the
middle-school library. It's the likes of Daniel Penny, who sought to protect
his fellow subway riders and faced decades behind bars. And of course, it's
countless Americans who dared challenge the progressive regime's insistence

on locking down our society, closing schools, masking toddlers, and imposing vaccine mandates. Since 2020—with that year's triple crises of a pandemic, racial unrest, and a disputed election—the left has cranked the handle of the Vise with ever-greater ruthlessness. These are only a handful of instances of the Progressive Political Vise in action. Each day's news brings new and troubling examples of the progressive left's relentless effort to transform American society by transforming the American people. Anyone who opposes the agenda is either crushed—or cowed into compliance.

I am likely not telling you much you do not already know. What we do all need to know is how we can *retake* the Vise, *restore* it to its intended use, and *reclaim* our country. The good news is that the election of 2024 showed that the American people have begun taking back our liberty. Let's join them on this worthy journey!

Chapter 2

LEARNING TO WIN

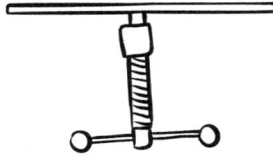

June 27, 2018
United States Supreme Court
Washington, DC

It *had* to be today. It was Wednesday, the last day for opinions. We'd come on Monday and Tuesday, just in case, but we had a feeling that our case would be among the very last to be decided. As I took my seat in the middle of the august and stately chamber, I reminded myself to keep breathing. *The next time you stand up,* I told myself, *you'll know. The next time you stand up, we may have won.* I willed myself not to contemplate the other possibility.

I had barely slept the night before. I thought of the countless plaintiffs who had come before this highest American court in its history. How had they coped with the anticipation and anxiety? I figured many of them had to have been as nervous as I was. For at least a generation, it's been customary for the Supreme Court to hand down decisions in its most important cases in the final week of the term—generally at the end of June. (Some of my friends, devoted court watchers, consider the end of the SCOTUS term—and not the solstice or Memorial Day—as the "real" start of summer.) It was no accident that ours was among the very last cases to be decided this year. Whatever came down from the bench would surely be a landmark.

Our case was called *Janus v. AFSCME*. Mark Janus worked as a child support specialist for the State of Illinois. Mark devoted his career to ensuring that often vulnerable kids got their needs met. When he was hired in 2007, Mark was stunned to find that a public-sector union—the American Federation of State, County, and Municipal Employees—deducted money from his paycheck. Mark wasn't inherently anti-union, but he did not share AFSCME's left-wing political agenda. He soon discovered that his preferences were irrelevant. Illinois law—and Supreme Court precedent—allowed public-sector unions to collect dues from anyone covered by their collective bargaining agreements, even if those employees did not want to join or support those unions.

Mark is a brave and principled man. He had long chafed at forking over dues to a union that he believed acted against the interests of its own members, the public they served, and the State of Illinois. The union's contract demands were always wildly out of proportion to what Mark felt was fair. Mark knew a basic truth: you can't be for big government, big taxes, and big bureaucracy and still be for the little guy. A deeply compassionate advocate for vulnerable kids, Mark was all about the "little guy." He was also tough: he'd been an Eagle Scout and later a Scoutmaster. He had the character and the determination to buck the nation's largest public employee union and take them all the way to the Supreme Court.

The Supreme Court is famously reluctant to overturn its own precedents. Mark Janus was not only asking them to overturn a precedent but to reverse what had been a unanimous decision—and one made within living memory. Reluctance is not the same as refusal, however. The shame of *Plessy v. Ferguson* was corrected by the triumph of *Brown v. Board of Education*—and though none of us knew it yet, in a few short years, the tragedy of *Roe v. Wade* would be redressed by *Dobbs v. Jackson*. The

Supreme Court, as Trump's second term demonstrates, is not immune from the pressures of the Political Vise, for good and, sometimes, for ill. We had done everything we could to use the Vise for liberty. We would find out today if we'd been successful.

It was now nearly 9:00 a.m. We'd taken our seats at 8:15, veterans of the procedure after three straight days of anticipation. Cell phones are not allowed in the Supreme Court chamber, so we had to do what people in this same situation have done for eons: make small talk and check out the room while finding reasons to be as optimistic as possible. As we waited, I kept replaying an exchange from four months earlier, when the Court had heard Janus. During arguments, Justice Anthony Kennedy had asked the union lawyer, "If you do not prevail in this case, the unions will have less political influence. Yes or no?"

The AFSCME lawyer had replied, "Yes, they will have less political influence."

Kennedy had fixed him with a sharp stare. "Well, isn't that the end of this case?"

In narrowly decided cases, Kennedy was often the swing vote. Based on what he'd said back in February, I had had an inkling he might swing to our side. As I tried to calm my nerves, I noticed that Justice Kennedy's wife, Mary, was in the audience. It didn't occur to me that this was unusual. In just over an hour, I—like millions of Americans—would be shocked when Kennedy announced his retirement from the bench.

I saw another face I knew better: Charles Mitchell, then head of the Pennsylvania Commonwealth Foundation. Charles has a sterling track record of fighting for government employees to exercise their constitutional rights. We were glad to have him on our side. I also recognized a number of journalists who had been covering our case for years. They had their pads and pencils at the ready; the ban on electronic devices meant that even now, in 2018, reporters at the Supreme Court would take notes the exact same way their counterparts had done for over a century. Some of these journalists were friendly to our cause; we knew that most weren't.

The "we" I keep referring to included Mark Janus himself, of course. I sat to Mark's left; to his right was Illinois Governor Bruce Rauner. Sitting elsewhere in the court was Jacob Huebert, then senior counsel for the Liberty Justice Center. He was the one who set our legal strategy. We had other staff waiting eagerly outside. They had their phones with them and would know the outcome nearly as quickly as we did. More importantly, those on the outside would be able to read the reactions to the decision as they poured in. If the Janus decision was narrow, our colleagues with cell phones would be in a better position to interpret the ramifications than those of us in the chambers.

At exactly 9:00, the doors behind each of the nine chairs swung open, and the justices entered. For a moment, we could only see eight; Ruth Bader Ginsburg, already in poor health, was so tiny that we could only catch periodic glimpses of the top of her head. The seconds ticked by. Then, the firm, clear voice of Chief Justice John Roberts: "Justice Alito will read the first opinion."

Those seven words told me we had won. The opinion of the court is, of course, read by someone in the majority. Samuel Alito was a committed originalist, a steward of this area of jurisprudence. We had known from the start that he would be sympathetic to Mark Janus—what we didn't know was how many of his fellow justices he could convince to join him. And even as Alito started to read what would be a 5-4 opinion, we were unsure of the scope of our victory. Would it be narrow, tailored to the specifics of the Janus case? Or would it be what we desperately hoped for, a sweeping win for the cause of worker freedom?

In 1977, a unanimous Supreme Court held in *Abood v. Detroit Board of Education* that teachers who did not want to join a union could still be compelled to pay "agency fees" to support collective bargaining activities. The court had said that an employee union invariably has two fundamentally distinct purposes: political work and representation work. A public-sector employee could opt out of supporting the union's political activism, but not its representation.

Our argument had been that in practice, there is no wall of separation that divides a union's various activities. Everything the union did was political. As far as Mark Janus was concerned, when his union bargained with the government for higher salaries, excessive benefits, and bloated pensions, that was compelling the State of Illinois to raise taxes and increase spending. Taxation and spending are inherently political acts.

As Justice Alito read his decision, I strained to follow his words. The snippets I heard sounded good: "Forcing free and independent individuals to endorse ideas they find objectionable raises serious First Amendment concerns . . . The State's extraction of agency fees from nonconsenting public-sector employees violates the First Amendment. . . . *Abood* erred in concluding otherwise, and *stare decisis* cannot support it . . . . *Abood* is therefore overruled."

I did not yet fully grasp the scope and scale of our victory, but it was very clear that this wasn't a narrowly tailored opinion. This was a sweeping victory for, to use Alito's phrase, "free and independent individuals." It was a triumph for those of us who had been fighting for a long time to ensure that ordinary Americans had the basic liberty to choose the causes on which their money was spent. It was a major win for Governor Rauner, and the Liberty Justice Center I had cofounded; it was a major win for a foundational American principle; it was a major win for one brave child support worker named Mark Janus. And it was also a major vindication of the value of the Political Vise.

Bruce Rauner's election had been a political earthquake. By the 2010s, Illinois was widely regarded as the "bluest" state in the Midwest. It was where Barack Obama—the most left-wing president in American history—had cut his political teeth. The state legislature was firmly in the control of liberal Democrats. Pundits declared that there was no way a Republican could ever again win a statewide election in the Land of Lincoln. As is fortunately sometimes the case, in 2014 the pundits were proved wrong. Bruce Rauner, running on a pro-growth, pro-free-market, pro-liberty platform, defeated the Democrat incumbent, Pat Quinn, in a stunning political upset. Not long after being sworn in, the new governor set to work on fulfilling his promise to help Illinois flourish. As we at the Illinois Policy Institute knew well, there was no better way to encourage that flourishing than to try to rein in the colossal power of the state's public-sector unions.

In January 2015, just days into his term, Bruce Rauner launched an effort to stop unions from collecting dues from non-members. This wasn't a minor or arcane issue. It was a matter of fundamental principles. The governor knew there could be no lasting and meaningful education reform—a central issue in his campaign—without curbing the influence of the teachers' unions. He also believed, as we believed, that the only way to set the state's fiscal house in order was to ensure that Illinois taxpayers received genuine value from public employees. Perhaps most important of all, he understood that this was a basic issue of personal freedom.

The governor took a two-pronged approach. On February 9, 2015, Rauner issued an executive order that forbade state agencies from collecting union agency fees from non-member employees. At the exact same time, the governor sued in the US District Court for the Northern District of Illinois. He asked for a declaratory judgment: forcing non-union members to pay agency fees violated their First Amendment rights. Rauner also asked the court to validate his executive order. It was an audacious strategy that would force the other side to fight on multiple fronts.

I probably don't need to tell you that the left is very adept at fighting pitched political battles. With lightning speed, the big public-sector unions—AFSCME, the Chicago Teachers Union, Service Employees International Union (SEIU), and the Illinois Education Association—struck back. They launched sophisticated media campaigns against Governor Rauner. They vilified him in the press, trusting that sympathetic media would help them paint the governor as a monster who just wanted to hurt kids and poor people. The unions mobilized their members to post on social media with frantic, angry criticisms of the Rauner plan. When a much-anticipated—and frankly, long overdue—budget impasse began, partly over this issue of forced dues, union members flooded Springfield. Loudly and boisterously, they marched through the streets of the state capital, rallying and protesting against the governor and his supporters.

If the left in general is very good at operating the Political Vise, the public-sector unions are the absolute masters of the instrument. A four-sided vise needs intense pressure from three of those sides to produce a desired outcome. The unions mobilized their Democrat allies in the state legislature. They cajoled nonprofit organizations (many of which relied on state government largesse) to protest against the funding delays brought about by the impasse. The all-important wealthy, leftist influencers (what we once colloquially called the "pillars of the community") weighed in against the governor's plan. The media, the establishment influencers, and the marchers in the streets did their damndest to convey the impression that the vast majority of ordinary Illinoisans rejected Rauner's goal. The Vise was tightening.

At the Illinois Policy Institute (our education organization) and Illinois Policy (our advocacy organization), we knew a little about how to work the Vise. As CEO, I directed our staff to begin to work on a counternarrative using all the strategies and tools we had at our disposal. Remembering that the Traditional Political Vise is tightened by media, by influencers, and by the people, we rallied right-of-center support for Governor Rauner's reform agenda. This wasn't directly coordinated with Rauner; we were neither part of his administration nor his political campaign. We were working with the governor, not for him, knowing that maintaining our autonomy and independence was vital to our work.

I had cofounded the Liberty Justice Center (LJC), as I noted above, as a project of the Illinois Policy Institute. By this time, LJC was a fully independent public interest law firm, but it still worked closely with us. The excellent attorneys at LJC were fully on board with the Rauner plan, but they were concerned that the governor did not have the legal standing to carry his lawsuit forward. He was not a government worker paying agency fees to a public-sector union. We needed a plaintiff who met that criterion—and who had the courage to be the public face of our fight.

The hard truth is that the left is much better than the right at telling emotion-driven stories. Conservatives want to argue the facts and the law; liberals want to tug at heartstrings. The left understands the old adage usually attributed to a very great son of Illinois, Carl Sandburg: "If the facts are against you, argue the law. If the law is against you, argue the facts. If the law and the facts are against you, pound the table and yell like hell." (Ol' Carl may have grasped the basic mechanism of the Political Vise!) For liberals, yelling like hell often works all too effectively. Storytelling—usually featuring a highly sympathetic victim of some real or imagined injustice—is the left's favorite weapon when the facts and the law are against them.

We had the facts. We believed we had the law. Now we needed someone with standing to help us tell the story. In early 2015, we had over 100,000 people in Illinois fully engaged in our work. (That number is now more than 2.5 million). Surely someone knew a state worker who would be willing to join the lawsuit as a plaintiff? Enter the relentless Kristina Rasmussen, then our executive vice president at the Illinois Policy Institute. At the time, Kristina lived in Springfield—and through her longtime friend, civic leader Don Tracy, she was introduced to Mark Janus.

In their first conversation, Mark told Kristina about his devotion to his job as a state childcare specialist. He talked with pride about his work ensuring that vulnerable kids got the support they deserved. Mark also talked about his huge frustration with the organization that confiscated (or "shanghaied" as Justice Alito would later put it) so much of his money. Mark Janus knew what was happening was unfair, but he didn't feel he had the power to fight the colossal power of the unions.

Kristina introduced Mark to the lawyers at LJC, including its then senior attorney, Jacob Huebert. Jacob invited Bill Messenger of the National Right to Work Legal Defense Foundation to join the effort as well. Our team explained to Mark that he did indeed have a case, but that fighting for his rights would take time. It might not be easy, and there was no guarantee of victory. We wanted Mark to understand that the left would quickly grasp that this case was a near-existential threat to the power of public-sector unions. They would fight back hard, and they would almost certainly not fight fair. It could get ugly. He would find out just how intense the pressure of the Progressive Political Vise could be.

Mark didn't hesitate. He agreed to become a client of the Liberty Justice Center. In March 2015, we filed a motion to intervene on Mark's behalf. Governor Rauner was dropped from the case, which was now known as *Janus v. AFSCME*. We had standing—and the fight was on.

Though Mark was LJC's client, Jacob Huebert made the decision to have Bill Messenger take the first chair. Bill had a great track record and had already argued and won two cases before the Supreme Court. Jacob's decision to put Bill in that chair rather than himself was one of the most selfless professional acts I have ever observed. I am certain Jacob would have done a masterful job. But Jacob, a talented and yet modest man, wanted to ensure that Mark Janus had the most experienced attorney leading the charge on his behalf. That willingness to put the client and the cause ahead of his own ego is part of what makes Jacob Huebert such an outstanding attorney and person.

Though there are exceptions, it usually takes several years for a case to wind its way to the Supreme Court. *Janus v. AFSCME* began its journey in March 2015. We would not have oral arguments in front of the nine justices until February 26, 2018. Both the Supreme Court and the American political landscape changed dramatically over the course of the intervening three years. The legendary justice Antonin Scalia, perhaps the greatest conservative jurist of our era, died early in 2016—an election year. Resisting colossal pressure from the Progressive Political Vise, Senate Majority Leader Mitch McConnell and his fellow Republicans held the seat open, determined to let the next president appoint Scalia's successor. Donald Trump pulled off his extraordinary upset win that November and soon appointed Neil Gorsuch to fill Scalia's seat on the Supreme Court.

With the benefit of hindsight, we've found that Justice Gorsuch has proved a fairly reliable vote for the court's now-solid conservative majority. In early 2018, however, we did not know enough about the newest justice.

We *did* know all too well that even judges with lifetime appointments were not immune from the pressures of the Political Vise. Time and again, Republican presidents had appointed justices to the Supreme Court, sure of their conservative credentials. Indeed, every single Republican president from Eisenhower to the second President Bush had seen at least one of his Supreme Court appointees shift sharply to the left.

Think of the likes of William Brennan (appointed by Dwight Eisenhower), Harry Blackmun (appointed by Richard Nixon), John Paul Stevens (appointed by Gerald Ford), Sandra Day O'Connor and Anthony Kennedy (appointed by Ronald Reagan), David Souter (appointed by the first President Bush), and even Chief Justice John Roberts (appointed by George W. Bush.) Each, to one degree or another, would prove a huge disappointment to the right. Only a handful of Republican-appointed justices, like the late Antonin Scalia or Clarence Thomas (who famously endured the brutality of the Progressive Political Vise during his confirmation hearings), have proven consistently faithful to the Constitution.

The Political Vise doesn't just work on those who regularly face re-election. Supreme Court justices read the *New York Times*. They vacation with the influencers. They read the books written by legal historians, and they notice that it is always the liberal justices who are lionized. Mindful of the opinion of their friends and anxious about their legacies, once-conservative justices acquiesce, they shift, they "evolve"—and as a result, they betray not only the presidents who appointed them but the Constitution they pledged to defend. I'd seen it happen again and again and again.

I wanted to believe that President Trump was a shrewder judge of character than some of his Republican predecessors and that Neil Gorsuch would prove to be a reliable and consistent conservative vote. As we headed to the Supreme Court that cold February morning in 2018, it was still too soon to tell.

Before the arguments, we held a rally in support of Mark Janus on the front steps of the Supreme Court. The unions held their own rally right next to ours. We shouted dueling slogans and waved dueling signs. It was fun.

Our rally was composed of like-minded folks working in Washington, DC—government workers who shared Mark's situation and beliefs, and activists from across the country who understood the magnitude of this case. Something happened that day that still stays with me. In the least surprising tactic ever, the unions sent over infiltrators to disrupt our rally. A couple of women came up to me and my companions, waving their signs in the middle of our rally.

I asked the two women, "What are you protesting for today?"

They replied in unison, "Workers' rights!"

"Wow," I said, "We are too! Let me ask you, who should determine your relationship with your union? You or your union boss?"

It may have felt like a trick question to them at first, but it wasn't. I could see the wheels turning in their heads. "Well, I guess I should be able to decide," one of the women finally said, her tone reluctant and halting.

I gave her my most encouraging smile. "Exactly! We completely agree. That is what this case is about."

I could tell they "got it." You could see that their very reality had been challenged. Everything they had been told was turned upside down. It hit them that all we wanted to do was let the workers decide their own destiny, their own speech. None of us abandon our tribes easily, or at the first moment of doubt. Political persuasion is often more about sowing seeds than about creating sudden epiphanies. It takes patience to turn the Vise and let it start to work. The women returned to their rally—but with their enthusiasm markedly diminished.

Mark Janus himself soon appeared, walking toward the court to hear the arguments. We greeted him with ringing cheers and shouts of encouragement. Two members of the LJC team walked beside Mark, and I watched with pride and excitement as the trio walked up the steps and across the terrace. When the "other side" saw and recognized him, pandemonium ensued. There was no violence between the dueling rallies, but emotions ran high. The powerful government unions knew well that theatrics get media coverage, and media coverage turns the Vise. They got loud, and they drew nearer to him, intimidation on their minds. Our side—with our signs that read "We the People"—held our ground.

As the union crowd slowly backed away, Mark turned to one of my colleagues. "This is overwhelming. I am not sure I can go through with this." My colleague offered words of reassurance. I saw Mark scan the faces of the large crowd there to support him. Encouraged by what he saw, he took a deep breath, gathered himself, and resumed his journey into the court and into history.

Four months later, on that bright June morning, we could not get up and leave as soon as Justice Alito delivered the majority opinion in our case. We were itching to celebrate—and to begin to digest the sheer scale of our victory. Out of respect for the court's rules and traditions, we sat as patiently as we could (still without our phones) while three other opinions were read. (Later that day, when Justice Kennedy announced his retirement, I was excited that President Trump would get his second Supreme Court appointment. I had no idea how contentious that appointment would become, and how we would soon see the Progressive Political Vise at its cruelest and most destructive. That's a story for another chapter.)

The opinions had been released online well before we heard them read in court. Our friends outside were exulting while we were still filled with anxious nerves. When Governor Rauner, Mark, Jacob, and I finally left the chamber, we were greeted first by the ever poised and organized Sarah Keenan, from the State Policy Network. The State Policy Network, then led by the indefatigable Tracie Sharp, had been instrumental in organizing the rally back in February. They had also provided logistical support to us for many years. Sarah volunteered to help us navigate the exit from the Supreme Court, out the front doors, down the stairs, and to the press pit that awaited us. I think we floated down that famous staircase.

I started the press conference with brief remarks, thanking Governor Rauner for initiating the case. He stepped to the microphone, followed by Jacob, and then the man of the hour, Mark Janus.

In introducing Mark, I said, "Without a plaintiff, you have no case. Mark, it is an honor to have been with you on this journey. Thank you for your courage, for your commitment to worker freedom, and for your unwavering poise and professionalism throughout this entire process. You have won the admiration of thousands of people all over the country who have followed your story. Thank you so much."

More than seven years later, what I find so moving about the Mark Janus story is that it encapsulates a basic truth: the American system can still work for "the little guy." It is easy to believe that "We the People" has been replaced by "We the Elites" or "We the Corporations" or "We, Your Betters." The reality is that sometimes the good guys win, and those victories are not just luck. These victories are the consequence of courage, of commitment, and of cultivating a canny understanding of how to effectively use the Political Vise on the people's behalf. We can and will see more victories. Just as Mark fought successfully to get back his free speech rights that had been taken from him by elite union bosses, we must fight to take back our right to direct our own destinies, which has been taken from us by an ever-growing and hostile government. William F. Buckley Jr. often remarked that the best defense against a usurpatory government is an assertive citizenry. If we do not reassert control over our government to serve the people rather than the media, the influencers, and politicians, then our republic will continue to atrophy and eventually die.

In the years since Mark's courage was rewarded at the Supreme Court, the stakes have only grown larger. As the GOP victories in 2024 have shown yet again, leftist activists take defeats—either at the ballot box or in court—personally. They double down, they mobilize, they probe for further weaknesses. Above all, they do not give up on trying to crush the people in the Progressive Political Vise. Let me give them credit for their tenacity, their savvy, and their relentlessness. Rather than lament their success and their determination to win, we need to match them, then surpass them, then defeat them. I am not just optimistic that we can win; I am certain that we will win—if we have the clarity to understand how power is accumulated, how it is deployed, and how we can use it to reclaim our liberty.

I saw Mark Janus win, and I have seen more victories since. As dark as things may seem at this moment, with seemingly the entire federal government bureaucracy, most of the courts, the legacy media, and the vast progressive NGO infrastructure all aligned against the cause of liberty, we have passed an inflection point. I believe we are just now entering a renaissance of reverence for the Founding Principles. I believe we are a people in the process of rediscovering and reclaiming our natural rights. We are no longer content to allow the elite influencers, the media, and the entrenched political class to chip away at our freedoms. "Eternal vigilance is the price of liberty"—you may have learned that saying in school. The vigilance that will ensure our victory isn't just a general wariness or mistrust of those who would seize our liberties. The vigilance that ensures our liberty requires an awareness of how the Traditional Political Vise works—and a keen understanding of how to unleash its extraordinary power.

Chapter 3

THE TRASH COMPACTOR
AND COVID-19

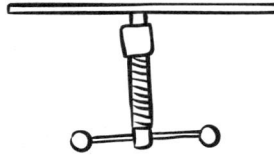

Politics is about pressure. If you cannot apply pressure, you have no power.

One of my favorite scenes in the very first *Star Wars* movie (retroactively titled "A New Hope") comes when our heroes are trapped in a huge trash compactor on the imperial Death Star. Luke Skywalker, Han Solo, Princess Leia, and Chewbacca find themselves stuck in a morass of space garbage. The walls start closing in, and as our heroes struggle desperately to slow the inexorable process, they are attacked from below by a primordial space creature. They are rescued from the masher at the last moment, with all (especially Luke) emerging considerably worse for wear.

Lots of *Star Wars* fans appreciate this scene, but I love it because it is such a powerful metaphor for what it feels like to be caught in the Traditional Political Vise. You can feel the pressure as the walls close in upon you. You start to panic—is that terrible smell your own fear or the trash around you? There is a fearsome creature—a "Dianoga" in the movie, perhaps a lobbyist in real life—who lives in the swampy cesspool beneath you. He wants to eat you alive. Welcome to politics, baby!

No one wants to be crushed in a trash compactor. It isn't fun to be caught in the Traditional Political Vise. But make no mistake. The Traditional Political Vise isn't a punishment. It is not a gruesome and smelly method of execution. It is the means by which the citizens of a constitutional republic guarantee that liberty survives. It is the best and most effective way to ensure that those who are granted temporary power use it wisely, and for the common good within our constitutional framework. The danger is not that human beings are going to get crushed in a literal trash compactor—or a vise. The danger to the republic is that either there is no Vise or that the wrong hands crank the handles.

Politics is like a sausage factory—a messy process with (ideally) a tasty result. We want, need, and deserve to have politicians who are under constant pressure from all three sides of the Traditional Political Vise: the *media*, the *people,* and *influencers.* Legislation and policy are squeezed out on the fourth side. The taste of that sausage (the palatability of the policy) depends on who exerts the most effective pressure.

I've been doing public policy work for more than twenty years. When I started, I had no idea that the Vise existed. As I've explained, a conversation with the late, great Senator Tom Coburn first helped me recognize the concept. But even as my eyes began to open, I was still fundamentally naïve. I still believed most politicians ran for office to advance a cause. They understood that the founding principles and free enterprise were the greatest force for good ever created to improve the human condition and were driven and guided by them. Public policy was about helping these well-intentioned, competent leaders implement wise and effective solutions to enduring problems.

When I first began to understand the Vise, I saw it as a means of getting and holding the attention of politicians who wanted to do the right thing. Perhaps they just needed those "right things" pointed out.

You may be smiling at my foolishness. It's okay, I laugh at myself too. Today's conservatives may not be "woke," but we are all awakened to the grim reality that far too many of our politicians respond only to the pressure of the Progressive Political Vise. In the previous chapter, I told the remarkable story of our Supreme Court victory in *Janus v. AFSCME*—an all-too-rare example of a defeat for the left. The seeds of that win were planted when my colleagues at Illinois Policy and the LJC and I finally let go of our illusions about how power really worked. We stopped wishing that things worked as the Founders intended and as we had been taught in school. We accepted the reality that in contemporary American society, the Political Vise is largely controlled by trial lawyers, public-sector unions, private-sector unions, nonprofits that get most of their money from government, and radical billionaires, like Tom Steyer, Peter Lewis, Mark Zuckerberg, Laurene Powell Jobs, and George Soros. As we'll discuss in another chapter, Big Tech and woke corporate America have recently joined this handful of left-wing billionaires. They have allied themselves with the traditional powers on the left (the unions and trial lawyers); together, they force not only politicians but ordinary citizens to do their bidding or be crushed in the Vise.

With the exception of the billionaires, progressive operators of the Political Vise have one thing in common: not one of them creates value on their own. Each, in their own way, extracts wealth and income from the private sector as part of their business models. To do that, they must use governmental power through the tax code and regulatory system. This cash extraction process—through collective bargaining, lawsuits, taxation, government grants, subsidies, and more—is what unifies the left. This commitment to taking as much as possible from the private sector is what holds the left together. Whatever ideological differences various progressive groups have among themselves are easily put aside for the common purpose of fleecing the taxpayer and taking wealth from its creators. This unity of purpose is a huge strategic advantage for the ideological left. This unity has allowed the left to both pursue their financial interests and enjoy the pleasure of wielding tremendous political and cultural power.

The left invariably portrays itself as the brave underdog, battling the forces of greed, oppression, and bigotry. Even as they skillfully and cynically deploy massive power against their perceived enemies, they depict themselves as a grassroots movement of plucky activists. They are always David, and the right is always Goliath. Because the left controls so much of the entertainment and cultural products we consume, this myth of the progressive heroic underdog insinuates itself into every corner of American life.

By contrast, the right-of-center movement does not have the assets to operate the Vise. In particular, the right lacks the fierce and relentless unity of the left. Conservatives generally share a political and economic philosophy, but it invariably proves challenging to build a movement based on personal responsibility—and the intense desire to be left alone. The think tanks and advocacy groups that promote conservative and libertarian ideas do excellent work. They convene important discussions. They attempt to influence legislation. But what they don't do enough is play hardball. Indeed, most are barred by the tax code and other laws from partisan politics, which is very much a hardball game.

Big business is not a reliable ally. Until recently, large corporations were studiously apolitical, eager to avoid offending consumers. They operated like Switzerland, with a predictable neutrality. When they lobbied, they sought tax code and regulatory relief, pursuing their own interests, careful to cultivate relationships with politicians across the entire ideological spectrum. The progressive left, with a combination of ruthlessness and patience, pushed big business to "go woke." From Disney to Coca-Cola to American Express to BlackRock, companies are engaging in politics more aggressively than ever before. Some of that is mere virtue signaling, which functions as a kind of blackmail payment to leftist groups. If a major corporation pays enough, it can stay out of the Vise. Some of that "wokeward" shift is pure economic self-interest. From the start of his presidency, Joe Biden provided massive government business subsidies through the likes of the CHIPs Act and the Investing in America Act. If your corporation wants to feed at the great big-government trough, you need to demonstrate that you are on board with the progressive agenda.

While the election of Trump and Republican majorities in 2024 has begun a broad pushback against these policies, the fight is not won. In many cases wokeness has gone underground, been renamed, and become less overt than before—but it is still present doing its destructive work.

Let me recap with three key points:

1. The left's use of the Political Vise has shifted our republic's sovereignty from the people to the elite influencers who seek to govern without interference from American citizens. The left has raised and deployed massive resources to work the Political Vise.

2. The greatest risk our republic faces today is that those who cherish the Founding Principles are not only underfunded and undermanned—but they also don't even know the Political Vise exists.

3. To save the republic, conservatives must first understand the Vise's capacities, orient the movement towards using the Vise effectively—and engage the American people for the cause of American liberty.

COVID-19: The Power of the Progressive Political Vise

While the attacks on DOGE have well illustrated the Progressive Political Vise at work, there is no bigger—and no more brutal—contemporary example of the Progressive Political Vise at work than the response to COVID-19. As I write this, we have just passed the fifth anniversary of the official beginning of the pandemic in March 2020. On social media, people repost images of empty store shelves, abandoned office buildings, and shuttered schools. Friends and family reminisce grimly about hoarding toilet paper, learning to bake bread, and trying (usually in vain) to keep bored children focused on "Zoom school."

As we share these alternately upsetting and hilarious memories, it is easy to forget that in the space of just a few days, the left deployed the Political Vise on a scope and scale never before seen in American life. They brought the Vise to bear upon President Trump, Congress, governors, local officials, journalists, and school boards. It was unprecedented in its speed and its effectiveness. A single, ruthlessly repetitive talking point emerged: *America needs to shut down. We need "two weeks to stop the spread." We are facing a deadly threat.* Another message was also clear: Failure to do whatever the Vise declared necessary to combat the coronavirus was to be complicit in mass murder.

Most of us remember that there was a great deal of confusion in the early days of the pandemic. We weren't entirely sure how the virus was spread. The government initially discouraged masking—but did insist we stay "six feet apart." The authorities insisted that COVID-19 was spread by droplets and warned that those droplets could live on surfaces. Stores ran out of hand sanitizer as well as toilet paper, and millions of Americans dutifully cleaned their groceries with disinfecting wipes.

While the advice of the public health authorities was confusing, make no mistake, the left was not confused. Some might not have been certain of the origins of COVID-19, or of exactly how the virus was spread. They were crystal clear, however, that this emergency presented them with an extraordinary opportunity to speed up and enhance the power of the Political Vise that they controlled and operated. You may have heard the infamous observation made by Rahm Emanuel, the Democrat former mayor of Chicago and chief of staff to Barack Obama: "You never let a serious crisis go to waste." It was a remarkably candid admission. Whatever else might be said of him, Emanuel was a skilled political operator. He couldn't resist bragging about his experience using the Political Vise.

What's quoted less often is Rahm's full remark, made a decade before COVID: "You never let a serious crisis go to waste—and what I mean by that is it's an opportunity to do things you think you could not do before." What the left has understood for decades is that every unexpected event opens the door to long-anticipated possibilities. When people are afraid or confused, they can often be convinced to trade their liberties for the promise of stability and safety. I do not believe that the left created the actual coronavirus, although questions have now been answered about its Chinese origin and US-funded "gain of function" research in that infamous Wuhan laboratory. What we also know now is that the moment the pandemic was declared in March 2020, the left knew the "serious crisis" for which they had been hoping had arrived at long last. They knew that they could not waste the moment, and they had to move quickly and ruthlessly to do the things they had not yet been able to do.

In the space of *less than a week*, the nation—and much of the world— ground to a halt. The public had the impression that everyone across the entire political spectrum agreed both about the scope of the threat and the need for urgent action. The truth is that the consensus was not organic—*it was manufactured*. With breathtaking speed, the left began to turn the handles of the Political Vise to force a single outcome: the largest and fastest transformation of American life in living memory. It would take a month for the first significant protests to begin. By mid-April 2020, when the pushback began, the Progressive Political Vise had already achieved some breathtakingly significant successes—and spent trillions of dollars.

It happened to me. I had spent years standing up to the progressive agenda, and yet with some embarrassment, I admit the Vise "got" me.

Like almost everyone, I wasn't sure what to make of this new virus. I accepted that it might pose a legitimate threat, particularly to the elderly. I also realized that we had a second "immunity problem." On March 15, I wrote an editorial suggesting that all the authorities making health-related recommendations (such as Deborah Birx, Anthony Fauci, and their state and local counterparts) were immune to the financial consequences of their decisions. I didn't yet know how far the authorities intended to go with their plans, but I knew that even a short shutdown would have a massive impact on business and the larger economy. I worried about the impact of a prolonged shutdown on communities, on children, on mental health. (I was right to be concerned. Cancer deaths would skyrocket because of delayed doctor visits; suicides and overdoses would dramatically increase; a generation of young children would fall behind in school.)

The elite influencers, like Bill Gates, were fully immune to the economic consequences of the prescribed shutdown. The doctors, infectious disease experts, epidemiologists, and thousands of other influencers promoting staying-at-home, social distancing, and other measures? They too were immune. Whether their recommendations were common sense or draconian overreach, they got paid regardless. Indeed, they had a very strong financial incentive to hype the pandemic's danger, as the hysteria they fostered guaranteed more readers, viewers, and listeners. To mix metaphors, politicians—feeling the pressure from the very rapid tightening of the Vise—rushed to the front of the paranoid parade and asserted leadership and took control. The media was all too happy to support that in breathless minute-by-minute reporting.

In my editorial, I argued that we needed to find a balance. We could work to protect public health while also ensuring that the economy continued to thrive. Under President Trump, the economy had been surging. The pandemic arrived at a moment of unprecedented American prosperity. I thought it would be dangerous and foolish to risk all that had been accomplished. I suggested that elite media voices, public health experts, and politicians everywhere should have their pay suspended for as long as the lockdowns lasted. That might ensure that "two weeks to stop the spread" really meant two weeks.

I saw all this happening, and I was worried. I thought of that Rahm Emanuel line, and the near certainty that the left would see the shutdown as a golden opportunity. I needed to speak out. But while some people loved the draft, other friends, colleagues, and media associates told me that my op-ed was too "mean-spirited" at a time like this. They said that to focus on anything other than the danger of the virus was callous. What was needed now was a single-minded focus on doing whatever was necessary to keep people safe. My friends were in the Vise, whether they knew it or not. And as it turned out, I was in the Vise as well. I decided not to pursue publication. I fell silent.

The American people are always generous in spirit. They are also instinctively trusting. With the media, the influencers, and the politicians united in their declaration that COVID-19 was a grave danger, the people acquiesced. President Trump had initially resisted the calls for extreme action. His characteristic optimism led him to insist that we could get through the crisis quickly. Yet as the pressure intensified, even a man famously resistant to the demands of the Vise began to shift his language.

When I consider that many of the wisest and most consistent conservatives I know found themselves unable to resist the hysteria of March 2020, I feel a little better about having fallen silent. Self-recriminations only get us so far—what matters is learning the lesson of our failures. What matters is making sure we are ready the next time. (There will be a "next time.")

The graph below reflects President Trump's evolution on COVID. It charts not only the spread of the virus, but also the effectiveness of the Vise upon his thinking and his pronouncements.[3]

Selected Donald Trump quotations and US COVID-19 cases

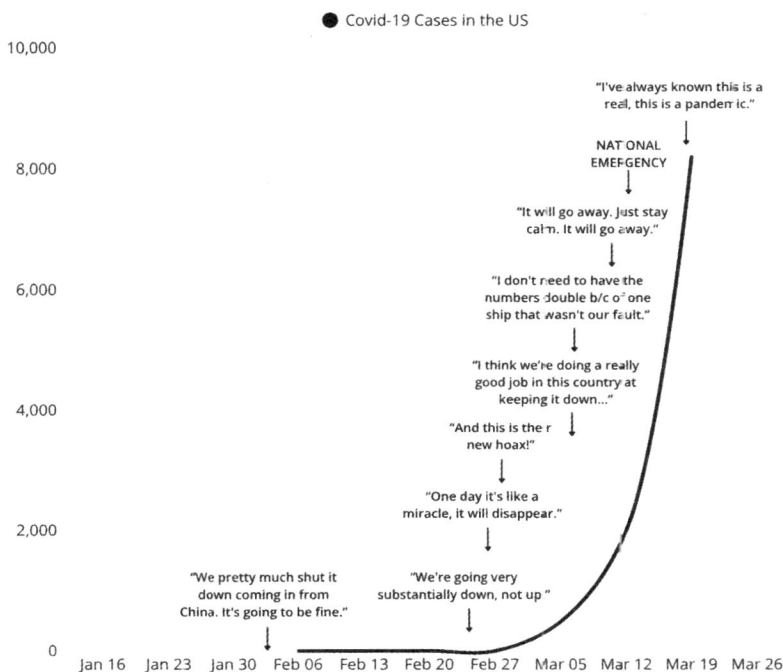

● Covid-19 Cases in the US

"I've always known this is a real, this is a pandemic."

NATIONAL EMERGENCY

"It will go away. Just stay calm. It will go away."

"I don't need to have the numbers double b/c of one ship that wasn't our fault."

"I think we're doing a really good job in this country at keeping it down..."

"And this is the r new hoax!"

"One day it's like a miracle, it will disappear."

"We pretty much shut it down coming in from China. It's going to be fine."

"We're going very substantially down, not up "

Jan 16   Jan 23   Jan 30   Feb 06   Feb 13   Feb 20   Feb 27   Mar 05   Mar 12   Mar 19   Mar 26

In hindsight, it is clear that President Trump's initial instincts were correct. When we compare the deaths and hospitalizations in New York—a state which locked down hard—with the deaths and hospitalizations in Florida, a state that did not abandon civil liberties, we see no evidence that the draconian approach saved more lives. Of course, evidence takes time to gather. The left was not interested in taking the time to assess the efficacy of various approaches. The left wanted lockdown, and they wanted it now. Under tremendous pressure from all sides of the Political Vise, the president gave in.

As the virus continued to spread both in the US and worldwide, the president, the COVID-19 Task Force, and others called for a "shelter in place" policy nationwide. Governors in numerous states followed, some even before the national policy was established. By March 21, across the vast expanse of the United States, people began to stay home, businesses closed, restaurants shut down, and service establishments from nail salons to fitness centers all shut their doors. Tens of millions of people began to lose income, and all too many permanently lost their jobs.

The stock market, with strong economic and job growth fueling it, had been at an all-time high. Employment was incredibly robust. In early 2020, there were more Americans working than ever before in history. We had the lowest unemployment since 1969, record-low African American unemployment, and record-low Hispanic unemployment. The income gap between the poor and middle class was closing. The American people were happily working, producing, and earning; together, we were building a brighter future for our country.

In a matter of just a few days, we destroyed all that hard-won progress. We committed economic self-immolation. The market crashed. Unemployment soared. Many called the virus a "black swan." (A black swan event is something very unexpected, often disastrously so, with lasting repercussions.) On April 24, 2020, the *Wall Street Journal*'s Holman Jenkins had the courage to tell the truth: "The black swan wasn't COVID-19. The black swan was the shutting down of the world's largest economy."[4] Just over a month into the pandemic, Jenkins was taking a considerable risk in resisting the Political Vise. I wish I had taken that same risk weeks earlier.

In the days that followed the initial declaration of the pandemic, new names and influencer personalities arrived in our living rooms and on our phones. Their message was always the same: if we did not bring our economy to a complete halt, countless Americans would die. President Trump chose Dr. Deborah Birx to head the coronavirus task force. Dr. Birx was a calm voice, disinclined to sensationalism. Realizing that she would not be a reliable ally in cranking the handle of the Vise, the media and influencers turned on her. Her measured approach was declared reckless, akin to "the builders of the Titanic saying the ship can't sink." The left quickly found someone whose alarmism was more suited to their agenda: Dr. Anthony Fauci. Fauci was promptly anointed as the scientist who best understood the threat of the virus. The media hung on his every word.

The elevation of Anthony Fauci to the rank of omnipotent and omniscient guru was a disaster. It was also quite deliberate. If you want to make sure that the opportunities created by crisis aren't wasted, you need to remind people that the crisis is both deadly and enduring. Fauci gave the left what it needed: a warning that the shutdowns would need to last much longer than two weeks, suggesting the threat posed by the virus would last for months, if not years.

The president was not so sure. No modern American leader has proven so immune to the pressures of the Political Vise as Donald Trump. He knew we needed to reopen the economy quickly. He could see the immense financial, psychological, social, and educational toll that even a brief shutdown would have. I do not fault the president for declaring an emergency or agreeing that we needed those famous "two weeks to stop the spread." Yet there is no escaping the unhappy truth that Trump's initial capitulation to the alarmists emboldened those who longed to take advantage of the crisis. The president gave them their proverbial inch—and they immediately demanded their mile.

When the president insisted it was up to him, not a group of doctors, to make decisions about reopening the economy, the press and progressive politicians would have none of it. Democrat governors, like J. B. Pritzker in Illinois, and local leaders, like Chicago Mayor Lori Lightfoot, called for the president—and all of us—to hand our autonomy over to the "professionals" instead of our elected representatives. Millions of Americans, successfully propagandized by the incessant fearmongering, went along, accepting the indefinite shutdowns and disruption as the only path to safety. Put another way, we were all in the Vise.

The shutting down of the economy was not the end goal of those turning the screws of the Vise. Saving lives wasn't the primary goal either, though it is certainly possible that many people did sincerely believe that lockdowns would slow or even stop the spread of COVID. For the left, the end goal was the opportunity to do what could only be done in a state of national emergency. Rahm Emanuel had advised never to let a crisis go to waste. It didn't matter whether the left had entirely manufactured the COVID threat or merely taken advantage of the emergence of a novel virus. Either way, they needed to plunge the nation into crisis in order to create the opportunity to do the heretofore unimaginable. COVID gave them the justification to destroy the economy—and then rebuild it on terms more to their liking. The immediate, colossal, and entirely predictable damage wrought by the shutdowns gave the Democrat politicians, the elite influencers, and their media allies the rationale to propose a radical solution to the devastating problem they themselves had created. That solution, of course, was the biggest stimulus bill in American history.

With the economy in freefall, many agreed that at least some federal stimulus was necessary. We could not force millions of Americans out of work, close down countless small businesses, and bring commerce to a halt without doing something to ameliorate the worst impacts of the shutdown. It would have been far better, of course, to avoid the lockdowns in the first place! As I've made clear, given the pressure of the Vise, that was an impossible argument to make. To my regret, I shelved my own attempt to make the case for keeping the country open. In politics, if you can't achieve the ideal thing, you do the next right thing. Once the shutdowns began, the next right thing was to limit the damage—and to try, as best we could, to restrain the left from taking full advantage of the crisis.

I was involved in a series of informal discussions with White House staff and policymakers from around the country. Our goal was to fashion a targeted stimulus that would help average Americans while restraining the left from inserting too many of their pet projects into the legislation. To be frank, we knew that it wasn't just the left that longed to spend recklessly. Plenty of Republicans as well as Democrats were putting forth some really dreadful ideas. The allure of a massive omnibus bill was too much temptation for most to resist. Both parties predictably delivered bad ideas, but even I was shocked by just how far Speaker Nancy Pelosi and Senate Minority Leader Chuck Schumer were willing to go. They certainly had no intention of letting a good crisis go to waste.

Here are just a handful of the outrageous things the Democrats inserted into the initial $2 trillion stimulus bill, none of which had anything to do with COVID-19:

- $25 million for the Kennedy Center
- Emission limitations for domestic airlines
- Up to three board seats on any airline that took stimulus money
- Impose collective bargaining rules upon the states
- A $15 per hour nationwide minimum wage
- $25 billion to the United States Postal Service (along with $11 million in debt forgiveness and, just for fun, authority to then borrow another $15 billion!)
- A bailout of underfunded pension systems to benefit coal miners, the Teamsters, and other labor unions
- Student loan reductions by $10,000 per student (which President Biden eventually attempted to do by executive fiat, later overturned by the US Supreme Court)

Kenneth Baer, the former communications director for President Obama's budget office, offered a rhetorical question to explain the Democrat strategy, telling *Politico*: "If you're going to Christmas-tree this up and spend $2 trillion, why not go big?" The Democrats knew perfectly well that some items on their wish list would not make it to President Trump's desk. They also knew that because of haste and a perceived sense of great urgency, many of those expensive goodies would slip through. Just to make certain that the bill got "Christmas-treed up," the powerful influencers—especially the public-employee unions, the Teamsters, and other special-interest groups—besieged Nancy Pelosi, Chuck Schumer, and every other member of Congress whom they thought they could pressure.[5] They called the final product the Coronavirus Aid, Relief, and Economic Security Act, or CARES Act. Combining the words "aid" and "relief" might seem redundant in other contexts, but given how much waste was crammed into the bill, it made perfect sense.

(Remember Senator Coburn's lament in the introduction that he was always asked for "one more thing" or "just this little request?" What happened with that initial COVID stimulus was Senator Coburn's experience, exponentially increased. Tom Coburn himself died of cancer on March 28, 2020, having lived just long enough to see his observations proven true once more.)

With both parties feeling the enormous pressure of the Vise—and its demand for a mammoth spending bill—very few in Washington had the courage to resist the crushing force coming from three sides. One who did was Representative Thomas Massie (R-KY). When he insisted that Congress hold an in-person vote on this massive bill, he was ridiculed and threatened. Massie wanted clarity and accountability. For his trouble, he got death threats and scorn. Even President Trump, caught up in the pervasive sense of crisis, excoriated Massie for daring to suggest that the bill was too big and too rushed. Like Luke Skywalker in the Death Star's trash compactor, Tom Massie got to feel just how intense and nasty the Vise's pressure can be.

Was all of this frantic effort on the part of politicians, elite influencers, and their media allies just to pass this one gargantuan bill? Was the hysteria and the fearmongering and the economic dislocation designed only to create the opportunity to decorate a single $2 trillion Christmas tree? No. The left made it clear that even this spending behemoth was a mere down payment. They had much more to spend, much more to change, much more to demand as part of their intended wholesale transformation of American society. Even as President Trump signed the CARES Act into law and the money began to flow, the Vise continued to tighten. Unfortunately, that initial bill became just the down payment on COVID-fueled deficit spending that drove our debt to over $35 trillion.

The theory of the Political Vise acknowledges that humans are often rational animals. When a certain behavior is rewarded, we want to repeat that behavior. As far as the left was concerned, the lesson of those early COVID days was that there are considerable rewards for generating a panic. Fortunately for America—and unfortunately for the progressives—conservatives and patriots began to resist those operating the Vise. President Trump pushed to reopen the country, while some red-state governors (led by Florida's Ron DeSantis) insisted on lifting the lockdowns, despite the dire warnings of the sainted Dr. Anthony Fauci.

By late April 2020, it was clear that the resistance had joined the battle. More and more Americans were holding out against the pressure of the Progressive Political Vise. With increasing courage, they started to question "the science" and the wisdom of a prolonged shutdown. Luke and Leia and the rest of their merry band were out of the trash compactor, as it were—but they were still on the Death Star. The left, having only accomplished a partial transformation of American society in that strange COVID spring, needed to find a new crisis through which to generate future opportunities. They would find it with the death of George Floyd. (More on that to come.)

The Political Vise is as old as America itself. As I explained in the introduction, our Founding Fathers understood how to use it. Thomas Jefferson and John Adams are not in living memory, but we all remember the COVID crisis, and we surely will for the rest of our lives. We have not yet had a reckoning over what we experienced—and we have not yet fully understood how the enemies of liberty took advantage of our fear. It is vital that we understand how the Progressive Political Vise was used so effectively against the American people just a few short years ago. It is even more imperative that we not only say "Never Again," but that we master the use of the Vise as our forefathers intended.

In the next few chapters, we'll explore each component of the Vise. We'll begin with, not surprisingly, the left side—the media.

Chapter 4

THE MEDIA, PART ONE:
CHANGE THE CHANNELS

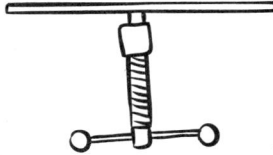

A truth: All media is biased. The question is whether the media is transparent and authentic about that bias.

In the first strange weeks of the COVID lockdowns, New York Governor Andrew Cuomo became a media superstar. With the Empire State suffering the worst effects of the coronavirus, Cuomo's daily press briefings became must-see TV for millions of house-bound Americans. On April 3, 2020, the *Times Union* declared Cuomo had become "the pandemic's most authoritative and trustworthy voice."[6] The paper reported that Cuomo enjoyed a 90% popularity rating, reflecting a nearly unimaginable consensus among normally curmudgeonly New Yorkers. It wasn't just his constituents taking part in the lovefest. Some Democrats suggested that the party should dump their shaky presumptive nominee, Joe Biden, and put the sure-handed Cuomo at the top of the ticket.

Just sixteen months later, Andrew Cuomo would resign in disgrace, undone by charges of sexual harassment, corruption, and lying about the staggering COVID death toll in nursing homes. Cuomo's fall was almost Shakespearean in its totality and rapidity. It was a reminder that the media has the power to create any narrative it likes and to elevate to super-stardom anyone it chooses. It can also ruin nearly anyone, including its former darlings. The media does these things without ever taking responsibility for their central role in creating and then destroying heroes. CNN, MSNBC, the *Washington Post,* the *New York Times*, and all the other outlets that constitute the media elite make the same claim: they impartially report the facts. When Andrew Cuomo ascended into the stratosphere, it was because of his competence and his leadership; when he fell from grace, it was because of his own misdeeds. The media claims to have had nothing to do with it.

You know better. We all know better. We know that the media—particularly at the elite levels—is heavily biased. What we don't always understand is just how effective the media is at turning the screws of the Political Vise in order to cajole, coerce, and crush the American people. We know that the media has always played a role in American politics. We do not yet fully grasp how dramatically that role has changed. The events of the last few years provide a case study in just how pernicious that influence has become. They also provide reasons to hope that the elite media's control of the Vise can be broken.

Various dictionaries define media as the means of communication, using newspapers, radio, television, and the internet. Most of the complaints about media bias refer to the news media—the institutions and platforms responsible for informing the public about what is happening in the world. I'm primarily focused on "the news" as well, but it bears noting that entertainment can have a tremendous impact on public opinion. Think, for example, how the popular television sitcoms *Will & Grace* and *Modern Family* advanced the cause of gay rights.

No matter how young you are, you've seen the media landscape transform in your lifetime. Particularly since the advent of social media within the last decade and a half, how we get our news has changed radically. As new platforms arrive to help us to connect, share, and inform, the efforts of the elites to control what we read and watch have become more intense, more dangerous, and—fortunately—more obvious. What you may not realize is that the news media is returning to what it was more than a century ago.

A History Lesson

In April 1896, thirty-eight-year-old Adolph Ochs purchased the struggling *New York Times*. In the 1890s, newspapers did not strive for impartiality. The two biggest papers in the city (and the nation) were Joseph Pulitzer's *New York World* and William Randolph Hearst's *New York Journal*. The *World* and the *Journal* were locked in a fierce circulation battle, each trying to outdo the other with coverage of scandal and corruption. Both papers were partisan and made no secret of their biases. Ochs figured he couldn't compete with Hearst and Pulitzer in sensationalism. He decided to try a novel marketing tactic for his new acquisition: objective journalism.

On April 18, 1896, Ochs published his first op-ed, laying out his agenda:

> It will be my earnest aim that THE NEW-YORK TIMES give the news, all the news, in concise and attractive form, in language that is parliamentary in good society, and give it as early, if not earlier, than it can be learned through any other reliable medium; to give the news impartially, without fear or favor, regardless of party, sect, or interests involved; to make the columns of THE NEW-YORK TIMES a forum for the consideration of all questions of public importance, and to that end to invite intelligent discussion from all shades of opinion.[7]

"To give the news impartially, without fear or favor" was, in the beginning, less a declaration of ethical intent than a shrewd marketing ploy. In the crowded marketplace, "objective journalism" could be a desirable niche. Over the years, Ochs and his descendants (who still own and publish the *Times*) would speak of this impartiality as a journalistic ideal to which all should aspire. What started as a clever strategy to differentiate the *Times* from its two main rivals morphed into a moral claim to which every other news outlet would, in time, be expected to declare allegiance.

Some thirty years after Ochs took over the *New York Times*, another inflection point: On November 15, 1926, the National Broadcasting Company launched itself with a gala radio event, carried on twenty-two stations across the East and the Midwest. Less than a year later, the second Gene Tunney/Jack Dempsey world heavyweight boxing match became the first truly national, coast-to-coast, live broadcast event. By the end of the decade, millions of Americans owned radios and tuned in to a rapidly increasing number of sports, news, and variety programs. All of this programming was sustained by advertising—and given the huge size of the audience on radio, advertisers were eager to ensure that the broadcasts were neither offensive nor partisan. Democrats and Republicans both use soap—and at the time, both Democrats and Republicans smoked cigarettes. There was no point in offending either. "Objectivity" made good marketing sense.

Over the following decades, America witnessed an extraordinary consolidation of news media. Newspapers merged or forced their rivals out of business. Cities that had once had a dozen morning papers now had only one. Broadcasting networks quickly grabbed control of almost all independent radio stations. Aided by both government and advertisers, a very small cadre of media elites soon exercised near-total narrative control over what Americans watched, read, and learned. This consolidation continued into nearly the end of the twentieth century. Three broadcast networks, two major newsweeklies, and a dozen or so major newspapers created *mass* communications for the first time in human history.

On the one hand, mass communication could bring people, communities, and an entire nation together. Watching a Super Bowl, the series finale of *M*A*S*H*, or coverage of the Challenger disaster gave Americans simultaneous shared experiences to a degree that had never been possible before. Witnessing history at the same time as everyone else can be incredibly unifying. On the other hand, consolidation meant that a very small group of very powerful people could decide what it was we all saw and heard. A handful of men in New York, Washington, DC, and Los Angeles decided what would get reported as the news of the day.

There's considerable nostalgia for what seems like a simple age. I run into people often who tell me that they remember fondly the golden age of network television news. They'd spent half an hour every evening as Walter Cronkite (CBS), Harry Reasoner (ABC), or John Chancellor (NBC) told them what they needed to know. When I remind them that the content of these broadcasts was carefully curated by a tiny elite, my friends nod. They get it intellectually. They still feel a fondness for what seemed like a more trusting era. It is hard to accept that even Walter Cronkite worked in the service of an agenda. Cronkite may have been a personally principled journalist, but he was, in the end, an employee of a particular media conglomerate—itself largely controlled by one man (the late mogul William S. Paley).

In a previous chapter, I noted that even Supreme Court justices with lifetime tenure are not immune from the pressures of the Vise. They care about what their friends think. They care about what their biographers will say. The same is true for the elites who ran the major newspapers and broadcast networks. They shaped the news to reflect their values and their priorities. They may have believed they were acting "without fear or favor," as Adolph Ochs had promised, but their courage was limited and hedged in by self-interest. The problem isn't that these elites allowed their own convictions to shape the news. The problem is that they denied that that's what they were doing. *They dressed up their bias as objectivity and denounced as irresponsible any suggestion otherwise.* There were very few gates through which information could flow. The gatekeepers were very powerful indeed.

Re-Fragmentation

By the late 1990s, widespread access to the Internet—along with the increasing popularity of cable television—began a process of what I call re-fragmentation of the media. The three major networks and a handful of influential urban papers began to lose their decades-long monopoly on the news. The Drudge Report began as a very simple website in 1995. Matt Drudge ran the site from his apartment in Los Angeles, collecting gossip and sharing insider information. On August 10, 1996, he scooped all the major networks and papers with the news that Republican presidential nominee Bob Dole had selected Jack Kemp as his running mate. It was the first time a website had been the first to break a major story. In February 1998, Drudge would get a much bigger scoop when his site became the first to report on President Clinton's affair with a staffer named Monica Lewinsky.

Over the next twenty years, this "re-fragmentation process" would result in an extraordinary proliferation of online and cable news outlets. Ratings for the major network news programs plummeted, as consumers now had a far greater array of options at their fingertips. I'll share just one data point: In 1981, Walter Cronkite's final year as anchor of the CBS Evening News, he garnered an average of 29 million nightly viewers from a total population of 220 million, meaning that 13.1% of the public tuned in to watch him. In 2024, CBS Evening News averaged 4.9 million viewers out of a population of 342 million. That's just 1.4%. Everyone knew who Walter Cronkite was. Do you know who the CBS Evening News anchor is today? (I didn't either. I had to look it up: Norah O'Donnell.)

Across the country, dozens of newspapers have ceased publication in recent years, unable to compete in the marketplace. These aren't just small-town papers; in 2024, even the venerable *Los Angeles Times* laid off half its newsroom. Two national papers, however, have bucked the trend. Almost entirely on the basis of digital subscriptions, the *New York Times* and *Washington Post* have increased circulation—and sustained their enormous influence. How have they done it? By overtly inserting left-wing opinion into their news content. Since 2016 and the election of Donald Trump, the *Post* and the *Times* have positioned themselves as the voice of the resistance to the MAGA movement. They recognize that their progressive subscribers are hungrier for "blue meat" than for sober analysis, and they have adapted to meet that demand.

When challenged on their increasingly obvious partisanship, legacy media like the *Post* and the *Times* shift back and forth between two different responses. The first is to claim that they have not abandoned objectivity at all. They insist that they are still practicing journalism as Adolph Ochs declared it should be practiced, "without fear or favor." When it becomes unbearably obvious that the *Times*, or the *Post*, or CNN is showing "favor" to one side, the legacy journalists declare that Donald Trump and the MAGA movement pose a threat so great that objectivity itself is an unaffordable luxury. As left-wing journalist Sean Illing wrote in a widely circulated 2020 column, "The obsession with 'objectivity' in particular has led to an obsession with 'balance' or 'fairness' that makes it easy for bad-faith actors to get away with pushing falsehoods."[8] Putting "balance" and "fairness" in scare quotes makes it clear: the progressive media believe that if they want to wield power—and turn the screws of the Political Vise—then old-fashioned objectivity is for losers. In the de-fragmented marketplace, and with the existential urgency of confronting the terrifying specter of Donald Trump and his supporters, you can only survive through ever more naked partisanship.

The biggest risk to the likes of the *Times* and the *Post* is not that they will be perceived as abandoning objectivity. The biggest risk is that their affluent, progressive readership will complain that they are too timid and too eager to engage in "both-sidesism." (That's a neologism created by the left. You can probably tell it's a slur.) In June 2020, the *New York Times* published an op-ed by Senator Tom Cotton, a Republican from Arkansas. The senator suggested we should send in federal troops to secure cities ravaged by days of looting and destruction in the aftermath of the death of George Floyd. The decision to publish the op-ed was met with howls of indignation, staff resignations, and canceled subscriptions. How dare the *Times* allow anyone to suggest that the rioting wasn't entirely justified?

The "paper of record" repented quickly. They attached a long disclaimer to the online version of the Cotton op-ed, confessing "the essay fell short of our standards and should not have been published."[9] James Bennet, the *Times* editorial page editor who approved the essay, was forced to resign in disgrace. Bennet's cancellation was both a *mea culpa* on the part of the *Times* and a warning to other journalists about the professional risks of continuing to embrace objectivity.

The legacy media's commitment to pandering to their progressive readership goes far beyond apologizing for daring to publish a conservative essayist. What happened to Tom Cotton and James Bennet may have been infuriating and cowardly, but it did not amount to outright journalistic malfeasance. It did not constitute election interference. The suppression of the Hunter Biden laptop story, on the other hand, was a striking reminder of the brazen collusion between the left and the media. In October 2020, less than a month before the presidential election, the media and the Biden campaign conspired to suppress a scandal. They kept Americans in the dark about a major scandal that, had it been more thoroughly exposed, might very well have changed the outcome of what turned out to be a very close election.

On October 14, 2020, the *New York Post* (founded by Alexander Hamilton in 1801 but now derided by the left as an unserious tabloid) published an article detailing emails that had been found on Hunter Biden's personal computer.[10] The emails revealed that in 2015, the younger Biden had introduced his father—then the vice president—to the head of the Ukrainian firm Burisma. Burisma later hired Hunter to serve on its board, paying him $50,000 per month. The elder Biden later pressured Ukrainian government officials to fire a state prosecutor who was investigating Burisma for corruption. As the *Post* reported (tactfully), other contents of the laptop included images and videos of Hunter engaged in sexual activity and smoking crack.

I probably don't need to remind you what happened next. As the *Post* wrote in an unsigned editorial a year later on October 12, 2021:

> One year ago, The Post revealed that Hunter Biden's abandoned laptop carried proof he sold influence while his father served

as vice president—and his dad, now president, knew it. Yet most other media treated the story itself as the scandal, reporting only on vague claims that sought to undermine it rather than rushing (as they would've under the last president) to advance it themselves.[11]

The bold emphasis is mine. The *Post's* editors had a right to be angry, but frankly, their reaction undersells the scale of the elite suppression of this important story.

The Progressive Political Vise can move very swiftly. Within days, some fifty members of the intelligence community (overwhelmingly Democrats) published an open letter, declaring that the laptop story bore all the signs of a Russian disinformation campaign. They produced no evidence. The left-wing media, eager to discredit a story that could prove hugely damaging to the Biden campaign, treated this open letter as if it were the final word on the matter. The *Post* reporters who broke the story were mocked, and the paper that Hamilton had founded was dismissed as a partisan gossip rag. (A fairly obvious instance of the proverbial pot calling the kettle black.)

That the Biden campaign would collude with legacy papers like the *New York Times* was not a surprise. Far more troubling and surprising was the active role that pre-Elon Musk Twitter, YouTube, and Facebook took in suppressing the Hunter Biden laptop story. For days, it was impossible to find a link to the *Post* story on Twitter—which by 2020 represented itself as the indispensable site for breaking news. Twitter executives actively suppressed the link, offering only the implausible excuse that the original *Post* article violated their site policy on hacked materials. It quickly became clear that the social media behemoths were acting in concert with legacy media and the wishes of the Biden campaign.

Perhaps the most important result of the blatant quashing of the laptop story was that it ended any remaining illusion that the giants of "new" media were non-partisan. Facebook, originally a site only available to college students, opened its digital doors to the general public in 2007.

Facebook made no declaration of objectivity, a la Adolph Ochs. After all, all the content was user-created. Whether you leaned left or right, you could post your views, your recipes, and lists of your favorite songs when you were in high school. Twitter appeared in 2008, and it too seemed radically neutral. You tweeted what you liked, you found folks to follow whose tweets you enjoyed, and when you opened up your phone or your laptop, you found those tweets listed in reverse chronological order.

Social media's promise was immense: instant connection with friends old and new, and unfettered discussions of culture, sports, and politics. It was understood that these new social media platforms would censor illegal material. No one objected to Twitter deleting child pornography. Few complained when Facebook refused to allow ISIS to post their gruesome beheading videos. Many, especially conservatives, saw social media as a precious opportunity to provide a counternarrative to the progressive legacy media. Frankly, we on the right were naïve in our enthusiasm for these new platforms. We assumed that the tech executives in Silicon Valley were mostly free-thinking libertarians, gleefully immune to the pressures of the Vise. Few of us anticipated that not only were these tech leaders not immune to pressure, but they would also themselves become enthusiastic turners of the Vise.

After Elon Musk purchased Twitter in 2022, he coordinated the release of what became known as the Twitter Files. Released in a series of install-ments, the files provided damning evidence of a years-long pattern of bias against conservative viewpoints. Right-wing voices were subject to "shadow-banning" if not outright de-platforming. The files revealed that despite some internal dissent, Twitter executives decided to actively suppress the Hunter Biden laptop story in October 2020. Less than three months later, that same leadership would ban President Donald Trump from the platform. Musk revealed a truth that had become obvious to many: Twitter, the site that had become the indispensable global forum for breaking news and conversation, was neither neutral nor objective. The platform that marketed itself as a place safe from the pressures of the Vise was actively engaged in crushing viewpoints it didn't like. Even cynical observers of the political scene were shaken by the scope and scale of the bias that the Twitter Files revealed.

The left was quick to note that the Twitter Files revealed no clear evidence that the Biden campaign had asked social media sites to suppress the story about Hunter's laptop. I'm not sure that's quite true—as any lawyer can tell you, absence of evidence is not evidence of absence. It's possible to maintain plausible deniability while also exerting real pressure. Think of a mob boss, musing about a rival. "Sure would be sad if something happened to that guy." The mob boss doesn't need to spell out what he wants done; his henchmen understand that what seems like an idle musing is in fact an order to whack someone.

But let's stipulate that no one from the Biden campaign called Twitter executives and demanded they block links to that *New York Post* story. The Progressive Political Vise doesn't work because left-wing politicians browbeat the media into compliance. The legacy media has long been the Democratic Party's willing accomplice, needing no coercion or prodding to advance a particular agenda. The Twitter Files exposed the simple reality that Silicon Valley tech executives were no different than the editorial staff at the *New York Times* or CNN.

If the Biden *campaign* was willing to use political pressure to stop a story they didn't like, the Biden *administration* proved far more ruthless in its commitment to controlling the narrative. In early 2022, without any public notification, the administration created the Orwellian-sounding "Disinformation Governance Board." Officially just an advisory panel nested in the Department of Homeland Security, the board was headed by Nina Jankowicz, a Bryn Mawr graduate whose chief claim to fame was writing a book entitled *How to Be a Woman Online: Surviving Abuse and Harassment, and How to Fight Back*. Under Jankowicz's direction, the Disinformation Governance Board claimed to be focused primarily on Russian meddling. In reality, when questioned by Congress, Jankowicz declared "there was a broad vision for what the board would do but (refused) to offer specifics."[12] It was clear to virtually everyone that the Board had no intention of limiting its brief to combatting foreign propaganda. Fortunately, after tremendous backlash, Homeland Security Director Alejandro Mayorkas reluctantly agreed to disband the board.

The Biden administration did not rely on a single Disinformation Board to pressure the media. In 2024 the Supreme Court heard *Murthy v. Missouri* (originally known as *Missouri v. Biden*). The case was a consolidation of a series of suits filed by Eric Schmitt, the one-time Missouri attorney general who now serves as the state's junior United States senator. Schmitt filed suit against "President Biden and other top-ranking government officials for allegedly working with social media giants such as Meta, Twitter, and YouTube to censor and suppress free speech, including truthful information, related to COVID-19, election integrity, and other topics, under the guise of combating 'misinformation.'"[13]

Many people, including me, hoped and expected the court to rule in favor of the plaintiffs and find the government had in fact compelled a curtailing of speech. The 6-3 ruling said that the plaintiffs had not established that there was a controversy in question, nor did they have standing. Months later Mark Zuckerberg, the founder of Facebook, issued a letter noting that Facebook was, in fact, compelled by the government to curtail free speech. Too little too late, when it came to Murthy.

The Murthy decision does not end the debate. While the circumstances of the government trampling on the speech rights of its citizens, either through proxies or directly, did not meet the court's threshold this time, the issue is not fading away. The government has developed a rapacious appetite to control our speech. They will not stop. In fact, their hubris will only grow.

Our efforts to protect speech must meet this challenge. To use a phrase of which I am fond, we cannot cede the commanding heights of culture to one political party or to one ideology. Culture is largely shaped and defined by speech, and media communications are core to that speech. Regardless of the Supreme Court's ruling in the Missouri case, those of us who are committed to liberty and to American ideals still must fight. When the legacy media and most social media platforms are entirely under the control of the left, it isn't enough to push back against the government's attempts to control what we read, watch, say, and hear. As in the example of the mob boss, if the worldview of deep-state bureaucrats is fundamentally aligned with that of those who own and manage media outlets, it's not always necessary for the state to spell out its desires.

Barring a Biden administration from directly instructing tech platforms to take down information they don't like is, of course, important. Unfortunately, too often, the platforms will censor and shadow-ban without any prompting. Further, shadow-banning comes in many forms—just search Google to find out how conservative news outlets are pushed pages down in the results that people submit. Those outlets are being shadow-banned and de-monetized by that purposeful algorithm. Remember the diagram of the Progressive Political Vise? The media, the politicians, and the powerful influencers put the squeeze on the American people. *It's not enough to point out that the media and the left-wing politicians are coordinating their efforts. To return the Political Vise to its original intent, we must build independent channels of media distribution.*

Elon Musk's bold decision to purchase Twitter (now renamed X) was a rare and welcome victory for free speech. He paid a high price, literally and figuratively, to acquire the social media site. Though his tenure at X has been controversial to people on the left, there's no question that he has done much to restore the platform to its original purpose. Musk's willingness to disclose the details of Twitter's own acquiescence to government pressure—especially regarding the Biden laptop story and a host of issues related to COVID-19—has validated and verified the suspicions of many conservatives.

Like many, I'm grateful to Elon Musk for all he has done and continues to do. At the same time, I know we cannot rely on a single wealthy visionary, no matter how dedicated and inspired he may be. There is no substitute for building our own enduring, flexible media institutions—institutions that can effectively work the Political Vise for "We the People." To do that in the long term, we cannot depend on a single individual. That's true even in the case of an even more influential figure than Elon Musk: Donald Trump. He has been a singular target for the media for the past decade. No human being in our recent political history has been so relentlessly squeezed by the Progressive Political Vise—and no one living has better demonstrated not only how to *resist* the pressure but to *apply* it.

I began this chapter with the story of Andrew Cuomo, who in that strange spring of 2020 enjoyed a few blissful weeks as the media's anointed hero. When they were done with him, they cast him down. Andrew Cuomo has now re-emerged as a news anchor for his second act in American public life—he is making strides back because he is a creature of the left. By contrast, the media has spent a decade trying to destroy Donald Trump. To a degree that they themselves cannot explain, they have failed time and time again. Like him or despise him, President Trump is a singular individual. Just as we cannot rely on Elon Musk to singlehandedly defend liberty, we cannot rely on Donald Trump alone to guide us in better deploying the Political Vise. What we can and must do, however, is learn the valuable lesson that Trump's example teaches about the media and power.

From cable news to search engines to podcasts to film to music to the arts and culture, it is the media that informs the people, the politicians, and the elite influencers. For the people to regain control of the Vise and its awesome power, we must invest in building media capacity.

While building liberty-loyal media capacity is essential, it is still not sufficient. We must also force reform upon those using media to attack the people's sovereignty. For those that refuse to reform, we must neuter their ability to have outsized influence and, in some cases, destroy their ability to garner audience.

One way to do this is to reveal the inherent biases in all media practitioners. As noted, the era of objective journalism was never actually true. Media has returned to its true nature—filled with opinion, advocacy and, all too often, gaslighting distortions and lies. But the solution is not the censorship complex now all too familiar; the solution is transparency on the biases all media practitioners possess.

Perhaps you are familiar with IMDb, the central warehouse of all things in film. Every writer, actor, director, producer, and more is listed there. An interested party can see the body of work of a given person or can look at a film and see who all was involved in it. For film buffs, it is a wonderful information tool that enlightens and educates the user.

Shouldn't we have a version of that for media? A go-to site listing every reporter, editor, producer, podcaster, on-air talent, booker (bookers are those who find guests for news shows; whom you choose to book largely determines the content you will see), and more.

Such a site should rate these media practitioners by their transparency versus opaqueness. A progressive reporter who is overtly progressive would receive a high transparency rating, as would a conservative reporter who is overtly conservative. But hide who you are, and your transparency rating will be negative. This should be part of a system that rewards authenticity and punishes the posers, the fabricators, the fellow travelers, and all who hide their true selves. (I'm thinking of you, Jake Tapper.)

With such a site, news consumers can take in news with a better understanding of the sources they choose. Over time, it is my belief that the progressive news outlets that are dishonest will be de-trafficked and thus neutered.

Wouldn't it be great if someone built this? It is a massive, audacious undertaking, to be sure, but the value it would provide to the American news consumer would be transformational. Well, I believe in this so much that I founded MediaPedia.org. We have a long way to go to bring the full vision to life, but we are well on our way. Please go to the site and subscribe—it's free, but the news enlightenment you will receive is priceless!

Chapter 5

THE MEDIA, PART TWO: REACHING THE MASSES, ONE BY ONE

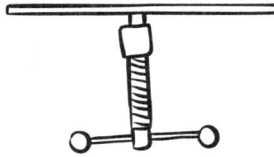

Consider the following: Donald Trump got 65 million votes in 2016. He got 75 million four years later. (He surpassed 77 million in 2024, an extraordinary, rare achievement.) What matters to most, of course, is that he won in 2016—and lost in 2020. The question of whether the latter election was stolen or merely "rigged" (as Mollie Hemingway suggests in her indispensable post-mortem[14]) is beyond the scope of this book. What is undeniable is that in 2020 it took extraordinarily well-coordinated machinations in the midst of a pandemic to ensure that those 75 million votes weren't enough to win. What is so impressive to me is that despite the near-universal hostility of legacy media throughout his presidency, President Trump was able to substantially increase his voter outreach. Much of that was due to his instinctive understanding of how to deploy his own media.

Whatever one thinks of Donald Trump, conservatives have much to learn from him, both in terms of how best to use existing media and how, when necessary, to create our own. President Trump's record-high popularity is a testament to his indefatigable energy, but also a testament to the way he cultivates his relationship with his supporters. The Progressive Political Vise has never been weaponized quite as extensively as it has been against Donald Trump. That he has resisted the pressure so well for so long is astonishing. His re-election, while spending about one-third the money that Kamala Harris spent, shows how building your own media and connecting directly with your voters is a winning strategy.

When you think of Donald Trump's use of the media, you probably think of Twitter (now known as X). From the time he joined the social media site in May 2009 until he was banned in January 2021, Trump tweeted more than 57,000 times. He posted over 25,000 tweets over the course of his presidency, an average of more than 17 tweets per day. President Trump's tweets made news, and they offered him a direct channel to his supporters. Long before Twitter finally took away his account after the January 6 Capitol riots, many in the legacy media had been loudly pleading for the site to ban him. It wasn't just that they thought the tweets were "mean" or "racist"; it was that the president's skillful deployment of Twitter allowed him to sustain an unfettered connection with his base.

When Elon Musk bought X, he restored Donald Trump's account. Not until August of 2024 did Trump resume using X. Trump marked his return in the splashiest possible way: with a live interview on X with Musk himself. While estimates are all over the map, tens of millions saw some of the interview, a massive direct engagement with the public. Trump once again showed he knows how to reach voters and bypass the legacy players. Further, that appearance is but one example of his ability to influence and sometimes control the cultural narrative.

Trump continues to use his own platform, Truth Social, daily. Whatever the future of either platform, it's worth remembering that neither site is the only way to bypass traditional media. When it comes to Trump in particular, it's easy to forget that in addition to those famous tweets, his team connected with voters using a wide variety of traditional and emerging technologies. As it turns out, much of what Trump and his people did—with great success—was to follow a script that my team and I had developed years earlier in Illinois.

It's strange to think of 2012 as ancient history. Yet when you remember that in that year, a centrist like Mitt Romney—distrusted by legions of conservatives—could coast to the Republican nomination, you realize that the world has changed utterly. In 2012, Donald Trump still had three more seasons ahead of him hosting *The Celebrity Apprentice*. Barack Obama's divisive second term still lay ahead of us. Taylor Swift was still making country music. And at Illinois Policy, I hired Ryan Green, one of the first dedicated digital professionals in think tank history.

I brought on Ryan because I knew we needed help. We had just 8,000 emails in our database. Our "open rate" for emails was less than 10%. If you're not familiar with the industry, let me assure you that that is bad. You aim for 30% or above; an open rate below 20% is considered unacceptable in the marketing business. We were not even halfway to acceptable. Ryan had done some work in public policy, but he was primarily an expert on digital and social media in the private sector. I hired him with a plea: Turn this around. My vision was to build a twenty-first-century direct marketing channel down to individual people. We eventually called this our "owned audience strategy." This would allow us to bypass the legacy media as much as possible and more directly control our outreach. Ryan, and the team he built, succeeded. He went on to cofound our marketing agency, and he is also a highly regarded thought leader in digital and social media in the policy and advocacy community.

Today, in Illinois alone, we have more than 2.5 million people in our database with names, emails, and zip codes. We created a "data collection funnel" by putting compelling content in people's social media feeds. In return, they opted in by providing their name, zip code, email address, and sometimes their cell phone number. We continue to add millions more all across the nation. (Want to opt into our database and get some awesome content? Go to ThePoliticalVise.com to sign up!) We have matched most of them with the voter file and other consumer databases. Every single one of these people has "opted in" voluntarily (and can opt out anytime, of course). Our open rate is over 30% for our active members. *The reason*

*they are in and stay in is because our team continually creates compelling
content that appeals to them as individuals.*

Remember, the overarching goal is to be able to use the Political Vise
to advance the cause of liberty once again. That vital outcome is, at least
in part, the result of imaginative work to beat the operators of the Progressive Political Vise at their own game.

What we realized is that sometimes, the imaginative work of creating
compelling content is about the effective repackaging of legacy media. One
night in 2015, Michael Lucci—at the time, our vice president of policy—
appeared on the local CBS affiliate's 10:00 p.m. newscast. He was on the
show to discuss what was then a revelation, but which is now a familiar
story: Illinois was losing population. (As of the most recent census figures,
the Land of Lincoln has experienced net outmigration for an astonishing
ten years in a row.) About 186,000 households tuned in to that broadcast.
(Local news stations have shed even more viewers since.) It's hard to know
how many of those 186,000 actually paid attention to Michael's segment.
They may have been talking to a loved one, scrolling on their phones, or
getting a snack.

What we do know is that Ryan and his team packaged up that segment
and put it on Facebook. Over 600,000 people viewed that Facebook clip,
with well over 200,000 watching the segment in its entirety. As you know,
clicking through to watch a video clip online requires more active intent
than slumping on the couch in front of the tube. No matter how you think
of it, we got higher "ratings" than Chicago's CBS2. We have gone on to
repeat and adapt this packaging practice many times, giving Illinois Policy
in effect our own television station. Yes, to be fair, it's an apples-to-oranges
comparison. Illinois Policy did not film Lucci's interview. We didn't produce
his original appearance. What we did do is find a way to repurpose that
clip in order to help inform the media narrative.

Innovation and adaptation are critical to any political movement.
Repurposing the CBS2 clip onto our Facebook page was a successful innovation. The danger is that it is easy to look at that anecdote and say

reflexively, "This proves that social media is the way forward!" Social media is *one* way forward, of course. Yet we wouldn't have had the clip in the first place had Lucci not engaged with potentially hostile legacy media. We didn't rely on a local broadcast channel to be our sole means of getting out our message—but we also didn't turn down the opportunity to take advantage of the platform they offered.

As I argued in the last chapter, there's no question that legacy media is biased. Journalistic objectivity itself began more as a marketing strategy than as a foundational principle. Put simply, for conservatives, the legacy media is not our friend. That doesn't mean, however, that it's a wise idea to refuse to engage with the major television networks or the *New York Times*. To turn the screws of the Political Vise, you need to do more than offer encouragement to those who already share your principles. As the old saying goes, you don't just want to preach your sermons to the choir. You need to persuade people who may not have had the chance to consider your views. When legacy media offers that opening, you seize it.

Remember Senator Tom Cotton's June 2020 op-ed in the *New York Times?* Published just as dozens of American cities were under attack from looters and rioters, Cotton's plea for public safety and the restoration of order sparked howls of outrage from progressives on the *Times* staff. The opinion page editor resigned, and the *Times* issued a groveling apology for having run the piece. It was a bad look for the "paper of record" and further proof that the proverbial lunatics were running the asylum. But none of that means that Senator Cotton made a mistake by penning the piece. Regardless of whether he knew that his essay would attract intense blowback or not, he guessed—rightly—that he would persuade at least some readers. Just as importantly, he probably knew that the violent reaction to his op-ed would only prove the merit of his point.

I've heard friends ask questions like this one: "Why would a genuine conservative want to write for the *New York Times?* They hate us!" Believe me, I'm sympathetic to that view. At the same time, refusing to engage with biased media constitutes a missed opportunity. That opportunity isn't just about reaching the unpersuaded, either. "High value" media placements help with donors and activists. When CBS2 interviewed Lucci, they didn't just give him a platform—they legitimized him as an expert. Like it or not, when legacy media cites a scholar or an activist, even if they do so with thinly disguised hostility, they validate that person's credibility. That has enduring value—and that value can be leveraged.

Politicians place great value on media placements. That can be more complicated an observation than it first appears. For example, conservative Republican senator from Arkansas Tom Cotton doesn't care much about what the *New York Times* staff thinks of him. He does care, and rightly so, that the orgy of pearl-clutching disdain with which his op-ed was greeted by the left boosted his national reputation. To the average American, the left's hysterical reaction to his reasonable assertion (that mass violence should not be tolerated) helped prove a longstanding point about the bias and irrationality of the media elite.

To be fair, politicians loathe media placements that they perceive as hostile. In November 2017, the *National Review*—one of the flagship journals of American conservatism—ran a cover story on Illinois Governor Bruce Rauner, calling him the "Worst Republican Governor" in America.[15] Rauner, his wife, and his entire team were all livid—at me.

I had a long history with Governor Rauner. In an earlier chapter, I told the story of our Supreme Court win in *Janus v. AFSCME*. You might remember that the governor had played a role in getting that fight for worker freedom started. As head of Illinois Policy, I had been thrilled when Rauner had been elected in 2014—many people had thought it would be impossible to ever elect a Republican again to statewide office in Illinois. Rauner had proved them wrong, and I was happy to work—pro bono—for him in the middle of his first term. As was his prerogative, Rauner rejected much of my counsel, and it became untenable for me to continue.

It is very hard for any Republican governor to use the Political Vise effectively when the state legislature is in Democrat hands. This was especially true in Illinois, where we faced a state House of Representatives controlled by one of the most canny, crafty, and experienced politicians I've ever observed—Michael Madigan. I had a strategy for standing up to Madigan, but as time went on, Rauner decided on a different approach. In August 2017, the governor signed a bill into law that provided for taxpayer funding of abortion across the state. I had strongly urged Governor Rauner not to take that course, and he had initially given me his word that he wouldn't sign the abortion bill. More importantly, he gave his word to Cardinal Blaise Cupich, the Archbishop of Chicago. When the governor went back on his promise and signed the bill, the Cardinal was understandably furious—as were dozens of State House Republicans. The pro-choice advocates, of course, were over the moon.

Rauner's support on the right unraveled completely. Yet I got the blame for the *National Review* piece. Because I was a go-to on media placement, and because I—and other figures in Illinois Policy—had aligned with or served his administration in one capacity or another, Bruce Rauner's loyalists assumed that I'd planted that damning cover story. As a result, they ended up trying to use the Political Vise against me in early 2018, an unpleasant experience that is seared into my memory. (I suspect you already know that politics can be a dirty, nasty business!)

I survived the hits. Governor Rauner didn't. His flip-flop on abortion and a host of other issues had infuriated his conservative base. Generally, when incumbents run for re-election, they don't face serious primary challenges from their own party. Because of his perceived betrayals, Rauner had to fend off a very intense primary rival in Jeanne Ives, one of the most well-informed fighters for liberty I have ever observed. The governor barely prevailed in that primary, and then got clobbered in the November 2018 general election. Rauner got only 39% of the vote against Democrat billionaire J. B. Pritzker, the worst result for an Illinois Republican since 1912.

I am not writing this to settle an old score. I respect that Rauner entered the arena. He had major achievements that most people have forgotten. Of course, fallings-out happen all the time in politics for a host of reasons. What matters is that Rauner not only turned his back on the very people who elected him, he failed to engage voters in a meaningful and enduring way. Despite the advice and pleas from many (including me), Rauner's team never built the kind of successful alternate media machine to get his message out. The *National Review* piece did so much damage to Rauner not just because it pointed out his real faults—but because he had no platform upon which to place a compelling counter-narrative.

Because Rauner was a Republican, he could not count on any help from the legacy media. Because he had betrayed the base on abortion (and a series of other issues), he could not count on continued backing from conservative outlets. His situation was dire, but it was politically survivable if he had possessed the means to turn the screws of the Political Vise. Without them, his re-election bid was doomed.[16]

In the pre-internet age of elite media consolidation, it was very difficult to destroy a person's reputation overnight. That doesn't mean it was impossible. Ask the late Wisconsin Senator Joseph McCarthy, whose reputation continues to suffer excessively as a result of being scorned and sullied repeatedly in the national media. In 1953, when Edward R. Murrow, the hugely (some would say, blindly) trusted CBS news broadcaster decided it was time to take down Senator McCarthy and his campaign against Communism, the rest of the elite media swiftly jumped on to the bandwagon that Murrow was driving. McCarthy's career was destroyed very quickly, perhaps because he posed an unusually grave threat to the comfortable and the entrenched. Only decades later have historians begun to consider the possibility that the senator from Wisconsin was more right than wrong about the danger our nation faced, and that he was ill-treated by those who had a vested interest in pretending that danger was make-believe. McCarthy went too far in many ways, sometimes attacking people with little evidence. But his basic premise—that the Soviet-led effort to infiltrate our government was a dire threat—proved to be true. It was only after the fall of the Soviet Union that the archives vindicated McCarthy.

It is much easier to destroy someone today. Folks call it "cancel culture." Always hidden behind the guise of calling some truly awful person to account, cancel culture is a means of destroying reputations, careers, and lives with extraordinary rapidity. When we want to say that something momentous happens very fast, we often say it happened "overnight." That undersells the rapidity with which the Progressive Political Vise can ruin almost whoever it chooses. It's not overnight anymore—it's a matter, quite literally, of minutes.

As I have experienced personally and as I advise professionally, resisting cancel culture is about more than developing a thick skin (though a thick skin helps). It's about deploying your own media—and your own twenty-first-century direct-marketing machine—to hit back at the would-be cancellers. To circle back to where we began this chapter, no one has done this better than Donald Trump. I noted above that Trump was a devoted "tweeter," creating his own ongoing conversation with voters and bypassing the traditional media gatekeepers. Our latter-day Edward R. Murrows tried to do to Trump what they had done to the likes of Joe McCarthy, but they failed time and again. They failed both because their attacks were transparently political—and because their target was the most masterful deployer of direct marketing seen in our era.

Innovative direct marketers of content will find an audience. They will find ways to monetize that audience. And, because they are bypassing the elite media's attempts to control the narrative, those direct marketers can effectively defend themselves and their clients from the shamers, the cancellers, and the Progressive Political Vise. Donald Trump did not rely on CNN interviews or flattering profiles in the papers of record to reach his supporters. Though it sometimes seemed like it, he did not rely solely on Twitter. From the time he launched his run for president in 2015, through his years in the White House, and in his campaign to beat back the intense lawfare thrown at him, Donald Trump has been the unparalleled master of direct outreach. Of course, if not for a turn of his head, that strategy would have cost him his life in Butler, Pennsylvania, on July 13, 2024.

Donald Trump is a unique figure in our nation's history. Whether you like him or not, he's undeniably the most influential American of the twenty-first century. There are many lessons we can draw from his tenacity, his popularity, and his policies. The danger, however, is that by focusing on this one extremely famous and unusual politician, we forget that many of his most successful strategies are not his alone. There's no point in trying to be the next Trump or copy him. There is a lot of wisdom in recognizing that he and his advisors rely on some indispensable tools for fighting back against the left. Put simply, you don't have to be Donald Trump to use those tools.

I'm not Donald Trump, but years before he came down that famous escalator to change American politics forever, I was already developing the tools to turn the screws of the Political Vise. These ideas aren't mine alone; as a student of politics, marketing, and history, what I've done throughout my career is adapt old wisdom to meet new challenges—and take advantage of emerging opportunities. I've been helped by talented people, like the aforementioned Ryan Green. If our goal is to bypass the distribution channels dominated by the authoritarian left—and successfully defend ourselves and our movement against media distortions and attempts at cancellation—we will need to do three key things. These are the foundations for not only winning elections but for effective advocacy.

1. *Create* compelling content that can be sliced thinly for smaller and smaller audiences.
2. *Design* hybrid distribution channels that reach target audiences by using third-party channels or by creating channels to direct-market to each consumer of content.
3. Above all, *capture* more information (first names, last names, emails, snail mails, social media profiles, cell numbers, consumption history, and so forth) about the individuals we need to reach.

If you use a video streaming service like Netflix, Amazon Prime, or Apple TV, you'll soon realize that the platform is tailoring content for you based on your likes and dislikes. If you like rom-coms, you'll see romantic comedies showing up first among your suggestions. If you listen to Spotify, the world's largest music-streaming platform, the app will design playlists for you based on what they're able to discern about your taste. The more movies you watch and the more songs you listen to, the more these apps and platforms learn about you. This allows these media platforms to market entertainment to you based on an ever more exact understanding of your preferences. (As an aside, we shouldn't forget that media behemoths like Apple and Amazon and Spotify are not politically neutral. They censor and "shadow-ban" content regularly, invisibly deploying the Progressive Political Vise.)

I realized years ago that if advocates for liberty wanted to regain influence, we had to be able to design, create, and tailor content for specific audiences. That sounds like a dull abstraction, so let me illustrate what that means, using an only slightly silly example. A single House congressional district has about 700,000 citizens. If you are in charge of running House campaigns nationwide for either the Democrats or Republicans, there are not enough people in any single district to justify creating specialized content for those whose hobby is, say, soap carving. (Hey, it's good, clean fun!) There are simply not enough people who find soap-carving content compelling in the northern Chicago suburbs (my home is in the Ninth Congressional District of Illinois—a fairly liberal district where soap carvers would be shunned!). That's true of every other House district, be it in Texas or California or North Carolina: just not that many soap carvers.

Let's imagine you did create soap-carving content for those enthusiasts— and distributed it through Facebook, Instagram, X, Pinterest, and other channels. Soap carvers would be thrilled—and crucially, many of them would "opt in" and consent to receive more content from you. They then become part of your "owned audience"—people who have signaled to you that the content you offer is compelling and welcome.

The cost of creating soap-carving content for a single congressional district, or any other small market, is prohibitive. If we can find all (or at least most) of the soap-carving lovers in all 435 districts and aggregate them, then it becomes worthwhile to create soap-carving content. Through email, text, and social media, we can market this content to them in a viable and cost-effective way.

Once you have your soap carvers on board, you can find equestrians, golfers, quilter welders, hunters, knitters, and more. As you layer in ever more subject areas, you begin to get to scale in terms of overall audience size. The key remains being able to create varied content for small slices of the overall audience. While the mix of subject areas will vary district by district (we can expect more hunters in a rural district than an urban one), we can ensure that even someone with a very rare hobby for their district (say, a bull-riding enthusiast in inner-city Boston) can be connected to content they want.

Take a look at the pie chart below. If you are running a marketing campaign in that market segment, you can see that each small slice of the audience is not big enough on its own to get to the market share you want. But by adding up all those small slices, you can accumulate enough to exceed the market-share threshold you seek.

All of what I just wrote applies to lifestyle subjects like soap carving. But it also applies to policy and political issues such as abortion, border security, immigration, entitlements, tax policy, Israel policy, NATO, China, Russia, Iran, and much more. The same principles apply—slice to the smaller segments, find those interested, and aggregate a material audience.

Adding slices to build a majority

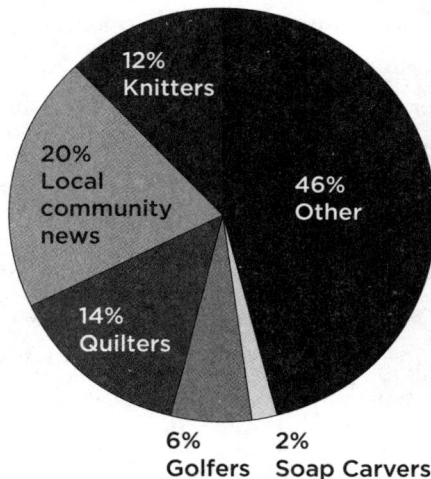

- 12% Knitters
- 20% Local community news
- 46% Other
- 14% Quilters
- 6% Golfers
- 2% Soap Carvers

Winning elections—and turning the Political Vise—requires building coalitions. That's not news. The art is to keep them together. The problem is that what engages one group in a larger coalition holds no interest for another. Economic conservatives might get very excited about proposals for further capital-gains tax cuts, but folks who are primarily focused on social issues like abortion and parental empowerment may not find capital-gains content to be compelling. Meanwhile, those fed up with our trade imbalances are receptive to Trump's use of tariffs to negotiate better deals while free-trade purists in his MAGA coalition are furious.

Recognizing the diversity of the coalition you're trying to assemble, the temptation is to focus on a handful of issues that you imagine unify almost everyone. That worked decades ago when people had very few media choices. In today's re-fragmented media environment, if it's not engaging, people will tune you out. They have too many other options available to hold their attention. There's no getting around the reality that it's essential to target each constituency within your coalition with specific, tailored content that will captivate and inspire.

This doesn't just apply in politics. It applies to any consumer-facing campaign for a product or service. Your goal is to get the person you're targeting to take an action: buy your soap, call their representatives, donate to your campaign. You need cost-effective, rapid content creation that calls the target to an action. You need to be able to test the content quickly (and repeatedly) to determine if it is successful in catalyzing that "call to action." And above all, you need to be both patient and relentless about acquiring the data to fuel that distribution. That's what Donald Trump has done—and what we have done at Illinois Policy, American Culture Project, MediaPedia, and my other organizations.

The key is remembering you aren't casting a wide net—you are designing thousands and thousands of unique nets, each designed to catch the attention and inspire the engagement of a single citizen. It is true that no one single person can turn the screws of the Political Vise. Individuals—if they are first engaged with as individuals—can be brought together into a cohesive, powerful force. A force, I know from experience, strong enough to resist the Progressive Political Vise, and strong enough to win the fight for liberty.

With an understanding of how media creates pressure on those inside the Political Vise, let's look at the opposite side of the Vise, the People.

Chapter 6

THE PEOPLE, PART ONE: LESSONS AND LEVERS

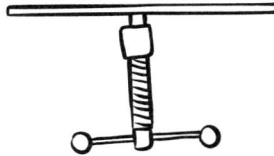

I saw the headline moments after it was posted. "California professor, writer of confidential Brett Kavanaugh letter, speaks out about her allegation of sexual assault." It was a story in the *Washington Post*, one of our three (along with the *New York Times* and *Wall Street Journal*) national papers of record. It was a Sunday morning—September 16, 2018—and I felt a knot in the pit of my stomach.

Here we go again, I thought. As I read the story, the accusations seemed incredibly thin. I was hopeful for a brief moment; surely a story this ancient—the allegations were decades old—would not gain traction. After a second, I laughed grimly. *They are gonna crush this guy,* I said to myself.

A few months earlier, on the same day that momentous decision came down in *Janus v. AFSCME*, Justice Anthony Kennedy had announced he was retiring from the Supreme Court. At the time, I was so caught up in the thrill of our historic victory for workers' rights that I didn't consider the significance of the Kennedy resignation. When President Trump declared on July 9, 2018, that he was nominating Brett Kavanaugh to fill the seat, I was cautiously optimistic. Kavanaugh had a solid conservative record after a decade on the US Court of Appeals for the District of Columbia Circuit. He was a member of the Federalist Society, an organization for which I had the highest respect. And though the Democrats in the Senate made their usual noises that the nominee was an "extremist" (a term the left regularly applies to anyone who doesn't think there's a constitutional right to abortion on demand up until the moment of birth), I figured the Republican majority would still have the votes to get Kavanaugh on to the Supreme Court.

Two and a half months later, when that *Washington Post* hit piece emerged, I felt sadly certain of how the story would go. There would be a growing chorus of demands for Judge Kavanaugh to step aside. The president would ask his political advisers what the next step would be, and those advisers—seasoned DC operatives—would tell him to give it up. Someone would place a call to Kavanaugh, and a statement would be drafted. Kavanaugh would hold a press conference where he would surely deny the allegations—and add that for the good of the nation, and out of respect for the president and for the Supreme Court, he was withdrawing his nomination.

That wasn't what I wanted to happen, of course. It was what I was afraid would happen. I had good reason to be concerned. While for decades, the left has deployed the Political Vise for a host of causes, they have used it with particular effectiveness on Supreme Court nominations. From the left's perspective, the high court has for decades been their most effective tool for advancing their agenda. Going back to Earl Warren's ascension as Chief Justice in 1953, the Supreme Court had steadily moved the country to the left. *Roe v. Wade*, the 1973 decision that removed the right of individual states to regulate abortion, was the paradigmatic triumph for the progressive movement. The left's great fear was that conservative presidents would appoint justices to undo all of this supposed progress. And so they mobilized with particular intensity every time a Republican president made a Supreme Court nomination.

As I noted, Brett Kavanaugh had been nominated to replace Justice Anthony Kennedy. Kennedy himself had only ended up on the Supreme

Court after the left's use of the Traditional Political Vise claimed one of its most notorious victories. In September 2018, I was afraid (as Yogi Berra famously put it) that we were about to have "déjà vu all over again." As it turned out, I would be pleasantly surprised. The left would fail to derail the Kavanaugh nomination, and against all odds and expectations, he would win Senate confirmation to the high court. You know this part of the story—what you have likely not considered is that Kavanaugh's ultimate triumph was the result of lessons learned from past confirmation battles. The survival of this particular nomination can be attributed to one thing: When it came down to the battle between the Progressive and the Traditional Political Vises, the good guys found a way to squeeze just a little bit harder.

To best illustrate this, we need to go back more than thirty years before the Kavanaugh nomination. On June 27, 1987, Justice Lewis Powell announced his retirement. Powell had been appointed by Richard Nixon, but like so many justices named to the court by Republican presidents, Powell had consistently voted with the liberals. In particular, Powell had joined the majority in *Roe v. Wade*. For conservatives, Powell's retirement was a crucial opportunity. President Ronald Reagan, more than halfway through his second term, would get a rare opportunity to name a third justice to the Supreme Court. If Powell's replacement was a strict constitutionalist, there was a chance Roe could be overturned—and some of the extreme excesses of the Warren-court era might also be rolled back.

Four days after Powell announced he was stepping down, President Reagan nominated Robert Bork to join the high court. Conservatives were thrilled. Bork had been a legendary law professor at Yale before serving as Solicitor General in the Nixon administration. He had later joined the same DC Court of Appeals on which Brett Kavanaugh would one day sit. Bork was 60 years old, with an extraordinarily brilliant track record. He had a first-rate legal mind and all of the requisite education and experience. Nearly two centuries of tradition indicated a nominee this qualified would have no problem winning Senate confirmation.

Until quite recently, it was considered very rare to have the Senate refuse to confirm a Supreme Court nomination. It was true that it had happened twice in living memory when the Senate rejected consecutive Nixon nominations in 1969 and 1970: Clement Haynsworth and G. Harrold Carswell. The Senate was troubled that as a lower court judge, Haynsworth had engaged in a demonstrable pattern of impropriety—ruling in cases in which he had a financial interest. Carswell, on the other hand, was a remarkably undistinguished nominee, with a reputation for laziness and mediocrity. Years later I read a noteworthy line from Nebraska Senator Roman Hruska, telling reporters while unsuccessfully lobbying for Carswell's confirmation: "Even if he were mediocre, there are a lot of mediocre judges and people and lawyers. They are entitled to a little representation, aren't they, and a little chance?"

Haynsworth had serious ethical problems. Despite Roman Hruska's plea, most of the rest of his Senate colleagues did not think that the Supreme Court was the ideal venue for celebrating mediocrity. (There have been plenty of mediocre justices confirmed over the years. Some of them are on the high court right now. Carswell's shortcomings, however, were particularly obvious.) No one had ever accused Robert Bork of either impropriety or mediocrity; his intellectual reputation, his judicial temperament, and his personal conduct were all above reproach. The only thing "wrong" with Robert Bork was that he was clearly a strict constitutional conservative. Established precedent said that philosophical differences over the law were not sufficient grounds for rejecting a Supreme Court nominee. As we would soon find out, "established precedent" was no match for the left's use of the Political Vise.

Remember the schema of the Progressive Political Vise? The media, powerful influencers, and left-wing politicians work together to squeeze the American people—and the people's conservative advocates. Ronald Reagan announced he had chosen Robert Bork on the morning of July 1, 1987—and within a matter of minutes, the Progressive Political Vise began to apply pressure to derail the nomination of one of the most gifted and qualified jurists of the modern era. Teddy Kennedy—later dubbed the "Lion of the Senate" and one of the most adept and cynical deployers of the Vise—took to the Senate floor barely an hour after news broke of Bork's nomination. That night, all the major networks aired Kennedy's fiery words:

> Robert Bork's America is a land in which women would be forced into back-alley abortions, Blacks would sit at segregated lunch counters, rogue police could break down citizens' doors in midnight raids, schoolchildren could not be taught about evolution, writers and artists would be censored at the whim of government, and the doors of the federal courts would be shut on the fingers of millions of citizens for whom the judiciary is often the only protector of the individual rights that are the heart of our democracy.[17]

In vain, Bork protested that none of this was true. Conservatives knew Kennedy's speech was a litany of lies, but they were caught flat-footed by the speed of the progressive response to the nomination. Teddy Kennedy didn't rush to make his speech to persuade a few wavering senators. He made his eloquently dishonest address for the nightly news, for the influencers, and for the liberal pressure groups that would quickly join the fight to stop the Bork nomination. A famously undisciplined man in his private life, Kennedy (like many in his family) had a keen grasp of how to create and maintain "message discipline." His speech was designed to be quoted endlessly, recycled daily, and deployed relentlessly to destroy one good man's reputation. It worked. In the pre-Internet age, the news media was a mass communications system controlled by a few dozen like-minded people. Those in the media and among the influencers were on Ted Kennedy's side and sealed the narrative. The minds of the American people followed as well.

On October 23, 1987, the Senate voted 58-42 against confirming Robert Bork to the Supreme Court. By the time the vote was held, the outcome was, sadly, a foregone conclusion.

Though Senator Kennedy's speech had marked the first turn of the Vise to crush the nomination, the left spent months ensuring that the reputation of this brilliant and decent man was destroyed. Very famously, the media even tracked down Bork's video rental history, hoping to find evidence that the nominee liked pornography. They discovered he had a taste for nothing more salacious than old James Bond and Alfred Hitchcock movies (as do I!). Even though the judge didn't have a single X- or R-rated film on his rental history, the papers printed the list anyway. Political observers had no trouble figuring out why. It was an unsubtle warning to future conservative nominees: We will do everything we can to crush you. Nothing is off-limits.

The Senate did finally approve a Reagan nominee: Anthony Kennedy. In his thirty years on the court, Kennedy would go on to be a reliable ally to the left on the biggest issues of the day, voting to keep the Roe decision the law of the land and authoring several majority opinions on gay rights. Regardless of what one's views were on gay marriage, it should have been decided by legislation, not judicial diktat. As far as progressives were concerned, Anthony Kennedy's liberalism proved Teddy Kennedy's strategy right: If they used the Vise to crush genuinely conservative nominees, they would be rewarded with (at worst) a milquetoast centrist.

Four years later, when Thurgood Marshall—the nation's first and only Black Supreme Court Justice—stepped down from the court, President George H. W. Bush nominated in his place a distinguished young Black judge named Clarence Thomas. Thomas, who had replaced Robert Bork himself on the DC Court of Appeals, had an exemplary judicial and academic record despite his relative youth. He was also, like Bork, unmistakably conservative: in legal terms, a "strict constructionist." With their focus on protecting the abortion franchise front and center in their minds, the media, the influential pressure groups, and Democratic politicians promptly launched a rerun of their successful campaign from four years earlier. By this point, "Bork" had become a verb—and the left intended to "Bork" Clarence Thomas by crushing him in the Vise.

The problem for the left was the obvious one: Thomas was only the second Black nominee ever. As a result, progressives, fearful of appearing racist, struggled to demonize him. Liberal pressure groups launched ever more extreme attacks on his judicial philosophy, but the Thomas nomination seemed assured. The nominee himself had learned from Bork's example, refusing to engage in lengthy debates during his nomination hearings while being careful and deliberate in his words. As hard as the left cranked the screws of the Vise, Thomas held firm.

The left was able to use the Political Vise to crush Robert Bork by painting him as a dangerous radical. They had accessed his video rental history as a "backup" in case their primary strategy failed. In the Thomas case, the effort to paint the young Black judge as an extremist had failed. After the Bork case, Congress had passed the Video Privacy Protection Act in 1988, making it a crime to disclose someone's rental history to the public. (Clearly, even some Democrats who had participated gleefully in "borking" a qualified nominee worried about what would happen if someone published the records of their own viewing habits.) Unable to derail Clarence Thomas in the same way that they had Robert Bork, the left upped the ante dramatically with a last-minute, surprise witness.

On October 6, 1991, NPR's Nina Totenberg reported that the FBI had interviewed Anita Hill, a former colleague of Clarence Thomas. Hill, Totenberg said, had accused Thomas of sexual harassment. Less than a week later, a series of prime-time televised hearings—featuring Anita Hill—began. The nation was treated to an unprecedented spectacle of "he said/she said" testimony, presided over by a Senate Judiciary Committee chair with plenty of skeletons in his own closet: Joe Biden. A few years later, during the impeachment trial of President Bill Clinton, Americans would hear about semen-stained dresses and oral sex in the Oval Office. In 1991, the graphic nature of Hill's testimony—including references to pornography and pubic hair—stunned and scandalized the public.

Clarence Thomas had many supporters and advisers, but it was impossible to prepare the nominee for the kind of intensely personal, probing

questions that the Senate Judiciary Committee asked. The entire nightmar-
ish process was completely unprecedented. In the end, Thomas decided to
let his own anger and indignation emerge. Staring a group of white senators
in the eye, his voice contained but furious, Thomas called the proceedings
"a high-tech lynching for uppity Blacks."

The nominee was correct—and he was also smart. Everyone in the
Senate knew the tragic history of lynching in this country. Most Black men
who were lynched had been falsely accused of sexual impropriety, just as
Thomas was. The shame of that dark chapter in the story of America
echoed in the Senate chambers—and the echo was just loud enough to
shame a handful of the wavering. By the extremely narrow margin of 52-48,
Thomas was confirmed. He has gone on to be perhaps the most consistent
and reliable defender of judicial restraint the modern court has seen.

The left was furious and anguished over their unsuccessful effort to
"bork" Clarence Thomas. For years afterward, it was common to see but-
tons and bumper stickers declaring, "I Believe Anita Hill." In the 1992
elections, the Democrats tapped into that resentment over the Thomas
confirmation. Several Democratic women who ran for Senate from blue
states campaigned explicitly on support for Hill. So many of them won that
a fawning media quickly dubbed 1992 "The Year of the Woman." Some
of those new senators would serve for decades, including the likes of Dianne
Feinstein, Barbara Boxer, and Patty Murray. (My own Illinois elected Carol
Moseley Braun, who proved even less competent and more radical than her
counterparts from California and Washington. She—blessedly—lasted only
a single term.) The message to conservatives was not subtle. "You may have
won the battle," the left said. "But we are going to win the war."

That Thomas had somehow survived the pressure of the Progressive
Political Vise frustrated and enraged Democrats. Some on the left decided
that even after his confirmation, an air of illegitimacy should hang over the
remainder of his tenure on the court. They have dangled the specter of Anita
Hill again and again. Even now, well over thirty years after the confirmation hearings, embittered progressives still search for ways to destroy Justice

Thomas. With predictable regularity, they attack his rulings, his judicial philosophy, his interviews, his vacation habits—and, most contemptibly of all, the political activities of his wife. Thomas's ability to maintain grace and amiability in the face of decades of relentless, venomous animus is inspiring. Few of us could do it nearly as well.

The left is wrong about many things, but their elite operatives are excellent students of failure. While some would continue to try to delegitimize Clarence Thomas, others focused on making sure that future efforts to "bork" a nominee would be more successful. They framed the Thomas nomination as a dangerous example of what happens when powerful men refuse to listen to vulnerable, victimized women. They worked hard to ensure that the senators who questioned Anita Hill repented for their tactics. They also used Hill's legacy to put Joe Biden, the Judiciary Chair, in the Vise. Feeling the pressure to demonstrate his regret at not doing more to stop Clarence Thomas, Biden became the Senate's most vociferous male advocate for the 1994 Violence Against Women Act. Before he ran for president in 2020, Biden made an obligatory phone call to Anita Hill, begging her forgiveness. The Vise demanded no less.

And then came 2018 and Brett Kavanaugh. In the twenty-seven years since the Thomas hearings, the left had refined its tactics—and transformed the culture. In 2018, the #MeToo movement was still sweeping the nation and upending workplace relationships. Let me be very clear: Sexual harassment and misconduct obviously do happen. They are wrong. Yet the #MeToo movement showed no interest in differentiating between rape and an awkward invitation to lunch. The only deciding factor in whether or not abuse had occurred was if a woman had felt uncomfortable. Her feelings were the only tool needed to measure misconduct. The #MeToo movement as a whole? That lies well beyond the scope of this book. But the way in which the left used #MeToo as a weapon against political opponents is a vital part of the story of the Political Vise. It is a potent weapon to animate the American people to apply pressure through the Political Vise.

As I said, I figured the Kavanaugh nomination was toast. Yes, the allegations themselves were incredibly flimsy. As you'll no doubt remember,

Christine Blasey Ford hazily remembered being assaulted by Brett Kavanaugh at a high school party some thirty-six years earlier. She could not remember the date of the party or the address of the house. She could produce no corroborating witnesses. Famously, even Blasey Ford's close friends—and her own father!—publicly expressed doubt about aspects of her story. Anita Hill had accused Clarence Thomas of repeatedly harassing her just a few years prior to his nomination while both were sober adults. Blasey Ford accused Kavanaugh of trying to rape her decades earlier when both were intoxicated teenagers.

My less politically aware friends couldn't see how allegations that ancient and vague could possibly be a problem for Kavanaugh. I replied that my friends were underestimating the power of the Progressive Political Vise. By 2018, good men regularly saw their careers derailed for even less.

Just as Anita Hill had done, Christine Blasey Ford testified before the Senate Judiciary Committee. Leaving nothing to chance, progressive activists urged Blasey Ford to hire Ricki Seidman to help her prepare for the hearings. In 1987, Seidman had worked as an aide to Teddy Kennedy during the Robert Bork hearings; four years later, she had assisted Anita Hill during the Clarence Thomas hearings. Seidman was a master political operator, keenly aware of what notes to play and what tone to strike for maximum effect. When Blasey Ford agreed to work with Seidman, any lingering doubt about the legitimacy of the allegations vanished. This was nothing but the Progressive Political Vise in action, bringing all hands on deck (or hands on the lever) to win a nasty fight.

Blasey Ford's testimony was broadcast live (during the day rather than in prime time.) In 1991, the major networks and legacy newspapers still had near-total control of what Americans read and watched. In 2018, people could stream the testimony on innumerable platforms—and react and comment in real time on Twitter, Facebook, and other sites. During the Thomas hearings, the media had treated Anita Hill with deference bordering on reverence. No one except the beleaguered nominee himself dared question any of her testimony. There was no conservative media presence in 1991; Fox News wouldn't launch for another five years. In contrast, by 2018 media defragmentation meant that the public not only had far more choices for how to watch the hearings but at last had the opportunity to hear pushback about the veracity and believability of the chief accuser.

To his great credit, President Trump refused to consider asking Kavanaugh to withdraw. Our forty-fifth (and now forty-seventh) president was and is a fighter. He does not shy away from battle, as far too many on our side have done far too many times. The president's team also advised Brett Kavanaugh to fight back hard. Where Clarence Thomas had conducted himself with quiet—but intense—dignity, Kavanaugh allowed himself to display his understandable anger at the absurd accusations against him. Both President Trump and Brett Kavanaugh understood instinctively that when the left tries to squeeze you in the Vise, the wisest strategy is to fight like hell to free yourself and clear your good name.

In addition to a pugnacious president and a nominee willing and able to raise his voice, conservatives had something else we hadn't had in 1991: the organizational capacity to use the Political Vise for ourselves. In 2005—roughly halfway in between the Thomas and Kavanaugh confirmations—a small group of determined activists formed the Judicial Crisis Network. Carrie Severino, a former law clerk to Clarence Thomas himself, created the network to support the nominations of John Roberts and Samuel Alito to the high court. Despite opposition from the left, each of George W. Bush's nominees was confirmed without the kind of rancor witnessed with Bork and Thomas. Those of us who supported the Judicial Crisis Network knew, however, it would only be a matter of time before we'd have a real "Bork- and Thomas-style" battle royale on our hands. With Brett Kavanaugh's nomination to the Supreme Court, we got that fight, in part because Kavanaugh would be replacing the left's key swing vote on major issues.

The Judicial Crisis Network—and many other conservative policy groups—used email, text, phone, and social media to activate supporters across the nation. The Senate was almost evenly divided between the parties, and it was clear the vote was going to be very, very close. It was particularly important to target vulnerable Democrats who were up for re-election later that fall. The network and allied organizations were able to mobilize hundreds of thousands of citizens across the nation, and they flooded the offices and phone lines of those wavering senators. In the end, with two senators not voting, Kavanaugh made it on to the court by a margin of 50-48—eclipsing the Thomas confirmation vote for the closest in American history. The people spoke, and righteousness prevailed.

As with Clarence Thomas, the Progressive Political Vise succeeded in tormenting a decent public servant—but could not deny his confirmation to the Supreme Court. The success the left had enjoyed in derailing Robert Bork could not be repeated because our side had learned its lessons. In the Thomas case, confirmation was won in part because of the issue of race, and the nominee's dignified but impassioned appeal to be saved from a "high-tech lynching." With Brett Kavanaugh, we won by tapping into a wellspring of public anger at what was transparently a partisan hit job. We won because both Kavanaugh and the president who nominated him were willing to fight. And above all, we won because we were able to use the technology and tools at our disposal to mobilize conservatives across the country. All sides of the Traditional Political Vise were operating to support Kavanaugh by applying pressure to the politicians in the Senate.

Remember 1992, the "Year of the Woman"? The year after Clarence Thomas was confirmed, the Democrats very effectively used the alleged mistreatment of Anita Hill to elect several women to the US Senate. Many wondered if the 2018 midterm election would see a similar outcome. Would the Democrats turn out huge numbers of angry liberal women and pick up more Senate seats? No. In fact, the opposite happened.

Even before Christine Blasey Ford's allegations dropped, conservative activists focused hard on putting four moderate, red-state Democrat senators in the Political Vise: Joe Donnelly of Indiana, Heidi Heitkamp of North Dakota, Joe Manchin of West Virginia, and Claire McCaskill of Missouri.

From the moment that President Trump announced his choice to replace Justice Kennedy, conservative messaging made it clear to those four senators that their states' voters wanted them to support Brett Kavanaugh. Once the accusations of sexual misconduct appeared, conservative groups redoubled their efforts. In the end, only Joe Manchin responded to the Vise, casting a pivotal vote to confirm.

A casual observer might assume that this meant that the Judicial Crisis Network (soon to be renamed the Concord Fund) and other conservative groups had failed to use the Political Vise effectively. Only one of the four targets actually switched his vote; in baseball terms, we were batting what appeared to be a weak .250.

But here's a basic rule about the Political Vise: sometimes, the squeeze just takes a little longer to arrive. When the November 2018 midterms came, Donnelly, Heitkamp, and McCaskill were all ousted by Republican challengers. Manchin, who had responded to the pressure, survived. What made this especially astounding was that these three huge wins came in an otherwise disappointing midterm cycle for Republicans. (To be fair, whichever party holds the White House usually does poorly in the midterms, and Trump's first term was no exception.) Voters in Indiana, Missouri, and North Dakota were angry that their senators had ignored their wishes, and GOP activists were able to harness and direct that anger to turn the screws of the Vise, throw out three liberals, and put three pro-liberty Republicans into office.

As an American with a deep reverence for our constitution, I look back with disgust on what was done to Robert Bork, Clarence Thomas, and Brett Kavanaugh. I hope that no Supreme Court nominee of either party ever endures anything comparable. Character assassination may be an ancient tactic, but it is beneath us as patriots and as citizens of an honorable republic. Yet even while we work towards a day when decency and civility are common once again in public life, we need to be clear-eyed about the battles that lie ahead—and the tactics we will need to use to win them.

We have been discussing two versions of the Political Vise—the Traditional Political Vise that has been operating for over 200 years and the

Progressive Political Vise that is a more recent phenomenon. While it is difficult to declare a clear demarcation when the left began to shift the Vise's power to put the people in the Vise by collaboration with the media and leftist influencers and politicians, I see the Bork nomination as the beginning of that process. They succeeded in not only pressuring President Reagan and the GOP senators but they also pressured the American people to believe a fundamental lie: Judge Bork was a dangerous man, unworthy to sit on the Court.

The pro-liberty team learned from what was done to Robert Bork and Clarence Thomas. And while we could not protect Brett Kavanaugh from being painfully and shamefully squeezed by the Progressive Political Vise, in the end, we successfully deployed the Traditional Political Vise to secure his confirmation—and to deliver a crushing blow to many of those who sought to humiliate and block him. Drawing lessons from past experience and taking advantage of a rapidly changing media landscape, we can reclaim the Vise—and restore this country.

When it comes to the Vise's power—the people always have the trump card to play. It requires active engagement. That is the hardest part.

But when the people make politicians fear their voters more than they fear the media and elite influencers, the sovereignty of "We the People" will remain invincible. Let's see how that happens.

Chapter 7

THE PEOPLE, PART TWO: TURNING THE VISE TOWARD LIBERTY

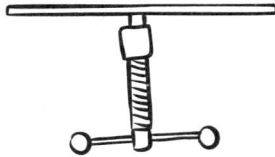

So long as We the People retain the tools of power, we cannot be denied our will when animated to a cause. It is what animates us that matters—truth or propaganda.

I had said that Brett Kavanaugh's nomination was "toast." I was rarely more glad to be wrong—and I was humbled, at least briefly, by the recognition that I had been wrong about the Political Vise itself. I hadn't been sure "the good guys" could deploy it as effectively as we did. As close as that final vote in the Senate was, it was an unmistakable win not only for President Trump, but for all of us eager to push back on the excesses and cruelties of the Progressive Political Vise.

Remember that the Traditional Political Vise involves the media, influencers, and the people putting the squeeze on policymakers. Brett Kavanaugh's confirmation was saved in part because liberty-driven media and influencers successfully activated the people. Outraged by what was happening and understanding the stakes, millions put their hands to the lever. Kavanaugh's win wasn't just a vindication for President Trump or for conservatives. It was a vindication of the principle that the citizens should be heard—and their pressure should be decisive.

"We the People." Those are the first three words of the preamble to the Constitution. The short phrase serves as a reminder that government derives its powers entirely from the people. It is the people who have inalienable rights, and a government's first responsibility is to safeguard those rights. You may have first read (or heard recited) these words when you were a child in school. What you may not have considered until now is that "We the People" is also a declaration about the nature of the Political Vise. If government is, as Abraham Lincoln wrote, "of the people, by the people, [and] for the people," then the people must always be the ones applying the pressure. If the people are in the grip of the Vise rather than turning its screws, then the system is not working as intended.

Newsflash: The system is *not* always working as intended.

Progressives are diligent about proclaiming great love for the people. All totalitarian philosophies declare that the government should serve the people's interests. Indeed, it's right there in the names: the *People's* Republic of China, or the Democratic *People's* Republic of North Korea. These are, of course, two of the most repressive regimes on planet earth! Yet their respective constitutions are filled with references to the central importance of serving the people. The North Korean constitution declares that its leaders "believe in the people as in heaven" and declares the state to be a "people-centered system." The reality is that North Koreans suffer under perhaps the cruelest regime on the planet. Yet even that most sadistic and bizarre of governments pays flowery lip service to the idea of the people.

The progressive elites who dominate our politics and our public life do not have the same total authority as Kim Jong Un in North Korea or Xi Jinping in China. For the most part, the left in this country insists that it does not want to establish the kind of one-party dictatorship that we see elsewhere. When folks on the right call our lefty friends "Communists," those friends sometimes get indignant. They insist that they believe in democracy and American values, and they generally repudiate the cruelties of the Chinese and North Korean governments. I have many good friends on the "other side of the aisle," and I know that, in their hearts, they don't want to create a Communist dictatorship. I also know that whether they like it or not, they share one fundamental precept with totalitarians everywhere. That precept is the idea that it is more important for the government to be *for* the people than *by* the people.

This is not an abstract distinction. Those two different prepositions have real meaning and power. When Abraham Lincoln wrote the Gettysburg Address, he put those prepositions in correct order—not alphabetically, but philosophically. "For" the people comes after "of" and "by," serving as a reminder that the government's role in protecting the people is only legitimate when that government is responsive to the people. In China and North Korea, the government claims to act in the best interests of the people—but the people themselves are presumed insufficiently capable, insufficiently wise, or insufficiently trustworthy to determine what those interests are. In these dictatorships, the government claims to play the role of a benevolent parent. In real life, children grow up, but in leftist regimes, the people remain perpetual children, always in need of direction, guidance, and care.

It will take us many more years to fully understand the impact of the COVID-19 pandemic on American society. It took many of us just a few days to understand that the pandemic would reveal the paternalistic contempt that so many politicians and media elites had for the American people. I have mentioned before Chicago Mayor Rahm Emanuel's advice to "never let a crisis go to waste." For the Biden administration and the Democratic governors of many blue states, the pandemic was an opportunity to reinforce in the public mind a fundamental lie: that government's most important function is to ensure the collective good and safety. In many ways, the government response to the pandemic functioned as a test: How much fear do we need to generate in order to get the people to surrender their liberty? How quickly can we move to curtail economic and physical freedom? What are the tools we have to compel submission, and how long can we use them without engendering backlash?

I'm not saying that the coronavirus wasn't real. I am not saying elected officials were consciously perpetuating a hoax in order to gain more power. But remember the nature of the left is to always assume that problems are best solved through the expansion of state power. It doesn't matter if a crisis is real or imagined. All that matters is leveraging that crisis. In the case of the Progressive Political Vise, that leveraging is literal—the more fear you can instill, the more you can turn the screws of the Vise, and the more you squeeze the people towards your desired outcome.

When COVID-19 arrived, several states with Democrat governors locked down hard. California and New York got most of the national press, thanks to the antics of Andrew Cuomo and Gavin Newsom, but my own Illinois followed much the same disastrous course. Our governor, J. B. Pritzker, would keep the Land of Lincoln in a state of emergency for an astonishing 1,155 days. As you might remember, particularly if you were in a "blue" state, the earliest weeks of the lockdowns were the harshest. At Illinois Policy Institute, we saw the devastation that these lockdowns created. Small business owners were losing their livelihoods. Children were isolated, lonely, and absolutely not learning. We wanted to collect and share the stories of ordinary people who were suffering.

In response to our work, Governor Pritzker's spokesperson issued a statement: "The [Illinois Policy Institute] has lobbied for some atrocious policies in the past, but this time their efforts could mean the difference between life and death for many Illinoisans. They need to stop lying to people about what's at stake in this crisis and own up to the public responsibility we all have to be committed to a truthful and honest conversation about our collective public health."[18]

In other words, merely collecting stories about the disastrous consequences of lockdowns was tantamount to killing people! To Governor Pritzker's office, "public responsibility" meant quiet obedience to the state's diktats. To the state's chief executive, the people of Illinois were vulnerable (and in our case, disobedient) children who needed to be protected not only from the virus itself but from frank discussions about the best way to respond to that virus. The government was, in essence, telling us to sit down and shut up. We might be sharing the voices *of* the people, but we were not acting *for* the people and their best interests—at least not as the State of Illinois defined those terms. Left unrestrained, the administrative state will always, always, insist it knows better.

As you probably remember from high school civics class, government by the people doesn't mean a free-for-all. We live in a republic, not a direct democracy. Our Constitution provides the structure and the system through which the people are heard. To put it another way, there's a difference between the Political Vise and a mob riot. In the latter, the mob uses force to get whatever the majority in the crowd wants at any given moment. Anyone who opposes the crowd gets trampled. The Political Vise leverages the power of the people to achieve wise outcomes; the mob just burns everything down.

The problem is that the authoritarian left—which does not want to be subject to the pressures of the Vise—maligns any attempt to question their decisions as an existential danger. Governor Pritzker said it was irresponsible for us to report the honest truth about the impact of his COVID policies. His spokespeople made clear we were threatening the lives of ordinary citizens. What the pandemic revealed was that the left was all too willing to exaggerate the dangers of the virus in order to move towards their constant goal: an ever-more-powerful government. An ever-more powerful government always *claims* to be acting in the best interests of the people, even as it ignores the plight and pleas of actual citizens.

To overcome resistance, the authoritarian left will declare a threat to be so immediate and so terrible that it justifies temporarily limiting (or indefinitely removing) the freedom of ordinary people. In 2020, hysteria about COVID became an exceptionally effective diagnostic tool. How much liberty could people be induced to surrender? How long would they comply? How effectively could resistance be quashed?

This raises an all-important question: How effectively can the "resistance" fight back? If the Progressive Political Vise is trying to squeeze the people, and the Traditional Political Vise is working to squeeze the politicians, how does one side prevail? The obvious answer is that the Vise that "squeezes harder" will win. In order to understand how the liberty side can out-exert and out-squeeze authoritarian progressives, we must first understand the vital distinction between the two kinds of pressure the different Vises provide.

Orchestrated Pressure and Organic Pressure

An orchestra is a coordinated event that can create beautiful, pleasing music. It can work in politics, too. The progressives are maestros at this.

On Valentine's Day, 2018, a deeply disturbed former student shot and killed seventeen people at Marjory Stoneman Douglas High School in Parkland, Florida. It was a devastating tragedy, made all the worse by the reality that the shooting should have been prevented. The killer was on the FBI's radar as a threat, but the Bureau had neglected to question him. During the rampage, an armed school safety officer waited outside the building, too fearful to engage and confront the killer. In the hours after the massacre, however, even while the bodies of the slain still lay in their classrooms, the left began a familiar, orchestrated pressure campaign. No one needed to know the shooter's motive; no one needed to examine the school's failings. All the left needed to know was that the murderer had used an AR-15. Politicians, influencers, and the media began their familiar chorus: The only solution is to ban guns.

The Parkland shooting happened on a Wednesday afternoon. The first funerals were held that Friday. But by Thursday evening—barely 24 hours after the shooting—Democratic political activists were already on the ground in South Florida, coordinating and orchestrating a "student-led" movement for gun control. Just *six days* after the shooting, one hundred students from Marjory Stoneman Douglas and fifteen parents were bussed 450 miles from Parkland to the state capital in Tallahassee. The buses and hotel accommodations were organized by Congresswoman Debbie Wasserman Schultz, the former head of the Democratic National Committee.

All the expenses for the students and their families were paid. The families who had lost children in the shooting were offered cash payments to join that lobbying trip—and to travel to the "March for Our Lives" rally held in Washington a few weeks later.

Remember the three sides of the Progressive Political Vise: left-wing politicians, influencers, and the media. After the Parkland shooting, all three worked together with extraordinary speed and effectiveness to orchestrate an intense campaign for "gun reform." As is often the case, what *seemed* like a spontaneous student-led effort was instead coordinated by political operatives working hand-in-hand with a cooperative and sympathetic media. This was classic astroturfing. Just as Astroturf mimics natural grass, astroturfing mimics an organic pressure campaign. Astroturfing creates the illusion that a movement that actually originated with the elites instead began with the people. March for Our Lives was a perfect example of an orchestrated pressure campaign masquerading as something rooted in the passions and convictions of ordinary citizens.

Whatever your views on gun control and how best to prevent school shootings, there's no doubt that in the aftermath of tragedy, the politicians, the influencers, and the media declare that there's just one simple answer to a complex problem. The free travel, the media coaching, and the lucrative book deals lavished on the Parkland survivors worked on two levels: first, to channel the anguish of grieving families in the desired direction, and second, to pressure the public to blame guns rather than a toxic culture. Orchestrated pressure is designed to ensure that the public's outrage only flows where the elites want it to flow.

It's hard to even imagine losing your child. Now imagine that your child has been killed in a high-profile shooting. Imagine that in your shock and your grief, politicians and activists and media figures descend on your street. Anderson Cooper knocks on your front door and wants to know how you feel about the laws that allowed the person who shot your child to acquire a gun. A Democratic congressperson calls, murmurs sympathies, and offers you an all-expenses-paid trip to Capitol Hill to lobby. "If there's anything you need," the politician says, "we'll make sure you have it. Your activism is the best way you have to honor the memory of your dead child."

This orchestrated pressure on a handful of bereaved and vulnerable people turns victims into influencers. It's incredibly cynical—and incredibly common. Orchestrated pressure is the hijacking of legitimate outrage or justified fear. The Progressive Political Vise takes this very real pain and directs it toward a specific end. The Vise tightens from three sides—and scared, vulnerable, grieving, and angry people are squeezed in the direction the elites want them to go.

Critical race theory, or CRT, has been around for decades. It began as an academic fad, and it has proven extraordinarily effective at becoming accepted doctrine at many colleges and universities. Simply put, CRT is the notion that America was founded not as an experiment in human liberty but as a ruthless capitalist business. CRT teaches that the desire to build a slave-based economy was the sole impetus behind the creation of our republic. CRT claims that racism—specifically against Black people—is at the very root of American values. Justice will only come when Americans accept this truth and commit themselves to building a radically new society centered on racial diversity, inclusion, and equity. Billions of dollars in reparations will, of course, be required.

CRT had captured the imaginations of the elites, but it was obviously unpalatable to millions of Americans. Then came the killing of George Floyd in May 2020. Within days, the gruesome viral video of Floyd's death beneath the knee of a Minneapolis police officer spawned violent riots in cities across the nation. In previous years, there had been civil unrest after the killings of other Black men, like Trayvon Martin or Mike Brown—but the death of George Floyd was the first such tragedy so masterfully and extensively hijacked by the Progressive Political Vise. In the summer of 2020, the American people were subjected to an unprecedented campaign of orchestrated pressure. The goal was to force an entire nation to embrace and accept critical race theory.

In a matter of just a few weeks, virtually every major organization in the country issued a statement denouncing systemic racism, pledging support for the Black Lives Matter movement, and promising "to do better." One of the goals of CRT was to defund the police; a number of major cities did vote to cut funding to law enforcement. Another goal was to tear down statues of "enslavers" and rechristen buildings that carried the names of those accused of racism. (In San Francisco, that included banning the names not just of Confederate generals but of Abraham Lincoln and Dianne Feinstein.) Above all else, the goal was to hire a vast army of administrators and bureaucrats to ensure that CRT was taught to children as young as kindergarteners—and that CRT's principles of diversity, equity, and inclusion were mandated in every American workplace.

This was all orchestrated pressure. The media, the influencers, and the politicians didn't just capitalize on the anger generated by the George Floyd killing; they fanned the flames of that rage. The video ran over and over again, as did endless interviews with left-wing activists who explained that Floyd's death wasn't the result of excessive force used by one rogue cop but a part of a pattern of racist violence that was endemic in American society. That racism had to be ripped out of American society—and that meant ripping up the very foundations of our republic.

In Washington, DC, House Speaker Nancy Pelosi and Senate Minority Leader Chuck Schumer knelt in public, draped in African *kente* cloth. The virtue-signaling was laughable, but the consequences for America were anything but.

The elites were keenly aware of the particularly fragile state of American democracy in the summer of 2020. They had already harnessed the alarm over COVID-19 to shutter millions of businesses, close down schools, and expand the power of the state to surveil the public. Unable to work, hundreds of millions—especially in "blue states"—were now dependent on government handouts to survive. The success of the lockdowns emboldened the progressive elites; if the public could be induced to accept such a vast expansion of government power because of fear of a virus, perhaps they could be persuaded to accept another such expansion because of outrage over racial injustice. Perhaps they could be persuaded to look at the world through the lens of CRT.

One way to recognize an orchestrated progressive pressure campaign is by the way it demonizes its opponents. The politicians, the media, and the influencers began to turn the vise in that strange and violent summer, trying to crush the livelihoods of anyone who dared question the notion that America was fundamentally racist and the police needed to be defunded. The Foundation for Individual Rights and Expression (FIRE) found "that attempts to punish college and university scholars for their speech skyrocketed" immediately after the death of George Floyd. Writing in 2023, FIRE noted "the number of scholars punished in the past three years nearly matches the number of scholars sanctioned in the *20 years* prior to 2020." The Foundation went on to note that 75% of attempts to silence and cancel came from the political left rather than the right.[19] Orchestrated pressure campaigns work by setting examples: the Progressive Political Vise assumes that once you see someone disciplined and humiliated for their views, you'll think twice before expressing your own doubts about the Black Lives Matter movement, the saintliness of George Floyd, or the necessity of imposing critical race theory.

The events of 2020 left an indelible mark on American public life. We are still coming to terms with the economic, cultural, and social consequences of the prolonged lockdowns. We are still trying to reckon with the scope of political and financial malfeasance that took place under the guise of keeping Americans safe. And we are still trying to push back against the extraordinary tightening of the Progressive Political Vise. Here's the good news: There are plenty of Americans remaining who still love liberty, who still embrace common sense, and who recoil at the excesses of the political left. It is from those citizens that the organic pushback against orchestrated pressure begins.

Organic pressure bubbles up spontaneously. It originates with the people. It doesn't need to be astroturfed. It cannot easily be hijacked, and it is not easy to manage from above. If you've worked in politics as long as

I have, there are few feelings as exhilarating as the recognition that the organic pressure is on your side. It's like sailing with the wind at your back. When organic pressure is against you, it's like steering directly into a gale. I know which side I'd rather be on. All of the great successes on the right of my adult life—from the age of Reagan to the era of Trump—have begun as organic protests against the crushing burdens and injustices of the progressive status quo.

The frustrating reality for conservatives is that so many of our organic, grassroots movements have been unable to turn the screws of the Political Vise. For all the successes we on the liberty side have enjoyed, there have been too many times where our movement has been co-opted or fragmented or crushed. Going up against the progressive elites is never easy. The organic feeling of the people is a powerful force, but if it isn't supported effectively, it can all too easily dissipate.

The school choice movement has worked for decades to empower parents. Until recently, the successes had been few, frankly, in the face of the sustained and intense pressure exerted by the teachers' unions and their political and media allies. Then came the double whammy of 2020— pandemic-driven school closures and the left's colossal cultural overreach after the death of George Floyd. Egged on by left-wing activists and responding to the orchestrated pressure from progressive elites, school boards across the country began to integrate CRT into their curriculums. As students returned to in-person learning, often after months (or even years) of ineffective Zoom school, they found their lessons had been transformed in the interim.

In Loudoun County, Virginia, parents fought back. The district had created the "Student Equity Ambassador Program." The job of these "Equity Ambassadors" was, as you might suspect, to snitch on students whose language or views did not conform to the now-compulsory view that America was an irredeemably racist nation. When a few parents complained, the school board dismissed them as a disgruntled (and bigoted) minority. Very quickly—and organically—a movement grew. It was a small army, led mostly (but not entirely) by moms. Many of these mothers had been exasperated by how long the schools had been shut; now, they were horrified to discover that the curriculum had transformed during the pandemic. Students were reporting other students (and teachers) for wrongthink. The lesson plans left many students upset and embarrassed and ashamed. Outraged parents didn't need to have their anger orchestrated. They just needed allies to help them fight back.

I cofounded the Liberty Justice Center in 2011 and was its chairman for many years. (I was chair when we won *Janus v. AFSCME*.) In June 2021, Liberty Justice Center (LJC) filed a lawsuit challenging the Student Equity Ambassador Program. LJC lost in federal district court, but in April 2023, the Fourth Circuit Court of Appeals ruled that the parents were right to express concerns, declaring that the Equity Ambassador Program "caused the parents' children to experience a non-speculative and objectively reasonable chilling effect on their speech."[20] It was at least a partial victory, and there have been many more since.

The aftermath of the Parkland high school shooting saw the media, Democrat politicians, and influencers descending on grief-stricken parents and students. The elites took advantage of exceptionally vulnerable people, channeling their grief and anger towards a predetermined response. By contrast, when parents in Loudoun County, Virginia—and dozens of other jurisdictions across the country—rose up in protest against the excesses of critical race theory, transgenderism, and pornography in school libraries, groups like the Liberty Justice Center asked a simple question: *How can we help?*

There are few things as powerful as the energy of the people, rising up organically in support of a cause. That energy alone is not enough to win lasting victories. The Progressive Political Vise is adept at defusing and discouraging organic conservative movements. The key to ensuring the success of an organic campaign—one that enables the people themselves to turn the Vise—is focusing that energy like the proverbial laser beam. It's not about co-opting the energy of the people. It's about ensuring that energy grows, endures, and triumphs.

Today, from Iowa to Texas and throughout many more states, school choice legislation is passing. At every bill signing, the politicians are front and center. But it is the organic, focused-like-a-laser activism of parents and advocates that creates those wins for "We the People"—in this case, the children.

The school choice movement has all the elements of what it takes for the good guys and gals to win: a motivated and informed citizenry, a policy solution that has the moral high ground in helping people, and, most importantly, leadership that emerged to harness that citizen energy into a coherent strategy and campaign. Together, people are reasserting their sovereignty within the public and private education systems of this country.

That's what our Founders wanted for our system—We the People to be sovereign within the constitutional framework of our founding as a republic. It's the cause to which I've dedicated my public career. In the next chapter, we'll look more closely at how we conservatives can meet the challenge of these "organic moments." And I'll explain how we on the movement right can act not just *for* the people, but *with* the people—and how together, we can use the Vise as the Founders intended.

Chapter 8

THE INFLUENCERS, PART ONE: A POWERFUL FEW

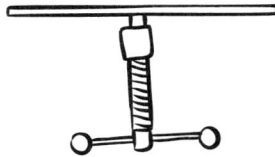

Influencers are elites, the insiders and the powerful. It is easier than you think to become an influencer. Earlier in the book I shared with you my journey in public policy and politics. Part of the reason I shared that was because I want you to know that you, too, can become an influencer.

On TikTok, YouTube, and other social media platforms, "influencers" are minor celebrities. They hustle and hawk beauty supplies, fitness gear, and food delivery apps. These influencers have an astonishing, unhealthy control over the buying habits of young people. Too many teenagers cannot distinguish between an apparent peer selling them something on Instagram and an actual expert who can offer real guidance. These online influencers are benign at best, downright dangerous at worst. Yet their baleful impact on our society is nothing compared to the true influencers of our society, a group that constitutes a vital—and malign—side of the Progressive Political Vise.

These influencers are the trial bar, public-sector unions, private-sector unions, and government-funded nonprofits. What do all of these different organizations have in common? None create value on their own. Not one.

It's important to remember exactly how the Political Vise works. In the Traditional Political Vise, the politicians feel the pressure applied by the media, the influencers, and the people. What makes the bottom side of the Vise—in this case, the influencer side—so vital is that it applies pressure not just on those in the Vise's grip, but on everyone else who turns a handle. In the diagram on the next page, the black arrows pointing up on either side of the influencers indicate that even as the influencers put the squeeze on the politicians, they also impact the other two sides of the Vise. They influence how the media reports on issues, people, politicians, business, culture, and much more. They also influence how the people form opinions and how well their organic pressure is focused and amplified or how effectively the people are orchestrated to create pressure.

Even in the Traditional Political Vise, the elite influencers exert an outsized force relative to their numbers. The left, of course, has succeeded in all too often putting the people rather than the politicians in the grip of the Progressive Political Vise. The media and the politicians now respond to the ever-more powerful influencers, joining with them (and often, following their commands) in the unhappy task of further subjugating the American people.

Who are these influencers? They fall into several distinct categories.

The trial bar extracts tremendous wealth from the private sector through litigation. They extort even more income through the mere threat of litigation. They do not build anything or create anything—but they stop many things from being built and created. The trial bar has a parasitical relationship with the private sector. The same is true of government unions. The government employs them to extract wealth and income from taxpayers to fund government salaries, benefits, and pensions. Worse, most of that money goes to politics to help elect the very politicians they will soon be negotiating with over pay and benefits. It is an immoral, insidious, and incestuous relationship that must end.

It is true of private-sector unions as well; these use favorable labor laws (created and imposed by government) to extract wealth and income from private-sector employers. Private-sector unions need government labor laws

THE TRADITIONAL POLITICAL VISE

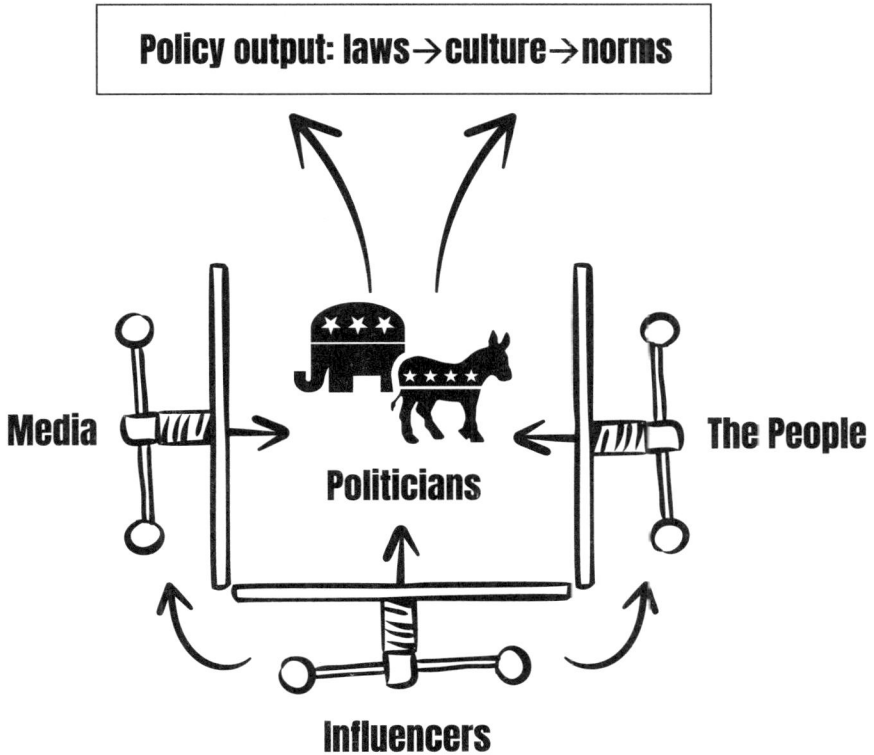

Policy output: laws→culture→norms

Media

Politicians

The People

Influencers

to protect their collective bargaining privileges—allowing them to become a monopoly labor provider to employers.

Many nonprofits get no government funding, but an astonishing number do—often in the form of grants. Many of the most powerful nonprofits in this country only survive because of legislation granting them funding and fees to operate. Many of these nonprofits do incredible, meaningful work. Others, though, function primarily to extract money in what is little more than a wealth transfer scam. What unifies them, both the worthy and unworthy, is that they require government to provide their core revenue stream.

Among the most powerful of the progressive nonprofits are the "extreme greens." These aren't just traditional conservation groups of the sort that advocate setting aside open space, or that encourage Americans to visit our national parks. The extreme greens focus on applying pressure to government to pass legislation—or simply impose regulations—to advance their "environmental" agenda. Some of these extreme greens do get government funding; others collect money from small donors and corporations. Their entire purpose is to influence politicians and administration officials to impose ever-stricter regulations. They raise money by campaigning for ever more draconian restrictions on private enterprise, restrictions that only the government can impose.

One of the more outrageous stories is that after the November 2024 election, the Biden administration transferred $2 billion from the Environmental Protection Agency to a group of green nonprofits called the Power Forward Communities. This transfer made news for its size, its timing, and that former Georgia gubernatorial candidate Stacy Abrams was associated with the recipients. *The Washington Post* "fact-checked" this claim and downplayed it while the EPA counterpunched with its own fact check of the *Post*.[21]

What made this massive grant so alarming was that it was given to a group that only had $100 in previous revenue. The theoretical goal of the grant was to help people obtain more efficient appliances, but is this really the best way to advance a green agenda even if you are a radical climate zealot? Who gives $2 billion to a group with no expertise and no experience? Suspicious minds want to know.

I should mention an ancillary arm of the extreme green movement: the for-profit environmental companies. These corporations do not want to compete in an open market. Rather, these companies (certain automakers, solar panel manufacturers, and many others) have built their business models not on delivering a quality product but on collecting ever-greater government subsidies. Unlike the other progressive influencers, these for-profit "green" companies do actually produce things. But they rely entirely on the taxpayers' largesse to do so.

Of course, early in Trump's second term, the Department of Government Efficiency (DOGE) exposed the corruption of NGOs funded through

United States Agency for International Development (USAID). DOGE revealed the flow of taxpayer money through USAID to unaccountable NGOs and others doing work behind an opaque curtain. That work was often to influence popular culture, news, entertainment, and the very idea of what is true and real—to control the narrative so as to shape how We the People think. In other words, to control how we think.

As those dependent on USAID funding learned, influencers understand that their survival hinges on a ceaseless flow of government money—and favorable regulations. Over the past half century, these groups have become ruthlessly expert at lobbying politicians, mustering votes, shaping public opinion, suppressing contrary views, and turning the levers of the Vise. The pushback against DOGE is the best contemporary example.

Among the many amazing revelations that DOGE uncovered was the long hidden fact that the US government had an old limestone mine deep in Pennsylvania in which all the paperwork was housed and processed when a government employee retired. Retirement applications were processed by hand and kept in manilla envelopes. It could take months to process a single person's retirement because it all still operated by the standards of the 1950s.

Another favorite DOGE hit is that the now notorious USAID spent $20 million to bring a version of *Sesame Street* to Iraq. And yet DOGE was attacked over and over again. You know that the corporate media and Democrats have jumped the shark when they are defending government waste and government bureaucrats!

We are making real progress, however. Since 2010 and the rise of the Tea Party—and later, the emergence of Donald Trump—the leftist or statist influencers have found themselves on the defensive. Despite their best efforts, they have not been able to gain total control over twenty-first-century communication strategies, including social media. What threatens their grip on the Vise is a resurgent engagement by the people. (I recommend Martin Gurri's 2018 book *The Revolt of the Public* for more on this.) Understandably unwilling to relinquish so great a power—and terrified at the thought of getting kicked off the proverbial "gravy train" and power position—the influencers have fought back. We can win that battle, but it requires being more clear-eyed than ever about the opponent we face.

This elite defensiveness often manifests as nostalgia for an imagined era of bipartisan civility. In December 2022, the *Daily Beast* (an online news site immensely popular with the progressive left) lamented that

> . . . members of Congress, in the House in particular, have seen their bipartisan camaraderie drop dramatically in recent years . . . four years of Trump have already driven a nasty, MAGA-tinged wedge between the two parties. (Members of both parties say) it is hard to hold the once casual conversations they had with opposing members.[22]

To a great extent, this is a false nostalgia. One senator badly beat another with a cane on the Senate floor in the 1860s, and the early twentieth century saw more than one fistfight in the House. The idea that enmity between members of our two political parties is somehow new—or somehow Donald Trump's fault—doesn't jibe with the historical facts! What this wistfulness for a more courteous past really reflects is an era where the left's elites could exert influence over both parties. When the substantive ideological differences are negligible, it is considerably easier to remain outwardly friendly.

I like to think of myself as a courteous man myself, and I think there's rarely an occasion to be rude or hostile, particularly in Congress! At the same time, I recognize that more than a little of the decline in "casual conversations" between members of the two parties comes down to the simple truth that a growing number in one of those parties now actively oppose the elite influencer agenda. When one party mostly capitulates and goes along, there is civility. When that party begins to respond to the people's desires, conflict rises, and that is a good thing.

We like to think of America as a meritocracy, a nation where people rise to power and prominence through their talents. The reality is that, at least for the influencers, power is largely a consequence of exploiting their role within closed, often secretive networks. These networks are rife with nepotism and almost incestuously interwoven. Let me name some names.

Did you know that Dr. Deborah Birx's husband, Paige Reffe, was an advance man for Hillary Clinton? Did you know that Senate Majority Leader Mitch McConnell is married to former Transportation Secretary Elaine Chao? Did you know that former North Dakota Senator (and Senate Majority Leader) Tom Daschle's wife, Linda, was a top airline lobbyist for twenty years? Did you know that Biden's former Chief of Staff, Ron Klain, is married to Monica Medina, the first ever ambassador to "plants and animals?" (I'm not making up that job. It is real—as are the connections.)

In May 2020, Michael Sussman went on trial for lying to the FBI. His case was a perfect illustration of the incestuous nature of politics in both Washington, DC, and the states. Fox News summed up the family and friendship ties that were woven through the case:

> US District Judge Christopher Cooper of the District of Columbia, who is presiding over the Sussmann case, is married to lawyer Amy Jeffress, who represented FBI lawyer Lisa Page in a civil case. Cooper, an Obama appointee, and Jeffress, a former top aide to Attorney General Eric Holder, are well connected in the Democratic Party. Current Attorney General Merrick Garland even presided over their 1999 wedding.[23]

At the staffer level, among reporters, and among elected officials and administration leaders and managers, relationships like these are common. They are intertwined, complex, and not always transparent. To some extent, this is natural. People live, work, and breathe politics in DC or in state capitals and major cities like Chicago, Dallas, Houston, and LA. Many of them come into the "business" of politics fresh out of college. They eat and drink and socialize together; they date and mate and marry. To some extent, this is inevitable. It only becomes dangerous to the republic when those informal and incestuous networks begin to work against the public interest.

These kinds of close connections don't just ensure perpetual employment for anyone lucky enough to be in these elite circles. They constitute a power center in and of themselves, in which favors are traded and deals concluded—and a lever of the Vise gets quietly, often secretly, turned tighter and tighter.

A far more obvious—and arguably even more pernicious—influence? The **public-sector unions,** which are in many respects the single most powerful political force in the United States today. The immense power of government employee unions is based on several factors:

- They are among the largest funders of political campaigns in the country. Ninety-one percent goes to Democrats and nine percent goes to Republicans, according to the Center for Responsive Politics.[24] The government unions fund the campaigns of the very people they then influence during contract negotiations.

- The public-sector unions operate our state, local, and federal governments. They are a powerful class of employees that form the permanent government. Even as politicians come and go, the government unions have members working in government for ten, twenty, thirty years and beyond. They hold the institutional memory that keeps the government running. They also ensure that government cares for them first, rather than ordinary citizens.

- The public-sector unions are financially immune to catastrophes that befall the rest of us. When the stock market goes up, they win. When the market goes down, they still win because taxes will be paid to replenish state coffers to pay their salaries and to the pension funds from which retirement payments are made.

- They are astonishingly wealthy. Many government workers that complete a full thirty-year career can retire while still in their fifties, often with free health care the rest of their lives and a guaranteed pension that will often range from $1.1 million to $2.5 million.
- They use the Vise to serve their interests, generating pressure that is quite literally bankrupting cities, states, and school districts across the nation.

The State of Illinois is among those most vulnerable to the abuse of the public-sector unions. Here, the union influencers have used the Vise to enrich its members at the expense of the poor and working class.

Illinois' career public employees pay little for excessive retirement benefits
Average benefits, retirement ages and employee contributions of career public employees with at least 30 years in five state retirement systems as of July 24, 2019.

System	Average lifetime payout	Average lifetime employee contribution	Average % covered by employee	Average retirement age	Average annual benefit
Teachers' Retirement System	$2,315,478	$113,526	5%	57.8	$82,222
State Universities Retirement System	$2,510,717	$121,328	5%	58.1	$90,154
State Employees' Retirement System	$1,697,078	$54,748	4%	56.9	$53,260
General Assembly Retirement System	$2,502,682	$199,605	12%	68.8	$147,933
Judges' Retirement System	$3,595,538	$171,200	8%	62.3	$146,057

Source: Freedom of Information Act request to state retirement systems

Note: Career employees are those with 30 years or more of service credit. GARS currently has only 12 career service retirees. Most SERS employees are also eligible for Social Security. Excludes 743 SURS retirees in self-managed plans. Excludes disability, survivor and other annuity types aside from normal retirement annuitants. Assumes average life expectancy of 85. Social Security life expectancy is 84 for men and 86.5 for women.

@illinoispolicy

Public-sector unions exert their greatest influence in Democrat-dominated "blue states," like Illinois, New York, New Jersey, Minnesota, and California. In these places, the insatiable demand for more and more pay and benefits has squeezed out spending for the genuinely disadvantaged. The average state government worker in Illinois earns about $66,000. The average Illinois career state retiree received $93,558 in pension payments in 2024, while the average worker in Illinois earned $69,020—$24,538 less.[25] Similar ratios are found in any state where public-sector unions dominate. The reality is that it is the working poor and middle class who fund millionaire retirement benefits for public-sector employees—employees who already receive salaries that are almost twice as high as the average private-sector worker. This is unjust and unsustainable, but it continues thanks to the tremendous influence of the public-sector unions.

Let me give you one example. The town of Harvey is a working-class suburb of Chicago that is more than 60% Black. In 2018, the city council was forced to lay off forty police and fire workers. The cuts amounted to 40% of Harvey's firefighters, 55% of regular police support personnel, and 25% of the unionized police force. It was a devastating blow to the people of Harvey. Why did it happen? The city could not meet its pension obligations to union retirees. Under Illinois law, that meant the state comptroller was required to confiscate revenues and redirect them to pay the pension funds first. This is the Progressive Political Vise in action: privileged elites, in this case public-sector unions, putting the squeeze on the residents of a working-class small town. For the unions, their pensions came before public safety. There are many other Harveys all across this country—and if we do not take back control of the Vise, there will be more.

How do the public-sector unions turn the lever? Massive campaign donations, reliable votes, and—in a close election—a small army of dedicated foot soldiers eager to ensure they don't lose their generous benefits. When a single lobbyist for Illinois AFSCME (the American Federation of State, County, and Municipal Employees, the nation's largest public-sector union) walks into the capitol in Springfield, every legislator knows that lobbyist has behind them some 35,000 active and involved members—as well as millions of dollars. That power influences. That power turns the lever. Government unions not only operate government, but they also give massive political contributions to their chosen candidates and incumbents, deploy ground-game canvassers and political organizers, and run one of the best propaganda machines in the business. They are a formidable, but not unconquerable, foe.

AFSCME is particularly noteworthy. You may recall they were the defendant in the *Janus v. AFSCME* US Supreme Court case I wrote about earlier. They are everywhere, in part because they are the largest government union in the country. In March 2025 they joined with the AFL-CIO and about a dozen other unions to stop President Trump from making cuts to an obscure agency, the Federal Mediation and Conciliation Services (FMCS).

Why would the unions want this agency to continue unfettered and unaccountable? The clue for you is in the word *conciliation*. Whenever unions reach an impasse with the government, they go to mediation. The tell is that the unions like this process because it sanctions much of what they had been negotiating for but were unable to secure with the government. The existence of the FMCS creates a wonderful dynamic for the unions: make outrageous demands that the government cannot accept, go to mediation, get conciliation, and attain 80 percent (my arbitrary estimate) of what they requested. Heads the union wins, tails the taxpayers lose—the mediation process *always* moves the ball in the union's direction.

That is why they sued—this agency is their partner in extracting more wealth and income from the American people.

Private-sector unions were once a hugely potent force in American politics, particularly on the left. Their numbers have declined substantially; in 1983, private-sector union members represented over 20% of the American labor force. Today, they are barely 6%. Compared to their brethren in the public sector, private-sector union members must live with the realities of the market. If they negotiate a contract that makes their business uncompetitive, their employer will soon go out of business—and unlike with public-sector retirees in Harvey, Illinois, the state won't intervene to make sure that generous benefits continue.

In the public-sector unions, leaders and members almost always share the same goals. They both overwhelmingly support Democrats. Since the advent of the Tea Party, the leadership of private-sector unions has remained loyally Democratic—but more and more ordinary members have turned to the right. While leaders of the United Auto Workers and the Teamsters endorse Democrats, Donald Trump has shown particular ability to win support from those unions' rank and file, a phenomenon that only seems to be accelerating with the results of the 2024 election. Unfortunately, while private-sector and public-sector workers often have very different interests, their respective leadership teams work in close coalition. The private-sector union bosses coordinate with public-sector unions, still supporting the progressive agenda, and still acting as a powerful elite influence on the Vise.

The **trial bar** collectively ranks as the fifth-largest funder of political campaigns. Unlike with the unions, the primary goal of the trial bar isn't to pressure elected officials to bestow generous salaries and pensions for its members. Their focus is on preventing tort reform. What the lawyers want to ensure is that the state does not impose limits on what can be awarded in personal injury, medical malpractice, or product liability suits. After all, the entire business model of the trial bar rests on collecting a substantial share of massive awards awarded by judges and juries.

The trial bar gives nearly 80% of its donations to Democrats. It uses the other 20% tactically, targeting a handful of important Republicans who might prove sympathetic to the bar's goals. While hugely bloated public-sector pensions are largely a phenomenon found in Democrat-dominated "blue states," tort reform faces obstacles even in many Republican-led "red states." It is easier to block reforms than it is to pass expensive pension enhancements, just as it is easier to spend money to elect a sympathetic county judge than it is to elect a state governor. The trial bar may not have the resources of the public-sector unions, but it uses its millions shrewdly. The consequence, of course, is the higher prices we pay for everything—as farmers, doctors, factories, and other productive businesses are forced to pay out millions in extravagant settlements—and spend millions more on defending themselves in wasteful and unjustified litigation. Just like the unions, both public and private, the trial bar influencers keep the squeeze on the American people.

One of the best examples of how the trial bar works the Political Vise occurred during the negotiation, writing, and implementation of

Obamacare. As many people pointed out, there was no way to reduce exorbitant medical costs without tort reform. The trial bar had made malpractice insurance unaffordable in many parts of the country; medical practices were closing, and patients were at risk of not receiving timely and competent care. There are many responsible ways to make medical care more affordable, but few were more attainable than medical tort reform. Attainable, of course, only as long as the politicians could withstand the squeeze from the trial bar.

Howard Dean—the former Vermont governor and later Democratic Party chair—was asked why no medical liability reforms were included in the "Affordable" Care Act. He replied that it was simple: "The people who wrote it did not want to take on the trial lawyers." President Barack Obama didn't want to be quite that candid. His administration wanted to sustain the illusion of reform by offering up "demonstration projects" to address some of the excesses of the trial bar. Supervising those projects? The Secretary of Health and Human Services (HHS), Kathleen Sebelius—the former governor of Kansas. Before she ran for office, Sebelius had served as a plaintiff's lawyer lobbyist. As HHS Secretary, her mandate was very clear: pretend to reform, but, as Dean had said, do not "take on the trial lawyers." Fifteen years after Obamacare passed into law, frivolous lawsuits continue to drive the cost of medical care higher and higher—driving doctors out of business and contributing to our nation's health crisis.

Another powerful lobby is certain **nonprofits**. Nonprofits are an essential ally of government. They provide much-needed services to the public. A key challenge for all players in the Political Vise is to distinguish those nonprofits that are run ethically and effectively (and many are!) from those that become a tool of a politician's political interests rather than the people's.

When he ran for re-election in 2010, then-Illinois Governor Pat Quinn, a Democrat, announced the creation of the $55 million Neighborhood Recovery Initiative (NRI). The NRI was designed to give money to community groups in the roughest urban neighborhoods with the ostensible goal of reducing violence and gang tensions. In reality, Governor Quinn simply funneled money through the NRI to turn out voters. Unemployed youth were paid with nonprofit funds to walk precincts and distribute fliers for the governor. It was a clear violation of the law—but also an example of how government funding of nonprofits can go astray. Though it's rarely as egregious as Governor Quinn and the NRI, the symbiotic relationship between government-funded nonprofits and political leaders rarely works out to the benefit of the people. Many nonprofits do exemplary and vital work, and most try to use the dollars they get from the state to serve their cause. As conservatives and advocates for limited government, we want charities to do what government can't and shouldn't do. Sometimes, that will mean ensuring those nonprofits get government support. The challenge is making sure that those nonprofits do not use the Vise against the very people they mean to serve.

As noted earlier, the entire efficacy of government funding nonprofits, or NGOs, has come under overdue scrutiny as a result of DOGE's deep dive into federal spending, including USAID. It is time to curtail this unaccountable, opaque spending that is out of reach of the people's accountability.

Over the past twenty years, the **Green Lobby** has emerged as a particularly powerful and influential force. My proverbial hat is off to them: "Big Green" has become a master of using orchestration to create pressure in the Vise. Ordinary Americans can feel that squeeze every day, as they cope with one unpopular "green" initiative after another. In recent years, the Green Lobby has:

- Regulated small gas cans to make them practically unusable
- Limited the amount of water to flush toilets
- Banned the incandescent light bulb (Trump has rescinded this!)
- Reduced the amount of water used in dishwashers and washing machines to the point that the results continue to deteriorate
- Imposed Corporate Average Fuel Economy (CAFE) standards to compel automakers to build ever smaller cars; the result is higher traffic fatalities

- Imposed, through lawsuits and regulations, so many restrictions that it now takes years to build roads, bridges, and buildings that once took a fraction of the time and cost; the result is that desperately needed housing doesn't get built
- Imposed electric vehicle mandates in several states, and effectively at the federal level through the CAFE standards, even as chargers remain scarce and often unusable

Big Green uses the Vise to extract money from government to run education and advocacy campaigns—campaigns that promote hysteria about climate change and call for ever greater governmental control of every aspect of our economy. The infamous Green New Deal, ridiculed when initially proposed, has largely been implemented through a piecemeal process. This progression—from ridicule to law—is a perfect illustration of the Political Vise at work.

Perhaps one of Big Green's most outrageous proposals is to eliminate the use of natural gas. Natural gas is the most abundant, clean-burning fuel available. It is easy to transport and use in almost every activity requiring energy. At one time the Green Lobby loved natural gas—at least, when we didn't have a lot of it. They promptly flipped to oppose its use just as the United States became the largest producer of natural gas with reserves sufficient to last hundreds of years. Big Green's opposition has stifled development of energy independence, rendering us ever more vulnerable to foreign adversaries.

Both the Obama and Biden administrations lavished subsidies on their favored Big Green companies. Not at all surprisingly, those companies were the ones that had the most effective influencers lobbying on their behalf. As president, Barack Obama gave more than $500 million in loan guarantees to Solyndra, a California solar company that soon went bankrupt. That was chump change compared to the $369 billion in Joe Biden's so-called Inflation Reduction Act. The public may not want electric cars and low-flow toilets and crummy, useless paper straws. It doesn't matter: Democrat administrations love their Big Green lobbyists. What the marketplace shuns, the government rewards.

TheHill.com publishes an annual list of the most influential Washington lobbyists. One thing has remained true for the past decade: The leaders of the nation's most powerful and wealthy Big Green organizations are invariably near the top of the list. The Natural Resources Defense Council, the Environmental Working Group, Earthjustice, the National Wildlife Federation, the League of Conservation Voters, and the Sierra Club—these are just the "apex predators" of the environmental lobby. As a collective, they hold extraordinary sway in DC and in state capitals. Big Green now rivals the public-sector unions as the most formidable deployer of the influencer side of the Political Vise.

In the beginning of this book, I explained how I came up with the concept of the Political Vise. I had asked the late Senator Tom Coburn why it was that almost everyone in public office moved leftwards after being elected. He explained the basic reason: The left wants to spend, the right wants to restrain spending, and the personal political rewards of spending almost invariably outweigh the rewards that come with restraint. This explains, of course, why there are relatively few powerful influencers on the right.

Relatively few, however, is not the same as none. There is the National Taxpayers Union (NTU), for example, with Brandon Arnold as its chief lobbyist. Brandon and NTU do a fantastic job of representing the interests of private-sector taxpayers, as does political veteran Grover Norquist of Americans for Tax Reform. Others deserving of mention include Tom Schatz of Americans Against Government Waste and Jessica Anderson of Sentinel Action Fund. Brooke Rollins, Director of Domestic Policy in President Trump's first term, built a highly influential team at the America First Policy Institute. She is now the Secretary of Agriculture in Trump's second term.

In recent years, perhaps the most effective of all conservative influencers has been Leonard Leo. Leo, a former executive at the Federalist Society and advisor to President Trump on judicial appointments, serves as principal at one of the largest conservative organizations in the country, the Marble Freedom Trust. His influence over lifetime judicial appointments, and now his stewardship of $1.6 billion in the Marble Freedom Trust means Leo will be an influencer for decades to come.

One of the great challenges our liberty movement faces is that we too often fracture rather than unify. In the late spring of 2025 President Trump posted a scathing, unwarranted criticism of Leo that well illustrates the breaches that too often happen on the right as compared to the more disciplined approach of the left. As a reminder, the left stays more disciplined because their unifying purpose is to control government and its spending to advance their business and ideological agendas.

There are other influencers I could name, but, in keeping with the first rule of Fight Club . . .

This table summarizes the problem of this imbalance.

	# ON HILL.COM LIST	# CONSERVATIVE	%
CORPORATIONS	90	3	3.3%
ASSOCIATIONS	132	3	2.3%
HIRED GUNS	194	0	0.0%
GRASS ROOTS	61	12	19.7%
TOTALS	477	18	3.8%

Source: TheHill.com 2019 Top Lobbying List

The Political Vise requires influencers. From the very beginning of our republic, various interest groups have lobbied their elected officials. When the

Vise works as intended, the influencers play a vital and helpful role. Yes, the influencers—corporations, unions, interest groups—are driven by the business and ideological interests of those they represent. That isn't the problem. Our republic is strong when various interests—businesspeople, farmers, scientists, and so forth—can come together to lobby the government for issues important to their particular group. It's much better to have these groups lobby for what they know they need than to have the government simply impose its own will. Influencers, the media, and the people all have a vital role to play in operating the Traditional Political Vise to achieve the best outcomes.

The problem is that in recent decades a handful of extremely powerful elite interests, like those I've mentioned in this chapter, have gained near total control of a lever of the Vise. Those who would restrict our freedoms and aggregate ever more power to the state? They have far more influence than those who campaign for liberty. We need influencers, yes—but "our team" has, to put it mildly, so far mounted insufficient countervailing force on behalf of the freedom agenda.

Consider the power of the Tesla protests following Elon Musk's installation as the head of DOGE. Why would anyone, left or right, object to the goal of identifying waste, fraud, and abuse? First, because the left cannot allow President Trump any successes that the public finds satisfying. Their goal of destroying him personally and politically did not end with his 2024 victory, it just entered a new phase. Second, the DOGE effort is attacking the root of the left's power—the deep, broad, and mostly unaccountable administrative state is quite real. The examination and exposure of all the insanity long normalized at USAID, the EPA, the Treasury, the Department of Education, and more, revealed to the public the truth about our government in the same way the pandemic and school lockdowns opened our eyes to what is actually going on in our schools.

In order to blunt Musk and DOGE's impact, he had to be attacked. Out of nowhere an anti-Musk, anti-Tesla protest began, including firebombing Tesla dealers and vandalism against Tesla cars and their owners. Protest signs declared "Burn a Tesla, Save Democracy." Tesla's sales and stock tanked as the protests grew. These protests are the classic example of an orchestrated effort to create the illusion of a grassroots uprising. Remember that organic (real, or natural) uprisings apply tremendous people pressure to the politicians inside the Traditional Political Vise. Orchestrated ones, when amplified by a compliant corporate media, can be almost as effective.

These Tesla protests were more out in the open than many such orchestrated efforts with its own, well-funded website, TeslaTakedown.com. All of this begs the question, who is funding this and similar efforts?

It is difficult to know for sure, but George Soros's Open Society Foundation, Project Indivisible, protest organizers Troublemakers and Disruption Project have all been reportedly involved.[26] But it is easier to ask *cui bono*—who benefits? Public- and private-sector unions, the trial bar, the Green Lobby, the Democratic Party—essentially the entire coalition of the left benefits. If we could do a forensic audit of the spending, I believe these are the places it would lead. (And perhaps all the way to the CCP in China—but that is a different book.)

Just how insidious and deep is the influencer corruption? For decades Thomas Hale Boggs Jr. headed the lobbying arm for one of the world's most powerful law firms: Squire, Patton, and Boggs. Few Americans in the last century understood how to deploy influence and use the Vise better than "Tommy" Boggs. Tommy's father was a long-time Louisiana congressman, while his mother served as United States ambassador to the Vatican. (The latter post is a coveted reward for the most elite of Roman Catholic influencers. I am thrilled that my good friend Brian Burch currently serves in that role.) Tommy's sister? None other than celebrated political reporter Cokie Roberts, once an enormously powerful figure at ABC News and, later, at NPR. Talk about incestuous political connections!

It would not be hyperbole to call Tommy Boggs the "godfather" of the Washington lobbying world. He thought of himself as entirely non-partisan, hiring former senators from both sides of the aisle to work for his firm. The political journalist Ken Silverstein wrote of Patton Boggs that "its past and current staff reads like an Encyclopedia of Contemporary Sociopaths and Miscreants."[27] Under Tommy, the Patton Boggs philosophy was to represent every well-heeled client who came through the door, regardless of their views, their agenda, or their decency. He lavished food, liquor, and campaign donations on anyone and everyone who would do his bidding.

When Tommy Boggs died in 2014, the distinguished guest list at his funeral was proof positive of the colossal power of influencers. Everyone in the swamp paid tribute to the amoral-yet-amiable master of his craft. Nancy Pelosi eulogized her friend as "a passionate advocate for American workers and middle-class families," which was a staggering lie. (To be fair, consider the source.) The truth is that few did more than Tommy Boggs to make it harder for American workers and families to prosper and live.

I often hear well-intentioned conservatives lament the pernicious influence of lobbyists like Tommy Boggs. That frustration is understandable. The truth is that we need *more*, not fewer lobbyists. We need *more* men and women committed to advancing human freedom and dignity—and with the political skill to get into the rooms where the decisions are made. To say that in an ideal America there would be no lobbyists is to misunderstand how our Founders thought of power and its rightful exercise.

If we are to be loyal to the Founders' vision, to the Constitution and to free enterprise, we need to do more than point out the reality that the left's influencers are a threat to our entire way of life. Instead, we need to marshal our resources to deploy a true counterbalance in Washington and in state capitals, an army of influencers committed to representing the people and the liberty agenda. The theory of the Political Vise provides the road map for how we can accomplish that goal. The question now is whether we in the freedom movement have the will to do what it takes to seize back that lever.

In the Traditional Political Vise, the three sides that we have now covered (media, the people and influencers) all apply pressure to political decision-makers—the politicians. Let's take a look at them.

Chapter 9

THE POLITICIANS: SETTING A NEW AGENDA

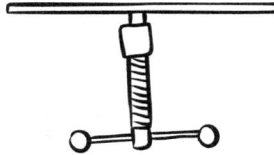

There are two types of politicians. There is the one who becomes a politician to advance a policy agenda. I would put Ronald Reagan, Barack Obama, and Donald Trump in that category. Then there is the politician that adopts a policy agenda to fuel his political ambitions. I would put Bill Clinton, Mitt Romney, and Joe Biden in that category. One is authentic, though their policies may be horrific. The other is useful if you can harness the power of the Political Vise for your cause—and maddening if the other side does so for theirs.

The COVID-19 panic laid bare that there are two other categories of politicians. There is the one that gains political power for the thrill of it, delighting in imposing their views on how you should live and how society should be structured. They are authoritarians. Then there is the politician that gains political power and may enjoy exercising it, but they use that power primarily to unleash the human spirit within each of us and they find joy when that liberty soars. Governors Gavin Newsom, Gretchen Whitmer, and J. B. Pritzker fall into the former category. Governors Ron DeSantis, Greg Abbott, Kim Reynolds, and Doug Ducey fall into the latter category.

If your kid comes home from school and announces, "Hey, Dad, I want to grow up to be president," you might—or might not—be pleased. But I am certain you hope he is the type of person that wants to be a politician to advance a worthy agenda!

Either way, I'm fairly sure you'd be a good deal less pleased if your child declared, "When I grow up, I want to be a politician and I will adopt whatever beliefs I need to win!"

We all probably have a favorite president. We may like our own member of Congress (see the box to the right). We may be fond of our own state governor. But affection and admiration for individual leaders rarely translate into respect for politicians as a class. We tend to speak of politicians with contempt, even to their faces. To some extent, of course, that contempt is earned. Yet, like it or not, politicians play a vital role in our society—and in the Political Vise.

The late Milton Friedman was perhaps the greatest economist of the twentieth century. He did not limit himself to the study of markets; like all truly influential economists, he knew his primary field was the study of human nature and incentives.

Friedman was a man of the right and a fierce defender of the free market. (He was Ronald Reagan's favorite economist, and it would not be unkind to suggest that the Gipper should have listened to Friedman even more closely than he did.) Yet Friedman understood that the real problem wasn't that too many liberals were winning federal and state office. The real problem was a misunderstanding of incentives and pressure:

> I do not believe that the solution to our problem is simply to elect the right people. The important thing is to establish a political climate of opinion which will make it politically profitable for the wrong people to do the right thing. Unless it is politically profitable for the wrong people to do the right thing, the right people will not do the right thing either, or if they try, they will shortly be out of office.[28]

Politicians Are People, Too!

According to a Gallup poll in April 2025, Congress remains unpopular with a 28 percent approval rating, actually up since October 2024 by about 12 points. Sixty-seven percent disapprove, down from 82 percent last year.

Even with this improvement, Congress remains deeply unpopular—and yet over 90 percent of incumbents are re-elected. What explains this?

People dislike Congress generally but seem to like their representative locally. It is similar to the teacher phenomenon—many teachers are terrible, but thankfully my child's teacher is terrific!

Part of the reason is that politicians are skilled at making people like them. I confess, I know many politicians, and I like most of them, even the ones with whom I disagree. They must possess some charm, or they can't stay elected.

I also confess to respecting their work ethic. I have found that most politicians work long hours, are under much stress and pressure, and miss many family events to advance their careers.

I do believe that most politicians start out with a policy interest and good intentions. But the Political Vise grinds and pulverizes those good intentions for all too many, all too quickly.

In the end, their virtue is judged by the two opening paragraphs at the beginning of this chapter and by their policy results. By those measures, most politicians are failing their constituents and America. Those who are succeeding should be respected and supported.

One final note on the high re-election rate: Politicians are also great mapmakers—most districts are drawn to not be competitive; only about 10 percent are vigorously contested each cycle.

This is, of course, a call for reinstating the Traditional Political Vise. Milton Friedman didn't use our image, but this idea of making it "politically profitable for the wrong people to do the right thing" gets to the very heart of why the Vise matters. I understand and empathize with the urge to "throw the bums out" and replace the current crop of bad politicians with better ones. But as Friedman says, if we do not change the system of pressures and incentives, changing the faces and names within the existing system will lead only to disappointment. To put it another way, we are angry at politicians for responding rationally to the system in which they operate.

The vast majority of politicians are neither particularly good nor bad. They are simply untethered to principle—and malleable in fact. When they find themselves in the Progressive Political Vise, with the left in full control of the screws, they automatically take the path of least resistance. Even the most principled politicians find it impossible to resist the pressure at times.

Think of the last few Republican House Speakers and Minority Leaders. Each one soon falls out of favor with the rank-and-file of the party, who declare they feel betrayed by the concessions and compromises the Speaker or Leader is forced to make. To modify a common expression in sports, conservatives keep "hating the player" rather than "hating the game." We don't need better quarterbacks; we need better rules for the sport. As Friedman says, we need to build a system that makes it easy for the mediocre, the malleable, and even the amoral politician to do the right thing.

We need to back up for a moment. What exactly is a politician? In one sense, the definition is simple: A politician is someone who makes political decisions as part of their job. The complicated part is that we have so very, very many of them. Presidents, governors, senators, state legislators, city council members, school board members, county supervisors, park district board members, county sheriffs, and, of course, the proverbial dog catchers. Each and every one is a politician. Add them all up, and according to the website Poliengine, there are more than 519,692 such politicians—elected officials—in the United States.

	NUMBER	%
Federal	537	0.1%
State	18,759	3.6%
Local	500,396	96.3%
Total	519,692	100.0%

Source: Poliengine.com

The media is obsessively focused on presidential elections. The reality is that even with Donald Trump's re-election, and Republican control of the House and Senate, the 537 federal elected officials together make up only one-tenth of one percent of the total number of politicians in this country. It is those other 519,155 state and local politicians who have a massive and often hidden impact on your life. They may not be household names, but they can make or break your household's quality of life.

By many estimates, my state of Illinois has the highest property taxes in the nation—when adjusted for the cost of living. It has one of the nation's highest state and local tax burdens. Illinois has land borders with five other states: Iowa, Missouri, Indiana, Kentucky, and Wisconsin. To one degree or another, each of our neighbors has considerably lower taxes. There's no passport control on state borders; it's not hard to see why the Land of Lincoln continues to lose population to all of its neighbors. It's not any presidential administration's fault that Illinois is hemorrhaging people. It's the decisions made by our own politicians, year after year after year.

President Trump was right to warn about the dangers of the "deep state." I am convinced that Donald Trump did the country a great service by shedding light on the near-absolute power wielded by unelected staff and bureaucrats in Washington, DC. The truth is, however, that if we are going to seize back our freedom from the "swamp," we will need to grasp how powerful the deep state has become not only in our nation's capital, but in cities and towns and counties across the nation.

I have a confession to make. Years ago, I too was a politician. My own village is tiny: 172 houses, seven streets, a post office, a train station, and a park—and a population of 500. Almost everyone in the village ends up eventually serving in our local government. I took my turn as a member of the village board and then spent four years as village president.

It was an eye-opening experience. Our jobs were fairly simple and obvious, such as making sure the sewers discharged to the treatment center and not into people's basements. If you want to start a revolution, let human waste regularly back up into people's finished basements. They will come after you with pitchforks—or, in our village, with empty bottles of bourbon or cabernet to knock you over the head! Fortunately, that only happened once, and no one was impaled or concussed. The town was neighborly and understanding about the occasional malodorous calamity.

And then, in my role as village president, I hired a new building inspector. He had excellent qualifications and performed well in his interview. I expected no problems with him. Yet as soon as he took over, he seemed to get drunk on the power given to him by ordinances and statutes. He was convinced he knew exactly how we should be living our lives. He was very clear we'd been doing it wrong, and he decided he was going to enforce a litany of long-neglected rules in our little community. Soon enough, complaints from homeowners trying to remodel their properties began to pour in. I had a mediation meeting with this inspector and one particularly frustrated homeowner. It was clear to me that the homeowner was in the right; I took the appropriate action, solved the problem, and put it behind me. Or so I thought. The building inspector stayed on after I stepped down. Sure enough, a few years later it was our turn to do a remodel and addition. We found ourselves at the mercy of that same building inspector for our permits and approvals. To say that he used his power to screw us would be an understatement. It was a reminder that the deep state is everywhere.

That building inspector was not a bad person. He was not trying to be vindictive. He took great pleasure in the power he wielded, but he genuinely believed he was exercising it for everyone's good. When he'd turn down yet another request, he'd repeat the same thing: "I am just making sure things are safe for your family." It sounds so reasonable. As we learned during the pandemic, safety is always the chief rationale the deep state uses to infringe on our liberties. I have no doubt that most of these overzealous code enforcers believe very much in the good that they are doing. But just because a bully believes the bullying is needed doesn't make him any less of a bully. A sincere autocrat is no less dangerous than a cynical one.

The building inspector was not an elected politician. For all the considerable power that those 519,692 elected officials wield, it pales in comparison to the millions of state and local workers whom those politicians appoint and hire.

According to the data-aggregating site Statista, there are more than 14 million state and local government employees. Add in the federal government's 2.6 million employees, and we have over 17 million workers who draw their salaries directly from taxpayers. The ratio of federal, state, and local government employees to elected officials? More than 33 to 1.

Obviously, not every politician hires exactly thirty-three full-time government workers. I hired far fewer—but the one building inspector I did hire did real damage. Extrapolate from that one anecdote, and you see the problem. It's not just the decisions our elected officials make—it's the decisions made by the people they hire. And rarely are the latter ever held accountable.

CATEGORY	NUMBER
Education	7,687,128
Hospitals	905,695
Police Protection	904,330
Corrections	690,001
Public Welfare	496,011
Highways	472,411
Health	413,868
Judicial & Legal	400,060
Finance Admin	391,256
Fire Protection	342,833
Transit	244,896
Parks & Rec	191,128
Water Supply	169,607
Natural Resources	157,484
Sewage	123,011
Housing & Community Development	100,278

Solid Waste Management	100,261
Libraries	89,945
Electric Power	76,053
Social Insurance Administration	65,700
Air Transportation	48,473
Water Transport Terminals	12,773
Gas Supply	11,265
State Liquor Stores	6,435
Other Government Administration	243,906
All Other	406,734
Total	14,741,542

Source: Statista.com

CATEGORY	NUMBER
Federal, State, Local	17,351,542
Elected	519,692
Ratio	33.4

Sources: Statista.com, Governing.com

The deep state isn't just the 519,692 for whom we voted, one way or another. It's the 17,351,542 for whom we didn't. If you want to know how freedom is being crushed and how our republic is at risk, all you have to understand is what that ratio of more than 33 to 1 means to your daily life. For every person for whom you voted, more than thirty-three people exercise unchecked influence over your life. We the People, the essence of a republic, have been replaced by this massive, entrenched, sclerotic deep state. These millions of government employees, many well-meaning and convinced they have our best interests at heart, wield near authoritarian control. We the People have little recourse for justice when we are mistreated by them. (For a great read on the subject, I highly recommend Jason Chaffetz's book *The Deep State*.)

Since 2020 we have all learned that the power of the deep state is nearly impossible to counter. From the grotesque abuses of power by public health professionals in federal, state, and local government to the revelations of the rogue FBI out to entrap Lieutenant General Michael Flynn, to the traitorous Russian collusion hoax targeting President Trump, to outsourced government censorship of social media during and after the 2020 election, the deep state has wielded its power with ever greater brazenness. They have dared the American people to say, "Enough." We can say "Enough" far more effectively if we first understand how to motivate the politicians who oversee the Deep State.

Whether they are elected officials or appointed bureaucrats, everything is "political" to politicians. As you will remember from the beginning of this book, the three primary motives for politicians are

- Expediency
- Fear
- Principle

If your goal is to use the Vise to pressure a politician to make a particular decision, it is vital to remember that the politician will invariably respond to that pressure based on their own particular mix of expediency, fear, and principle. It's worth examining each of those motives in turn. If we're going to put politicians in the Vise, we need to understand exactly what makes them "feel the squeeze."

Political Expediency

At its core, political expediency is all about the deal, or what's euphemistically called "horse-trading." I will scratch your back if you scratch mine, goes the saying; in Congress, for example, horse-trading means "I will vote for your bridge to nowhere if you will vote for my highway to hell." Notice that in practice, horse-trading means more spending, more waste, and ever greater government expansion. In order for one congressman to get his useless bridge, he must support another representative's unneeded highway. It is always easier to get two bad pieces of legislation passed than one. Look at the massive stimulus bills that emerged from Washington, DC, during the pandemic—each of them was stuffed with goodies that resulted from round after round of horse-trading.

Political expediency goes well beyond horse-trading. Politicians make choices based on both short- and long-term electoral imperatives. They think not only about how to get their bridge built but how they will win the next election. When you lobby a politician, you must make the case for your proposed legislation in terms of why and how it would be expedient for that politician to support it. Politicians may genuinely care about a policy's effect on people, but that care is almost always downstream from the political considerations. They first focus on the political impact. They will ask some basic questions: *Who will oppose this policy and why? Who will support this policy and why? Where will the bulk of my donors be on this issue? How will my grassroots supporters view this bill? How will it play in the media?* Those are politically expedient considerations. They affect every political decision-maker, including very good, principled ones. When you lobby them, you need to have ready answers to those questions. You must be able to frame your goal in terms of expediency.

The best way to sell a proposal is to first consider the political implications for the decision-maker. You should construct soothing—but compelling—arguments, using each of the main sides of the Political Vise.

"Your constituents (the **people**) support this policy. We surveyed your district, and we found that 73 percent are in favor of it."

"We spoke with Bob Smith, Sam Johnson, and David Wright (**donors and influencers**). They agree this is a good idea and a policy you should lead on.

"We've crafted a suggested opinion piece that your team could submit to the local paper. During our recent meeting with the paper's editors (**media**), they loved this idea."

Based upon my informal survey of hundreds of political decision-makers over the years, I estimate that about 65 percent of all policy decisions are made through this filter—political expediency. The successful citizen activist absolutely must understand this and craft sales pitches through the lens of expediency. That is not selling out—that is selling in the language politicians speak as their mother tongue. Once you close on that aspect of the sale, only then do you move on to how the policy will change people's lives for the better.

Political Fear

Political fear is real, it is powerful, and it is a vital component of the Vise. Think of former Senators Kyrsten Sinema of Arizona and Joe Manchin of West Virginia. Each was elected in a conservative state. Each was considerably more moderate than their fellow Democratic senators. Each became key to passing or blocking Senate legislation during the first two years of Joe Biden's presidency.

In 2021 and 2022, I participated in many discussions on how to ramp up pressure on Manchin and Sinema "to do the right thing" and stop radically leftist legislation. We appealed to each using arguments from expediency—but also by deploying fear. We made it clear that Arizona and West Virginia voters did not want the bloated spending of Build Back Better, they did not want the filibuster gutted, and they did not want to continue writing blank checks to the Ukrainian regime in Kiev. Though they didn't always vote our way, Sinema and Manchin responded to the very real anger of their own constituents. Rightly afraid for their political futures, they blocked many of the most extreme elements of the Biden agenda.

Tellingly, the left also tried to use fear to squeeze these two swing senators. They rolled out paid media campaigns, grassroots activation, social-media pressure, and more. Infamously, they overreached when a series of angry far-left protestors followed Sinema into the ladies' room, continuing to harass the senator as she did her business in a stall, emerged, and (thankfully) washed her hands. The protestor videoed the entire encounter. The general reaction was that the left had gone too far again—using physical intimidation as a substitute for political pressure. It was a humorous but dangerous overreach.

It is the left, too, that has issued far more sinister threats against Supreme Court justices. As I've noted before, the Supreme Court is also a political body. Despite the efforts to work both collegially and outside of the electoral arena, the justices have always been aware of the political nature of their decisions. In the spring of 2022, someone working within the Supreme Court leaked a draft of the decision in *Dobbs v. Jackson Women's Health Organization*. The draft indicated the Court would soon overturn 1973's controversial *Roe v. Wade* abortion decision. This leak was the ultimate act of betrayal of the Court as an institution. Privacy and trust had long governed the Court and its staff. Someone on the inside decided that tradition of comity was worth violating to create public pressure—and perhaps scare one of the justices away from overturning Roe.

Sometimes, the threats become very serious indeed. In June 2022—just two weeks before the *Dobbs* decision was released—an armed California man was arrested near the home of Justice Brett Kavanaugh. The suspect made it clear he intended to assassinate the conservative justice. (The left-leaning media offered almost no coverage of the case, wishing to avoid drawing attention to the consequences of their own hysterical coverage of the Court.)

Based upon my informal survey of hundreds of political decision makers over the years, I estimate that about **30 percent** of all policy decisions are made through the filter of political fear. The successful activist understands that deploying fear is risky. It is a strategy to be used with prudence and without malice. The other side can wield threats without much risk. The right does not have that luxury. We can and must make it clear that politicians who oppose a liberty agenda will pay a price at the ballot box. It is not wrong to threaten an official that you'll withhold your vote. It's not wrong to make it clear you'll primary a politician in the next election. It is wrong to threaten their physical safety, accost them at airports, and verbally abuse their children. We must distinguish between a warning to withdraw support and an actual intimation of violence. I know full well the left doesn't always draw that distinction, as Donald Trump knows better than anyone. For the sake of the republic, *we* must.

Political Principle

My informal survey of politicians led me to estimate that 65% of them act primarily on expedience and 30% primarily out of fear. I'll bet you can do the math: That leaves 5% who make policy decisions primarily on principle. I doubt that shocks anyone. President Trump won in 2016 and 2024 in no small part because of deep frustration with our political class. Millions of Americans are sick and tired of being governed by people untethered to a guiding philosophy.

I am often asked how I make policy decisions. What is my filter? The answer is simple: If a given policy empowers people and fits within the framework of the Constitution, I am generally for it. If it further empowers government, I am generally against it. Of course, I understand that even principles must be worked out within the system. For example, I think taxing labor is a form of slavery. One's labor should not be taxed, ever. It is servitude to the government, which is just as evil as forced labor to another person. I also recognize that is not yet the majority view. So, if I were a politician and a flat-income-tax proposal came before me, I would vote for it in a heartbeat. In a republic, we cannot allow the ideal to be the enemy of the good—or at least, of the better. If the goal is to empower a free people within the system the Framers intended, principle requires compromise.

A good way to learn about candidates, or politicians running for re-election, is to ask them about their decision-making filters. If they say something like "I consult my district, listen to my constituents and then make a decision," that is a politically expedient answer. It is also an invitation to a follow-up:

"But when you can't reach anyone, you are alone in the room and need to make a decision, what is your filter then?"

The moments that follow will likely include either awkward silence or (given that these are politicians) filled with a lot of words with little meaning. Ideally, you would hear something like, "I decide based upon the needs of my district filtered through my personal philosophy. My personal philosophy is that I want to grow government revenue by growing the economy, not raising rates or fees." Or, perhaps, "I want to find ways to get government to do more with less." What you don't want to hear is, "I'm not sure. What do you think it should be?" I had a candidate for office ask me that question. (That Republican candidate ran for governor in 2022 in Illinois; thankfully he lost badly in the primary!)

When we say that someone is principled, it sounds like a compliment. Surely someone acting out of principle is better than someone acting out of self-interest (be it self-preservation or expediency). The problem, of course, is that not all principles are equal. Vladimir Lenin was principled. Pol Pot was principled. They were each responsible for millions of deaths and monumental suffering, but they were each sincere believers in Communism. They were evil, but they were not frauds. When you wish for politicians with principles, make sure those principles are the right ones.

Why Are Democrats and Republicans Different?

It's fashionable on the right to describe the Democrats and the Republicans as two wings of a "uniparty." The casual observer looks at the horse-trading and the compromises, and laments that all politicians are essentially the same. I understand that view, but though there's some merit to the complaint, the accusations of a "uniparty" miss some vital distinctions. If we are to recapture the screws of the Vise, we need to understand the very real differences.

I mentioned earlier that there are two types of politicians. One type becomes a politician to advance a policy agenda. The second type adopts a policy agenda to advance his or her political ambition.

The Democrat Party attracts mostly the former. It is not that they are more virtuous, but rather that they have very clear ideas about using government to advance "progress."

The left's coalition is composed of two categories of people. The first group is the influencers we covered earlier: the trial bar, government unions, private-sector unions, nonprofits that get most of their money from government, and the green extremists. These powerful influencers do not create anything. Using government is their business model. They push for policies that empower them to extract wealth and income in the form of legal settlements, generous salaries, benefits, pensions, and government grants.

About Campaign Finance "Reform"

All campaign finance regulations are designed to protect the political class from being held accountable by the people. Whenever a politician is advocating for campaign finance limitations, what they really want to limit is not money. Incumbents always find the money (or it finds them).

What they really want to limit is you and your rights to redress your grievances. They want to take the power of the Political Vise away from you and keep it for themselves. They want to prevent you from marshalling enough resources to challenge them and take them out of office or hold them to account for a bad vote.

They will disguise this true goal in all kinds of high-sounding rhetoric about democracy, fairness, dark money, and more. All lies. They are lying to you every time. Don't be lied to. The Vise should be used every time to stop any campaign finance "reforms." In fact, those so-called reforms are an existential threat to the Vise and to you. After all, it takes money to operate the Vise.

The second group, which includes both some influencers and a great many Democrat politicians, is the ideological true believers. These social justice warriors intend to use government to create equity and fairness. They have embraced the woke doctrine, and they reject our nation's Founding Principles. This second group shares a common belief in using the power of government to achieve a better world. They draw many aspiring "change-makers," often recruited from elite college campuses. Many want to be the next Kamala Harris, the next Alexandria Ocasio-Cortez (a.k.a. AOC), the next Hakeem Jeffries.

On the other side of the aisle, contemporary Republicans don't have this same intense fervor about changing the world. They want lower taxes, less government, and the chance to pursue the American Dream through free enterprise. They don't want more laws or more spending. Other Republicans, particularly in rural and exurban areas, hold strong views on abortion, immigration, and guns. While views on these social issues vary widely from district to district, what unifies the Republican party is—still—a free-market economic agenda. People on the right generally want government to leave them alone: They want the government to do less, not more.

It requires actions to roll policies back. The influencers and the media howl that those nasty conservatives are trying to take precious things away. No politician likes to *take* things away. They assume, not wrongly, that the expedient and popular thing is to *give* the people things. Conservatives too often are ill-equipped to explain the basic truth: rolling back excessive government is giving the people something very precious: more freedom and individual empowerment.

Even as Washington politicians from both parties (and President Trump himself) supported a massive expansion of government spending during the COVID-19 panic, we saw a handful of brave Republican governors push back against the elite consensus. Instead of prolonged shutdowns, state leaders like Ron DeSantis, Greg Abbott, and Kristi Noem (among others) adopted a default question: "How quickly can we get the economy opened up?" Time has vindicated the wisdom of ending lockdowns as soon as possible, especially for the sake of small business owners and schoolchildren. Too few Republicans in Congress showed the same courage as these "red state" governors.

The "early" COVID reopenings were a reminder that Republicans are at their best when they prioritize rolling back government. Because the pandemic restrictions were so onerous and unreasonable, and the fiscal stimulus so wildly excessive, it was easy for voters to see the benefits of doing away with regulations. Mask mandates, for example, are a tangible reminder of the raw power of the government. Lifting those mandates invariably proved popular and helped the likes of Ron DeSantis and other liberty-oriented governors glide to re-election in the post-pandemic 2022 midterms. There's a lesson here: we can win by pushing back against government overreach. The trick is helping the public see other mandates and regulations the same way they saw the requirement to wear a piece of fabric on their faces!

Part of the problem is that politics attracts many of the left's best and brightest. On the right, the best and brightest tend to go into business and entrepreneurship. This makes sense: The left believes that government is the primary vehicle for building a better world. The right believes that free enterprise, faith, and family are the highest callings. The most gifted people gravitate to the professions where they believe they can have the greatest impact. What that means in practice is that the right invariably will attract fewer talented people interested in political careers.

Republican districts are rarely filled to the brim with potential candidates. The best option is often to recruit successful businesspeople to leave the private sector to go into public life. In our contentious political environment, that's often a very hard sell! Over the years, I've worked tirelessly to recruit excellent Republican candidates. My colleagues and I have had thousands of conversations, driven hundreds of thousands of miles, and swallowed a lot of bad coffee and an unhealthy number of Diet Cokes, all in pursuit of excellent candidates. Too often, the answer is, "I'm flattered, but no thanks." What keeps the recruiters going is the knowledge that one or two great finds—like former Illinois state representatives Tom Morrison and Jeanne Ives, or the brilliant Congressmen Jim Jordan and Tom Massie—can transform the political landscape.

Recruiting candidates will remain a great challenge for the right. To find a principled person who is available to run, with the financial where-withal, the temperament, the network, and the skills, is very, very difficult. And even when that person has been successfully recruited, all too often they end up moving left once in office. They find they like the game, the stature, the power. They too begin to choose expediency for the sake of ambition. Think of Arlen Specter, Charlie Crist, Mitt Romney, Liz Cheney, and Adam Kinzinger and a dozen more like them. They each felt the squeeze of the Progressive Political Vise—and each lacked the conviction to resist its pressure.

It is important to recruit excellent Republican candidates. Yet as Milton Friedman made so clear, we cannot build a better politics merely by electing better people. The system that the Framers designed was intended to pro-duce beneficial outcomes regardless of the character of individual politi-cians. The value of the Political Vise is that it works whether a given politician is motivated by principle, fear, expediency, or some mix of all three. The task before us is to be clear-eyed about human nature, resolute on policy, and above all else, to regain control of the Political Vise. Whether they are heroes or villains or simply ordinary men and women, whether elected or appointed, it is long past time to put the political class back where they belong: in the grip of that Vise.

With an understanding of the four key elements of the Vise (media, the people, influencers, and politicians), let's look at how the Vise is operating in contemporary America.

Chapter 10

HOW THE LEFT PUTS
THE AMERICAN PEOPLE IN THE VISE

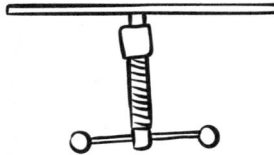

We live in the period of greatest risk to our republic since the Civil War. The radicalized progressive left aims to apply the power of the Political Vise to subjugate those Americans who dissent from their worldview.

The entire premise of the American Founding is that the people are sovereign. The Constitution empowers the people to live their lives freely. As the Framers designed it, the government must always be accountable to the people's will. The people—through the media, through civic institutions, through political participation, through elite influencers—hold politicians accountable. This is the Political Vise as designed. It is how it still can work. You already know the chief reason it doesn't work as well as it should: the countervailing and malevolent pressure of the Progressive Political Vise. Progressive in this context means centralized command and control within government, with the government replacing the people as the sovereign power. Instead of government being empowered, and yet limited, by the people, the government would have the power to dole out rights to the people.

Though most will not define it this way, as I see it, the 2024 election was the fifth consecutive election cycle in which the American people were faced with a simple choice. They weren't just choosing between a Democrat and a Republican. They were choosing which Vise they wanted to strengthen. They were deciding whether they wanted to be squeezed or whether they'd like to be among those doing the squeezing. Thankfully, the people chose to reassert their sovereignty in 2024.

Why do I say 2024 marks the fifth election cycle? The answer lies in an idea and a campaign that emerged in my adopted hometown.

Many good things have come out of Chicago. It's the home of the Illinois Policy Institute and the city to which I have devoted much of my professional life. It is the city where Barack Obama cut his political teeth and figured out how to leverage a modest career as a community organizer into an audacious and successful run for president. It is also the city from which one of the left's most pernicious and destructive concepts emerged. In April 2008, just as that junior senator from Illinois drew close to clinching the Democratic nomination, a University of Chicago professor named Richard Thaler coauthored a book called *Nudge: Improving Decisions about Health, Wealth, and Happiness*. It didn't quite zoom to the top of the *New York Times* bestseller list, but it proved enormously influential with many of the elites, particularly Barack Obama and the eager, ambitious coterie that surrounded him.

The basic idea of *Nudge* was that institutions could and should do more to change human behavior. Thaler argued that politicians, influencers, and the media should think of themselves as "choice architects," encouraging people to make better and healthier decisions for themselves and their families. That sounds benign, as do the examples Thaler provides. He suggests a cafeteria should offer both junk food and healthy options, so as to maximize individual choice—but should arrange the offerings so that the healthy food is what customers see first. Thaler called this "libertarian paternalism." In the cafeteria example, people could still choose unhealthy snacks, but they would have to exert more effort to get what they craved.

THE PROGRESSIVE POLITICAL VISE

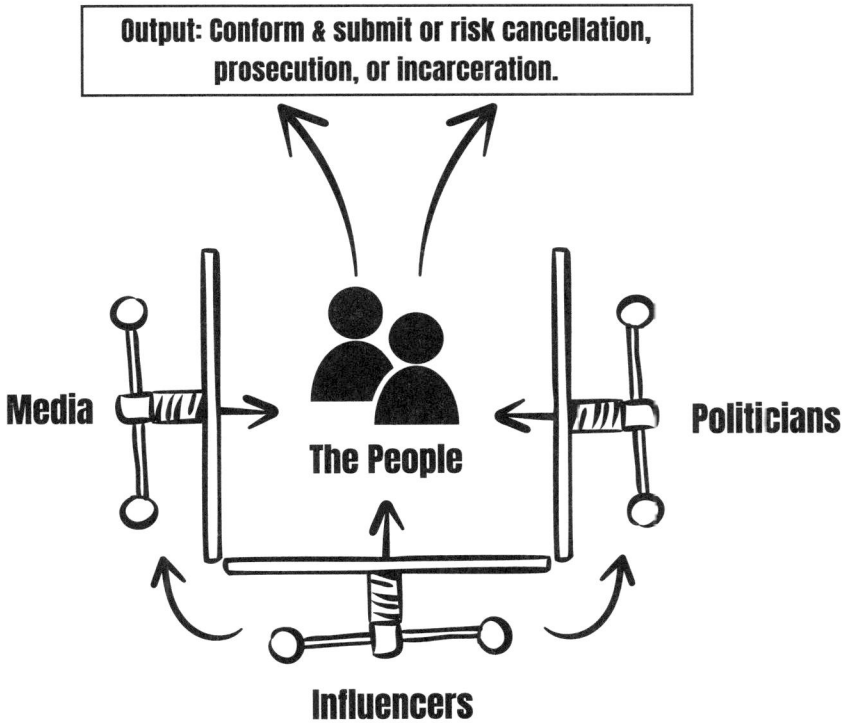

Output: Conform & submit or risk cancellation, prosecution, or incarceration.

Media

The People

Politicians

Influencers

People are compelled to make decisions based upon three criteria:
1. Personal Expediency
2. Personal Fear
3. Personal Principle

To put it in constitutional terms, *Nudge* paid lip service to the notion that the people were still sovereign—and at the same time, argued persuasively that a sovereign people could not be trusted to make the "right" choices without some gentle, subtle pressure.[29]

The reviews in the elite media were mixed. It wasn't that the critics found "libertarian paternalism" to be an obvious contradiction in terms. It wasn't that "choice architects" sounded Orwellian. It was that Thaler (and his coauthor, Harvard Law Professor and future Obama advisor Cass Sunstein) didn't go far enough. The *New Yorker* wrote in frustration:

> Many of the suggestions in "Nudge" seem like good ideas, and even, practical ones. The whole project, though, as Thaler and Sunstein acknowledge, raises some pretty awkward questions. If the "nudgee" can't be depended on to recognize his own best interests, why stop at a nudge? Why not offer a "push," or perhaps even a "shove"?[30]

Or, in the language I prefer, why not a very hard squeeze in the Vise? The *New Yorker* wasn't mocking the idea of libertarian paternalism. They were suggesting it would be wise for the state and influential institutions to consider dropping the adjective. Paternalism—for the good of the people—would be worth it. A little liberty surrendered for the sake of better health, longer life, and the elimination of prejudice and bigotry? Surely, an excellent trade-off.

Barack Obama and his team—including his incoming chief of staff, Rahm Emanuel (a son of the Windy City and, lamentably, its future mayor)—read *Nudge* and reviews like the one I cite here. It confirmed the wisdom of their impulse to use executive and legislative power to nudge, push, and squeeze the American people in order to make them "better." Many presidents in American history mistake comparatively narrow election victories as mandates to implement their vision. Barack Obama took that tradition to a new extreme; as far as he was concerned, the votes of 52 percent of the American people constituted authorization to launch a radical campaign to remake the citizenry.

If you're over thirty, you remember the adulation the media showered on this comparatively callow junior senator. They described him in almost messianic terms—something that Obama himself relished. (Upon clinching the Democratic nomination for president, he declared that history would remember "that this was the moment when the rise of the oceans began to slow, and our planet began to heal.") Obama believed his own hype, as many politicians do. Flush with a sense of purpose and goaded on by an adoring media, Barack Obama believed that his election conferred upon him the obligation to nudge the American people to abandon outdated principles and tired beliefs. The American people were long overdue to spend some time squeezed in the Vise. Perhaps, if the pressure was applied forcefully enough, we would become a better people—a people worthy of the likes of Barack Obama.

A number of American presidents have been lawyers. Barack Obama actually lectured on constitutional law. In both his classes and his speeches, he made clear his vision of the Constitution, particularly as it related to the courts. In a 2022 essay, the Federalist Society's Francis J. Menton summarized the distinction between the progressive and traditional visions of the court and the Constitution. It is worth quoting at length:

> The two visions . . . can be summarized in just a few sentences each:
>
> - **Vision 1.** The constitution allocates powers to the three branches of government, and also lists certain rights entitled to constitutional protection. The role of the courts is (1) to assure that the powers are exercised only by those to whom they are allocated, (2) to protect the enumerated rights, and (3) as to things claimed to be rights but not listed, to avoid getting involved.
> - **Vision 2.** The constitution is an archaic document adopted more than 200 years ago, and largely obsolete. The role of the courts is to implement the current priorities of the academic left and then somehow rationalize how that is consistent with the written document. If a right is enumerated in the constitution but disfavored by the current left (e.g., the right to "keep and bear arms"), then the courts should find a way to uphold enactments that minimize that right down to the point that it is a nullity. If a right is not enumerated in the constitution, but is a priority of the left (e.g., abortion), then that right can be

discovered in some vague and unspecific constitutional language ("due process"). **And if the left has a priority to transform the economy and the way the people live,** but the Congress
does not have sufficient majorities to enact that priority, then
the Executive agencies can implement that priority on their
own authority, and the role of the courts is to assist the agencies
in finding something in the tens of thousands of pages of federal
statutes, however vague and dubious, that can be claimed to
authorize the action.[31]

The bold emphasis is mine. As Menton knows, the left very much does
prioritize both the transformation of the economy and how we live. This
impulse existed long before Barack Obama and a book called *Nudge*, but
after the Democrat triumphs in the 2008 election, that impulse accelerated.
Obama was fond of quoting the phrase made famous by Martin Luther
King: "The fierce urgency of now." The left felt the urgency and the opportunity, and all three branches of government—cheered on by gleeful influencers and the media—turned the screws of the Progressive Political Vise
faster than ever before.

Let me collapse eight years of history into a few sentences. The courts,
Congress, and the president foisted endless progressive innovations onto
an increasingly frustrated and angry people. "Obamacare" made our
nation's expensive and unwieldy health care system worse; taxes rose,
states lost the freedom to decide the definition of marriage, and automakers—
bought with massive government bailouts—accepted ruinous fuel efficiency standards. In two consecutive midterm elections in 2010 and 2014,
the American people repudiated progressive excesses. They voted to
wriggle free from the Progressive Vise—and the Vise just squeezed back
harder.

You know the story. In the most remarkable upset in modern American political history, Donald Trump defeated Hillary Clinton in the 2016
election. I'll be the first to admit that I didn't see it coming, and I was

hardly alone. In retrospect, I probably should have given the American people just a bit more credit. They were fed up. They were angry. They still believed in American greatness. And those people pushed back at the ballot box.

The elites were stunned, and as soon as they had wiped away their tears and processed their grief, they fought back. When you've experienced a devastating shock—and to the left, the election of Donald Trump was the most devastating shock imaginable—you want to do all you can to make sure that nothing like that ever, ever happens again. That meant launching a far more intense battle against the American people, ensuring that the Progressive Political Vise crushed Trump and his supporters. By 2016, I knew how this would work. There would be less "nudging"—and a lot more "trampling."

I've been in politics long enough to know that there are two basic responses to a crushing defeat. The first is to accept that your message didn't carry the day and take responsibility for the loss. The second is to blame the people for rejecting you. When you take that second path, you avoid introspection. You avoid reassessing your beliefs. You simply decide that the people are wrong, and you need to make sure that they are never allowed to be that wrong again. The American people, having chosen wrongly and thus proven unworthy of the trust of the elites, must be controlled. After the election of Donald Trump, the media, left-wing politicians and influencers came together with a renewed and intensified purpose: to suppress dissent, to control information, and to change the rules of the American game.

If the entire premise of the American Founding is that the people are sovereign, it is profoundly and definitionally un-American to conspire against that sovereignty. Of course, that is exactly what the left has done, with ever more frantic urgency, since the first election of Donald Trump, during his four years out of office, and now once again with him in office. As far as the progressives are concerned, the American people cannot be permitted to make such terrible choices, but when they do, that choice must be nullified. The left is, at the present, unable to engineer an actual military coup d'etat. However, they are once again using a "whole of society" approach to blocking Trump in his second term.

They must continue to use the Vise to crush that pesky sovereignty of the people. Part of their strategy also includes convincing the public that our vaunted ideals of liberty are themselves "problematic." If popular sovereignty is at the heart of the American experiment, then perhaps the American experiment itself was a tragic, cruel mistake.

In 2015, the same year that Donald Trump launched his presidential campaign, a radical left-wing journalist named Nikole Hannah-Jones joined the *New York Times*. Hannah-Jones had already built a career lamenting American systemic racism and celebrating America's enemies. She spent a year in Cuba, scribbling effusive praise for the Castro regime. Hannah-Jones was now one of the media elites. She was ideally positioned to turn the screws of the Progressive Political Vise, and turn them she did. With the help and encouragement of her powerful handlers at the *Times*, Hannah-Jones composed her magnum opus: The 1619 Project. The project's audacious goal? Nothing short of forcing Americans to accept a new and dark narrative about the Founders.

Donald Trump had won two (three!?) elections with a simple slogan: *Make America Great Again.* The 1619 Project—and the enormous woke influencer apparatus that spread it—argued that America had *never* been great. Our very origins were steeped in racism and exploitation. The Revolutionary War was fought at the behest of slaveholders. The Constitution was not a guarantor of liberty but an instrument of oppression. White Americans owed reparations to Blacks, and those reparations could include everything from direct cash payments to abject apologies to racial preferences in hiring. Above all, reparations required building a new and "better" America, one with more focus on uplifting the marginalized than on ensuring the sovereignty of the people. Without using the term, Hannah-Jones and her allies identified the instrument necessary to "uplifting the marginalized:" the Progressive Political Vise.

In the aftermath of Trump's first election, the left began to weaponize two contradictory arguments about America. The first of these messages was that America needed to finally reckon with its evil, racist Founders. The second of these messages was that our precious democracy was in peril and needed to be saved. The discrepancy was obvious: If our democracy was rotten to the core, rooted in bigotry and oppression, why exert so much effort to save it? The left wasn't worried about intellectual inconsistencies. They were focused on deploying these arguments to kneecap the Trump agenda—and to ensure that the people were never allowed to make such a grave mistake again.

Both of these theories existed before Donald Trump, but during his first term, they became both the soundtrack and the screenplay for the progressive assault on the American people. The fact that the music didn't quite match the script didn't matter—what mattered was power. What mattered was the squeeze.

Nikole Hannah-Jones was the most visible face of an entire movement of leftist intellectuals, influencers, and politicians bent on exposing what they saw as the dark side of American history. Donald Trump had narrowly lost the popular vote to Hillary Clinton, but he'd decisively won the electoral college. To the left, that result was proof that the electoral college needed to be abandoned. The fastest way to accomplish that desired result was to pressure the American people to believe that the Founders had not been brilliant architects of a constitutional republic, but instead were nothing more than self-interested bigots hellbent on consolidating power for rich white slaveholders. (With Trump winning the popular vote in 2024, the left seems to have forgotten its obsession with abolishing the electoral college.)

Ironically, for so-called progressives, that insistence on revisiting old wounds meant reversing decades and decades of progress. As recently as 1978, a Democrat president from the Deep South, Jimmy Carter, had pardoned Confederate President Jefferson Davis. In his accompanying proclamation, Carter declared:

Our Nation needs to clear away the guilts and enmities and recriminations of the past, to finally set at rest the divisions that threatened to destroy our Nation and to discredit the principles on which it was founded. Our people need to turn their attention to the important tasks that still lie before us in establishing those principles for all people.[32]

The 1619 Project, the Black Lives Matter movement, and the violent insurrections that followed the death of George Floyd? They were gleeful, deliberate efforts to "discredit the principles" on which America was founded. If the Constitution, the law, and American tradition had somehow led to the election of Donald Trump, then the left considered those founding principles to be well worth discrediting. The destruction of Confederate monuments and the renaming of public buildings had begun under the Obama administration, but the process accelerated in reaction to President Trump. By the summer of 2020, as the nation was roiled by violence, the left succeeded in orchestrating a wild, tumultuous season of statue-smashing and history-erasing. The hands that turned the screws of the Progressive Political Vise might claim to revere ol' Jimmy Carter, but they rejected his plea "to clear away the guilts and enmities and recriminations of the past." They intended to weaponize those guilts and enmities and recriminations, and by any measure, they succeeded.

A Vise squeezes from more than one side. As they raged against Donald Trump, the left did not just focus on reviving old racial enmities. In the fall of 2017, exactly a year after Trump had upset Clinton, a new hashtag went viral on Twitter (now X): #MeToo. I have spent much of my career implementing successful campaigns, and I instantly recognized what was happening. Remember those "Parkland kids" who suddenly appeared in the Florida capital and the streets of Washington, DC? Their anguish was real, but their pain had been slickly packaged and promoted by the progressive left. The same thing was happening with #MeToo. What appeared to be an organic, spontaneous movement to call out sexual abuse was in fact a coordinated campaign to ruin lives and careers.

I will stipulate that Donald Trump has not always behaved like a perfect gentleman, though his temperament was quite different in 2024 than previously. I am not interested in the particulars of the president's private life. I was fascinated by the rage that his alleged conduct generated on the left. When that infamous "Access Hollywood" tape—featuring Trump's using crude language to describe women—failed to derail his campaign, the progressive left saw an opportunity. They saw that millions of white, liberal, Democratic women despised Trump. They might have failed to use his occasional boorishness to stop Trump from becoming president, but they could weaponize that rage against less powerful men.

It is ridiculous that I need to say this next sentence, but it remains necessary: My entire life, and the underlying philosophy of the freedom movement, is a belief in the requirement of consent in all relationships. That applies to people and their sexual lives, and that applies to people and their government.

I am glad that in recent years, powerful and violent abusers like Harvey Weinstein have seen real consequences for their gross and indefensible conduct. But in the early Trump years, the left made no distinction between rapists like Weinstein and men who made clumsy attempts to ask out colleagues, to flirt, and to otherwise behave as men (and women) have since the beginning of time. Nine months into the Trump presidency, Moira Donegan—an editor at the venerable left-wing outlet the *New Republic*—created a Google Doc called "Shitty Men in Media." She invited other women writers (almost all, like Donegan, young, white, liberal feminists in Manhattan and Brooklyn) to contribute stories of bad male behavior. The men who found themselves on the list were accused of such crimes as looking longingly at pretty coworkers or dating women whom the list's contributors considered too young. It wasn't just a petty way of airing grievances. The Shitty Men in Media list had the power to end careers; just days after the list appeared, the *Atlantic* fired once-respected editor Leon Wieseltier. Other terminations followed.

The #MeToo movement and the Shitty Men in Media list "captured the public imagination." By now, you should recognize that phrase doesn't refer to an idea or trend organically emerging out of nowhere. It refers to the outcome of a conscious and coordinated campaign by left-wing politicians, the media, and powerful influencers to pressure the American people to believe a certain thing. Once the influencers and the media have drawn the attention of the public, they apply the Vise to pressure toward a particular and desired result. In the case of the Black Lives Matter movement and the 1619 Project, that result was white guilt, reparations, and the rewriting of history. In the case of the #MeToo movement, the desired outcome was transforming gender dynamics in schools and workplaces to render men anxious and women suspicious. Above all, it was to remind the American public that even though Donald Trump was president, the mores, customs, and culture of our country would be dictated by the progressive elites.

By the time the 2018 midterms rolled around, the media had given us another term: cancel culture. The phrase had its origins in the Black community, where it was used innocuously to refer to a television show or a music artist whose popularity had suddenly dimmed. In Trump's first term and the years since, the progressive elites turned cancel culture into an everyday experience for anyone who dared embrace conservative values. People lost their jobs for pro-life activism or for defending traditional values. Conservative speakers were shouted down on college campuses. A Boeing executive lost his job because someone found an article he'd written in 1987 opposing women fighter pilots. A teacher was fired for refusing to use a student's preferred pronoun. In the late 2010s and early 2020s, these stories became as commonplace as they were terrifying.

Donald Trump is not a creature of the Progressive Political Vise. He has been elected twice despite the best efforts and expectations of the elites. His rise had upset an entire narrative of history. Barack Obama's 2008 victory was supposed to inaugurate a new Golden Age of progressivism, as ordinary Americans were "nudged," pressured, and squeezed to be a people worthy of their leaders. The rise of Trump taught the elites exactly the wrong lesson. They did not conclude they were wrong. They did not engage in critical self-examination. Instead, they decided to punish the American public for their outrageous temerity in electing the Orange Monster. Cancel culture, #MeToo, and the Great Racial Reckoning were all efforts to crush what the left found objectionable. Could they impose enough consequences on individuals and rewrite enough history? Perhaps they could look back at the Trump era as a brief and unpleasant detour on the Long March towards a Diverse, Equitable, Socialist Future.

The progressive left wanted to punish the American people for their error, but of course, they also wanted to crush the "Error" himself. From the time he was sworn in the first time until the present moment, Donald Trump has been subjected to unprecedented pressure. It started with the Russia Hoax and continued with an endless series of increasingly preposterous allegations against the forty-fifth and now forty-seventh president. Dilbert creator Scott Adams keeps a running list of all the hoaxes about Trump that have been proven to be false. At last count, that number was twenty, but it is sure to rise. Sadly, given that we are in a propaganda war, millions of Americans still think that these hoaxes are true.

I'll concede that President Trump's pugnacious demeanor often made it easy for his enemies to rally against him. Yet Trump's combative style in no way justified the extraordinary "lawfare" launched against him. To paraphrase Shakespeare, he was a man "more sinned against than sinning."

I've already explained how the corporate media long ago abandoned any pretense of objectivity. The rise of Donald Trump made that abandonment much more explicit. One cable network, MSNBC, cut virtually all other programming to campaign 24/7 against him. Night after night, the likes of Chris Hayes, Rachel Maddow, and Lawrence O'Donnell devoted their entire broadcast hours to ever shriller anti-Trump monologues. The goal was to whip their audience (heavily skewed toward aging liberals) into an absolute frenzy of anti-Trump fervor. Those viewers would then donate to the Democrat Party and other lefty organizations. That steady infusion of "rage donations" would fuel the engines that turned the Progressive Political Vise.

In 2020, as the Progressive Political Vise worked to constrain and crush both Donald Trump and those who supported him, the elites kept their focus on the most urgent goal of all: ensuring that the president was defeated for re-election. Using the pandemic as cover, they rewrote the rules for elections, all but guaranteeing mischief. Social-media platforms and Google cooperated, doing all they could (and they can do a lot) to suppress pro-Trump information. We may never know the full extent of the manipulations that took place before, during, and after the 2020 election. We do know that the vote was very close, and that time and again, in swing state after swing state, the Democrats found just enough votes to win. Perhaps that was mere coincidence.

January 6, 2021: Supporters of President Trump march on the Capitol in Washington, incensed and anguished over what they believed was a stolen election. Leave aside, if you can, the question of whether the election was stolen outright—or if, as Mollie Hemingway puts it, merely "rigged." The media, the influencers, and the left declared that even raising questions about ballot integrity was unacceptable. As it so often does, in the weeks between the November election and the formal congressional tabulation of electoral college votes, the Progressive Political Vise crushed any attempt to review or analyze the outcome.

As a lifelong political junkie, I know what it's like to be on the losing side. In a democracy, you take your share of defeats along with the victories. I had also heard Democrats complain about stolen elections, something they did loudly and vociferously in 2000, 2004, and 2016. (In other words, any time a Republican won.) Until 2020, though, I had never witnessed such a frantic and concerted effort to shut down debate and discussion about election integrity. I understood why an angry crowd marched on the halls of Congress that cold January day. Without excusing violence, I note that when you squeeze ordinary Americans in a Vise, not all of them will comply with your demands. Rebellion against tyranny is in our national DNA. We can and will fight back.

Those who entered the United States Capitol on January 6, 2021, were far less destructive than the Black Lives Matter rioters who had torched American cities the previous summer. It didn't matter to the elites and the media, who immediately framed the events of the day not only as an insurrection but an existential threat to our democracy. Within hours, we saw perhaps the most brazen example of the Progressive Political Vise at work: at the behest of the liberal media and the left, Silicon Valley tech executives shut down President Trump's Twitter account. The leader of the free world lost access to social media because an unelected and unaccountable elite decided the president represented a clear and present danger to the republic. If nothing else, it was an indication of both how much the elites feared Donald Trump—and how brazen they had become in their efforts both to destroy him and dispirit his supporters.

Make no mistake, the zealous and over-the-top prosecutions of the J6ers were intended to deter any will to fight after future election "irregularities." It was a direct attempt to put the American people inside the Political Vise, nudged, shoved, controlled, squeezed, and molded by those progressives in control of their version of the Vise.

How did it come to this? That's a common question asked in the aftermath of every upheaval. As I've tried to make clear, the acceleration toward crisis began in 2008, when Barack Obama decided it was his mandate to nudge Americans into becoming a people worthy of a leader like him. The Progressive Political Vise squeezed, and ordinary citizens squeezed back. To win this battle, we can and must rebuild the traditional Political Vise with one adaptation to be covered later.

We must also understand a little more about the language and the lies of the left. Those lies provide the fuel used to turn the screws on all three sides of the Vise. Let's take a look at one of the most pernicious big lies—Wokeism and Group Identity Politics.

Chapter 11

THE POWER OF WOKEISM

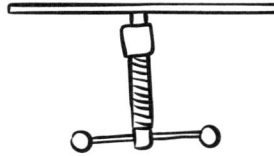

Group Identity Politics is dehumanizing to the very people advocates purport to care about. It tells individuals that your entire life and destiny are based upon one aspect of your humanity, be it your race, ethnicity, gender, sexuality, or immigration status. With white, mostly male oppressors in charge, you have little to no agency over your life. Only the government can come in to right the injustices you face. In return, you must give up your hope and aspiration to live your version of the American Dream. Group Identity Politics (a.k.a. GIP) is an immoral cancer that must be excised from the American culture.

Racist. It's among the most damaging and terrifying of contemporary accusations. It is a charge with a long history—but with a particularly powerful modern application. When someone who isn't a member of a protected group is called a racist, he quickly realizes he may have no defense. To the left, the accusation is always legitimate; the defense always inadequate; the punishment always deserved. I'll never forget being on the receiving end of that charge, which started with a simple political cartoon.

Political cartoons are a splendid part of the Anglo-American tradition. Since at least the seventeenth century, various participants in the fray have used cartoons to make incisive, memorable points. Even in today's digital world, a simple ink cartoon—or even a well-drawn sketch—can add far more heft to an argument than a long essay. The screws of the Traditional Political Vise have always been turned, at least in small part, by clever cartoons. Knowing this well, at Illinois Policy we've long had a talented staff cartoonist, Eric Allie (now at the marketing agency Iron Light).

In August 2017, we published a cartoon of Eric's. As you can see, it showed a young Black child panhandling for change on the sidewalk. A rich white man in a nice suit, cigar falling from his lips, shows the child one empty pocket and declares, "Sorry, kid, I'm broke." The white guy's other pocket, however, is stuffed with cash.

The rich white man represented real estate developers who get money controlled by the Chicago mayor through a scheme called Tax Increment Financing Districts, or TIFs. TIFs siphon property tax money into a mayoral-controlled fund that was (and is still) then given to these wealthy developers to build new developments in the tax district. Those developers then, in turn, donate money to the mayor and other politicians involved in allocating the funds.

The net effect is to subsidize wealthy white developers at the expense of the Chicago Public Schools, the library, the park district, Stroger Hospital (formerly Cook County Hospital) and more. In the cartoon the Black child represented the district's underserved students; the cash represented the untapped property-tax revenue that the mayor and city stubbornly refused to use for student needs. That same month, Chris Lentino of the Institute wrote a compelling op-ed pointing out that the very Chicago politicians demanding more taxpayer cash for schools were deliberately ignoring the vast resources they already had.

To be clear, spending on Chicago Public Schools was and is at record levels with abysmal results. Our point with the cartoon wasn't to mock Chicago's Black kids. Quite the opposite—we were mocking the wealthy developers! Eric's cartoon made the point that we were standing with those kids, asking a basic question about why the City of Chicago was ignoring their needs and getting such poor results despite all the spending. It didn't matter. The political left reserves for itself the right to decide what is and what isn't racist, and the judgment it passes is usually final. There is rarely a chance to appeal.

Timing matters. Long, hot summers are often not the best time to hold reasoned debate. The cartoon ran just days after ugly clashes over a Confederate monument in Charlottesville. The violence claimed one life and left that pretty Southern city badly shaken. The progressive media had pounced on President Trump's response to the unrest, falsely claiming that he had said that neo-Nazis were "very fine people." With anti-Trump fever running very high in August 2017, our enemies saw a chance to tie Illinois Policy to the president they hated—and to tar us with the brush of racism.

You'll recall Chicago Mayor Rahm Emanuel's infamous aphorism about the importance of never letting a good crisis go to waste. Hizzoner was and is an absolute master of manipulating the Progressive Political Vise, and he quickly linked our campaign for responsible tax policy to Charlottesville, telling the press:

> At the same time the president of the United States is throwing his arms around neo-Nazis and Klansmen, Governor [Bruce] Rauner's brain trust at the Illinois Policy Institute weighed in on the SB1 [education funding bill] debate by publishing an unambiguously racist cartoon.[33]

I admit I chuckled when I read that. Typical Rahm, cramming multiple falsehoods into a single sentence. Donald Trump never threw his arms around Klansmen. We were not Rauner's "brain trust," and never had been. And above all, the cartoon we published was not "unambiguously racist."

The mayor's words offer an excellent example of how the left uses language to crush their enemies in the Vise. For example, the addition of "unambiguously" is not just about inserting another adverb. It's about shutting down debate. What is "unambiguous" cannot be questioned. Whenever the left cries "racist," it intends the accusation to be unambiguous, unimpeachable, and undeniable. If you challenge them, you will prove yourself to be a racist as well.

We took the cartoon down; the Vise's pressure worked against us. In politics, you pick your battles. It was not an admission that the image was racist. It was a recognition of reality: The cartoon was a distraction from the real work, and we could not let the real conversation about school funding get hopelessly sidetracked. Our intent was clear to anyone who looked at the image in good faith. Money that should be flowing to schools filled with poor minority kids was instead lining the pockets of wealthy white developers—and Mayor Emanuel drove that process. I was rightly proud that the Institute had a long track record of advancing issues to benefit minority communities. I also knew that in 2017, that track record didn't matter. What mattered were angry soundbites.

A few weeks before, I had done a studio appearance on the WVON AM Morning Show with Charles Thomas and Maze Jackson, two respected and popular Black radio hosts in Chicago. It had gone well. Because of our pre-existing relationship, Jackson and Thomas agreed to let me come on their show the morning after the cartoon firestorm blew up. When it comes to race, you rarely get a second chance. This invitation to WVON was such a chance for me personally, and for the Institute. My appearance wasn't a brief spot—it was a sixty-minute high-wire performance. Put one foot wrong? Disaster and cancellation.

Thankfully, the hosts were completely fair. They discussed the cartoon among themselves, with me, and with two Black women who were in-studio guests. I was calling in, and so no one knew I was pacing around my dining room, beads of sweat on my forehead, as I did my best to make the case for the good intentions of the cartoon. To my great relief, neither Charles and Maze nor their female guests thought our cartoon was racist. The challenge came from Democrat state Representative Christian Mitchell, also a guest on WVON.

In the legislature, Mitchell had described what Eric Allie had drawn as a "Sambo cartoon." His colleague, Representative Jaime Andrade, called the comic "unacceptable"—and added a four-letter word as well. Andrade joined Mitchell on the call-in show. It was daunting to take on these legislators, but the hour-long format of the show allowed me to unpack the real issue. I was able to describe the policy in moral terms: money was being siphoned away from schools filled with minority kids. By the time the hour wrapped up, I had not only won over the hosts and the female guests, but I'd also won over Representative Andrade as well. Jaime agreed to work with Illinois Policy on other issues, and years later, he's been as good as his word.

Given time and a neutral platform, we can defend ourselves against spurious charges of racism. The problem is that too rarely are we given that time and space. We can't count on the rare (and welcome!) fairness of media outlets like WVON. We must create our own spaces—and equip our side to speak more effectively in this new and charged cultural landscape. That means learning to interpret, translate, and understand the language of Wokeism. It means understanding that Wokeism isn't about justice. It's about the raw exercise of power. It's about turning the screws of the Progressive Political Vise.

"Woke" began as Black slang. It referred originally to being awakened to deep structural inequities and committing to combatting the systemic injustices that flowed from them.

My goal is not to summarize the entire history and ideology of the woke movement. There are many excellent recent books on the scope and scale of Wokeism's influence on our culture; I especially recommend Mike Gonzalez's *The Plot to Change America: How Identity Politics Is Dividing the Land of the Free.* Mike's title captures a fundamental truth about Wokeism: it requires us to define ourselves not as individuals, but as members of a group. To the woke, what makes you who you are is not your soul, your intellect, your curiosity, and your capacity to love. What makes you who you are is the color of your skin and your sexual orientation. To be woke is to decide one's own unique human qualities are secondary to taking one's place in a particular battalion of the Oppressed and the Marginalized. To be woke is to see one's own struggles and travails not as the consequence of personal failings or bad luck, but entirely as the result of systemic racism, homophobia, or some other entrenched bigotry.

Wokeness is just the current manifestation of one of the oldest and most dangerous threats to our republic (which I noted at the beginning of this chapter): Group Identity Politics, or GIP. GIP always starts with a fundamental premise: the American Dream is unattainable for someone like you. It is unattainable because the system is stacked against someone of your skin color, your sexual orientation, your gender, or your religion. You cannot achieve success on your own, no matter how hard you try. Even here, in the supposed land of the free, "people like you" cannot make it on their own. Everything is rigged against you. Your only hope is to put your faith not in your own efforts, but in your group identity. Working together, perhaps your group can seize power, and yes, use that Political Vise on your behalf for a change.

The goal of anyone who believes in GIP is to expand state power in order to protect your group. Protection doesn't just mean being kept safe from physical harm. It means being given special access to opportunities. It means privileged access to everything from college admissions to government jobs to promotions in the private sector. It means insisting that the schools stop teaching America is exceptional and great, because how could a country be great if it once badly treated people like you? Instead, GIP demands that school curricula focus on the particular sufferings of your people and tell the story of your group's long and difficult slog to overcome oppression.

Above all else, GIP demands equity and justice—two goals that to the woke are of necessity *always* just out of reach. After all, if your group had achieved full parity with other Americans, you wouldn't need these special carve-outs, these special classes, these endless government-mandated boosts designed to elevate. Stories of success are dismissed as rare exceptions. I grew up hearing people on the left say that "Americans will never vote for a Black president." When Barack Obama was elected and then re-elected (both times by comfortable if not overwhelming margins) those committed to GIP insisted that Obama was an outlier. Neither narratives of individual success nor statistical proof of parity (or "equity") are ever sufficient to end the demands for special treatment and preferences.

Many of the criticisms of Wokeism and GIP are rooted in the assumption that they are nothing more than grifts. It is true that these ideologies are enormous money-machines. The Woke Industrial Complex employs a lot of people. It squeezes (or to be blunter, shakes down) corporations, generating personal fortunes for the most skilled and ambitious grievance peddlers. In 2023, one founder of the Black Lives Matter movement sued another. The flagship organization of the woke left—responsible for appalling acts of insurrection and violence in the summer of 2020—succeeded in shaking down millions from corporations eager to establish their own woke credentials. As the money flowed in, the grifters quarreled over the loot like pirates fighting over captured booty. Soon "Black Lives Matter, Grassroots Incorporated" sued "Black Lives Matter, Global Network Foundation" for $10 million. Some Black Lives Matter leaders bought multi-million-dollar homes; others put family members on their foundation payrolls. It would be amusing if it weren't so infuriating, sad, and predictable.

There is a danger in dismissing Wokeism and GIP as a simple grift. The real threat isn't just a motley assembly of charlatans fleecing corporate donors. The real threat is that Wokeism is much more than a scam. It is part and parcel of the left's longstanding and relentless campaign to aggregate power to the state—and away from individuals. This isn't just about getting rich. It's about building a culture of dependence. It's about teaching people to believe that fulfillment comes from submitting to the collective. It's about inculcating a worldview that it is the state *and only the state* that can right historic wrongs and ensure future flourishing. Individual hucksters may make fortunes promoting Wokeism and GIP, but the real goal is not just money. The real goal is total control.

The real goal is to crush your enemies in the Progressive Political Vise.

It was Karl Marx who conceived of history as an epic struggle between the classes. Sooner or later, Marx predicted, the working class would rise up and overthrow the tyrannical bourgeoisie. American progressives admired Marx, and they were envious when the Russian Revolution of 1917 ushered in a Communist state. For the next seven decades, patriotic Americans worried—rightly—about the threat of Communism reaching our shores. Abroad, we sought to contain the relentless expansion of the Soviet Union (and later, the People's Republic of China). At home, we fought hard to uncover the very real and pernicious influence of Communist sympathizers in the government, in higher education, and in the media.

We have never had a Communist revolution in this country. Part of that was because of our determination to combat the threat. Historians tell us that Thomas Jefferson never actually said "Eternal vigilance is the price of liberty," but the quotation captures his thinking. We fought off the Communist threat abroad, and we did our best to guard against it at home. The Soviet Union eventually collapsed, not just because they couldn't match our military superiority, but because they could not keep up with the economic dynamism of a free market democracy. The other, more important reason we never had a Communist revolution was because the success of capitalism completely undercut the fundamental appeal of Marxist ideology.

Communism failed because it doesn't work. Capitalism succeeds because it does.

Marx insisted that the workers could never attain the prosperity of the middle classes without a violent uprising. Generations of Americans saw that simply wasn't true. The American working class realized that with hard work, they too could enjoy the fruits of their labor—without destroying the system. Put simply, working-class Americans didn't want to *overthrow* the bourgeoisie. They wanted to *become* the bourgeoisie. They believed they could become the bourgeoisie, and the free-enterprise system provided the tools and opportunity for that happy upward mobility. For the first time in human history, millions and millions were able to escape poverty and find prosperity.

In the late twentieth century, as Communism began to sputter toward collapse, and as Americans consistently rejected the siren song of class warfare, the American left needed a new organizing principle. For fifty years, from the 1930s to the 1980s, the left had relied on Franklin Delano Roosevelt's venerable New Deal coalition. The coalition was a diverse alliance of urban racial and religious minorities (including Catholics, Jews, and Blacks) along with trade unions, white Southerners, and university professors. Ronald Reagan's landslide victories in 1980 and 1984 shattered what had already become an outdated and awkward Democratic coalition. To achieve power once again, the left needed to build a different series of alliances. They settled on an organizing principle of grievance.

Organizing the working class to fight capitalism had failed, for one obvious and happy reason: capitalism solves the problem of poverty. Organizing around racial, sexual, and cultural grievances would prove to be much more effective. The reason is also obvious, but not at all happy: resentment is a feeling, not an economic state. No matter how prosperous you become, you can still be made to believe that you have been held back by your sex or by the color of your skin.

Here are four basic principles about grievances:

- By their very nature, grievances cannot be soothed by prosperity.
- By their very nature, grievances fester.
- By their very nature, grievances can be both manufactured and sustained.
- By their very nature, grievances can become a glue that binds the resentful to a cause—or to a political party.

Though the roots of grievance politics go back to the fracturing of the New Deal coalition in the 1980s, it has been under Presidents Obama, Trump, and Biden that the left has centered those grievances in their organizing. The foundational principle is simple: Only the government can heal these old injuries. Only by expanding the power of the state can we bring that sweet and long-delayed justice! And if justice is still delayed, and grievances still fester, then the answer is always the same: expand the power of the state. Squeeze the enemies of progress in the Vise! Spend $10 billion here, $50 billion there, and a trillion or two over there, and maybe after the next election—if you vote Democrat—we'll be able to finally solve all the problems that have you so worried, angry, and resentful!

Am I being hyperbolic? I don't think you can look at the last decade and a half of American political history and say anything other than this is exactly how our system works now.

As it assiduously assembled this new coalition of the aggrieved and the entitled, the Democrat Party found it necessary to move further and further left. They did this on a host of fronts, starting with a concerted outreach to sexual minorities. In his first term, Bill Clinton had signed the Defense of Marriage Act. As late as 2008, Barack Obama ran for president declaring that marriage should remain between a man and a woman. Both presidents rapidly "evolved" (a verb Obama used to describe his own shift). Within a few short years, every major Democrat politician and candidate embraced not only marriage equality but the right of children to undergo sex-change surgeries. In a single decade, progressive politicians like Barack Obama, the Clintons, and Joe Biden went from considering same-sex marriage to be a bridge too far to embracing transgender sex workers on the White House lawn. In terms of embracing the foundational principles of Wokeism, there is no longer any daylight between older so-called "centrist" Democrats like Joe Biden, Nancy Pelosi and Chuck Schumer—and the radical young "squad" led by AOC, Ilhan Omar, Rashida Tlaib, and the newly favored Jasmine Crockett. The entire party is "all in" on Group Identity Politics (GIP).

In 1984, at their convention in San Francisco, the Democratic Party recognized their Gay and Lesbian Caucus for the first time. Today, the phrase "Gay and Lesbian" sounds almost quaint. Since 2000, the official Democratic caucus has evolved from "Gay and Lesbian" to "LGBTQ+." (That's "Lesbian, Gay, Bisexual, Transgendered, and Queer," with the plus sign symbolizing that other sexual minorities are welcome as well.) Conservatives often joke about the alphabet soup, but the ever-longer acronym reveals the left's strategy. Each time they add a letter, they enroll a new official member of the Grievance Coalition. They bind the dissatisfactions and the aspirations of sexual minorities to the agenda of the progressive left. They are building a "League of Lingering Resentments." That strange alliance is united in the conviction that only an ever-more powerful state can address their discontent and guarantee their protection.

A relatively small percentage of Americans are LGBTQ+. The number of young people who identify as LGBTQ+ is rapidly rising; a 2024 Gallup survey found that 22.3% of Generation Z adults consider themselves to be something other than heterosexual.[34] That's just about *ten times* the 2.3% of Baby Boomers who consider themselves LGBTQ+! That discrepancy says less about evolving sexual desires and much more about the social and cultural cachet that comes with identifying with a marginalized group. To be "queer" for the young is to be instantly enrolled in the ranks of those marching for justice. This is especially true for kids growing up in white, middle-class families. In the Olympic Games of GIP, they have no status.

By embracing queerness, young people can deftly and swiftly pivot from being one of the oppressors to being one of the oppressed. If you want to belong, you need to be aggrieved.

The progressive left doesn't just focus on the grievances of sexual minorities. For years, they've mobilized suburban women with a single-minded focus on protecting access to abortion. More recently, they've targeted white, middle-class professionals with endless promises of student loan bailouts. Anyone in politics understands the importance of micro-targeting, which is the tailoring of a message to meet the interests of a particular group. For the Democrat Party in particular and the progressive left more broadly, the micro-targeting isn't aimed at particular economic or racial demographics. It's aimed at stoking and cultivating a particular grievance. It's aimed at reminding even affluent, educated, white women that they too are members of a threatened group.

If necessary, the progressive left will also revive long-dormant conflicts. I noted at the beginning of this chapter the unfortunate timing of a cartoon that Illinois Policy published. It appeared just days after racial violence erupted in Charlottesville in August 2017. That unrest was rooted in the efforts by the liberal Virginia college town to remove a statue of Robert E. Lee.

It's important to understand that this obsession with cleansing the nation of Confederate monuments was new. As recently as the 1970s, politicians across the spectrum supported President Gerald Ford's official pardon of the great Southern general. In 1978, President Jimmy Carter had posthumously pardoned and restored the citizenship of Confederate President Jefferson Davis. During the 1992 presidential campaign, official Clinton-Gore campaign merchandise proudly featured the Confederate flag. (Both Democrat candidates were from Southern states, and at least initially, did not hide their pride in their heritage.) Twenty-five years later, in 2017, Democrats across the country were demanding the removal of any and all monuments to the Confederacy. There could be no healing, no progress, no equity, no inclusion as long as one single street or schoolhouse still bore the name of someone who fought on the wrong side.

I have no intention of relitigating the Civil War in this book. I simply note that for decades, the "War Between the States" was considered a tragic but necessary fight between two foes that each believed their fight was a just cause. (Obviously, the eradication of slavery was the truly just cause. I shouldn't have to say that since it is so obvious, but given how this could be parsed, I want to be explicit!)

On both sides of the aisle, politicians acknowledged that slavery was a great evil, and it was good and right that it be ended. They also acknowledged that those who fought for the Confederacy were good and decent men, certainly not by today's understanding of decency but in accordance with the times in which they lived. Bipartisan majorities could navigate all these nuances and see them as worthy of being remembered for their courage. The sudden pivot toward demonizing Confederate heritage—and the subsequent rush to take down statues and rename streets, schools, and military bases—was a manufactured effort to stoke racial grievance.

I note, too, that it is very inexpensive to topple a statue or tear down a flag. The left is happy to spend other people's money, but even progressive Democrats appreciate the chance to signal virtue on the cheap!

The left knew perfectly well that this effort to rewrite history would inflame rather than soothe old wounds. *That's what they wanted.* When a tiny number of virulent racists marched to protest the removal of the statue, the left magnified the threat exponentially. They blamed President Trump and accused him of standing in sympathy with the Ku Klux Klan and the neo-Nazis. Having created a conflagration, they declared a five-alarm fire. The woke arsonists didn't call the fire department, but they certainly called their reliable allies, the media. They warned their base that the "far right" was coming for every Black person, every LGBTQ+ person, and every woman.

The left understood the basic axiom of GIP: people are most aware of their "identity" when they feel that identity is under attack. For the progressive left, coalitions are built and sustained not just on grievance, but on anxiety. Someone—usually a white man—is always coming to take away your freedoms and deny you opportunities. The only way to stop him is to join us! Wokeism is sustained by resentment, entitlement, and fear. The left's revival of long-buried hostilities over the Civil War was cynical. In terms of agitating and uniting their base, it was all too successful.

State Representative Christian Mitchell, who attacked us over that cartoon? He framed his criticism in terms of racial grievance. It was only later that we discovered that from 2011 through 2018 Mitchell had received 122 donations totaling $176,895 to his committee from real estate developers, architectural and engineering firms, construction firms, and trade unions. Each and every one an elite influencer, benefiting from projects financed with TIF funds. We were advocating that that money should go, instead, to Chicago Public Schools. In the cartoon, the rich white man's left-side pocket was stuffed with cash. As it turned out, some of that cash was being shoveled into the Mitchell campaign. The angry politician used the rhetoric of racial grievance—the vocabulary of Wokeism—to attack us. His real motive was money and power.

Some people warned me that it was a mistake to go on that WVON morning program. Why walk into the lion's den? Some have warned me that I should delete this section of the book as well. The reality is that direct confrontation is the only way to defeat GIP. The reality is that we cannot restore America if we do not make fighting Wokeism our highest priority. If we are serious about regaining what I like to call "the commanding heights," we cannot cower at the accusations of racism and insensitivity that will invariably come our way. This doesn't mean tolerating bigotry in our own ranks. Our system of free enterprise, individual responsibility, and limitless opportunity is designed so that all may flourish. We need to be bolder about making that case, taking the fight directly to the corrupt and destructive peddlers of Wokeism.

One story makes me optimistic that we can move past GIP and the concept of systemic racism: the success of Central and West African immigrants. My friend, Dr. Orphe Divounguy, came from Gabon, Africa, and is living the American Dream. When I asked him why he was so successful and why so many from West Africa, especially nearby Nigeria, were successful, he revealed the truth. Paraphrasing, "Our culture is one of achievement, not victimization. I am African—we don't have time for grievance and we don't have time to worry about racism. Of course, there is some racism, but it is what we do about it that matters. We came here for opportunity. Unfortunately, the rhetoric I hear in some Black American communities often focuses on victimization rather than self-accountability and pursuit of opportunity."

Nigerian immigrants are among the most successful of all immigrants, in terms of income, in terms of education, in terms of family formation, and in terms of entrepreneurship.

The Nigerian story is one of not just Nigerian success, but American openness and opportunity. Those stories are the antidote to Wokeism and GIP.

With an understanding of the left's reliance on the grievance coalition, let's now take a look at how the left is trying to redefine what it means to find human flourishing and fulfillment.

Chapter 12

VICTIMHOOD VERSUS FULFILLMENT

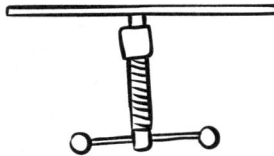

What is fulfillment? What does it mean to be fulfilled? Too many people on the right dismiss the left's very attractive appeal to the American people. We fail to understand it at our own peril.

No, I am not trying to turn this book into a college philosophy textbook. And no, there will not be a quiz at the end of the chapter. These are, of course, questions well worth asking. It's a basic truth of life that each of us should endeavor to discover what matters most to us. It is wise to regularly ask ourselves whether we're on the right track toward finding our deep fulfillment—and wise, too, to ask if that sense of what fulfills us is growing or changing over time. That self-examination is beyond the scope of my mission here—but the importance of how we find fulfillment is central to this project.

A few years ago, I realized that one of the greatest divides between the left and the right in contemporary America revolved around these deceptively simple questions. Virtually everyone at every point on the political spectrum wants their fellow citizens to find fulfillment. Virtually everyone wants to experience happiness. The problem is that today's left defines happiness and fulfillment differently. This isn't just a philosophical difference. They define happiness and fulfillment in ways that maximize the power of the state, and maximize the pressure exerted by the Progressive Political Vise. Worst of all, the means they propose to bring about that fulfillment invariably fail.

Let me back up for a moment, all the way back to a beautiful Saturday morning in the fall of 1988. I'm out early for my morning run through the Lincoln Park Zoo, along the lakefront and among the many soccer, football and softball fields. It is a chance to clear my head, center my mind, burn off some tension, and stay fit. As I jog past one of the athletic fields, out of the corner of my eye, I see a couple of guys waving at me, trying to get my attention. I stop. "Sorry, buddy," says a tall, fit man a few years my senior. "But just a quick question. Do you want to play touch football with us? We're down a man."

Sure, I figure. It might be a fun break from a solitary run. As it turns out, this will not be a one-off. I will end up playing in that informal league for the next twenty years.

From the weekend after Labor Day until the beginning of May, we played every single Saturday, rain or snow or shine. (We took off the weekend after Thanksgiving and Christmas—but only if the latter fell on Saturday.) We'd start showing up around 9:00 a.m. to warm up and banter; by 10:00, we were ready to play—two teams, six on six. At noon we'd retire to the River Shannon, the legendary Irish pub on Armitage Avenue. We would drink beer, eat hot dogs, and talk about . . . well, everything. Over the years, as new guys joined our informal league and others dropped out, I played, drank, and laughed with men from every imaginable walk of life. I threw passes to and "tackled" state prosecutors, defense lawyers, doctors, commodity traders, real estate developers, salesmen, construction workers, electricians, and budding venture capitalists. Though it's been many years since I last played a football game in Lincoln Park, some of the friendships I made on those fields survive to the present day.

I found deep and enduring fulfillment in those touch football games. I found community, and I found fun. In a sense, I also found purpose. The truth is that human beings are not meant to be alone. We flourish when we come together to play, to build, or to accomplish a goal. Of course, we all find that flourishing and sense of fulfillment in different ways. Not everyone wants to spend their Saturday mornings running around on the grass and falling down in mud! The deep joy I got from my Saturday touch football games was mine. It doesn't have to be yours. Perhaps you find that deep fulfillment in volunteering at the library, or in your Wednesday night book club, or in coaching your daughter's softball team. Perhaps you find it in teaching Sunday school, or in deer hunting with your buddies, or in playing the cello in an amateur chamber music group. There is no end to the possibilities for finding meaning and purpose.

Perhaps you're wondering why I've begun this chapter this way. Fear not—just as I'm not writing a philosophy text, I'm also not pivoting to writing a self-help book. I am not trying to recruit you to any particular sort of sport or public service activity. I am pointing out something that might seem obvious but correlates closely with the fundamental thesis of this book: *In contemporary America, fulfillment itself has become political.* Everyone across the ideological spectrum believes that fulfillment is a good thing. It is the progressive left, however, that insists that government institutions are responsible for providing that deep sense of purpose. It is the progressive left that dismisses the possibility that individuals can find that meaning on their own. *It is the progressive left that weaponizes the very absence of fulfillment in order to move the screws of the Vise.*

As I argued in the previous chapter, woke philosophy suggests that our system was set up only for the benefit of the few. Wokeism insists that our country's institutions are racist to their very foundations. The woke maintain that capitalism, far from being an engine for human flourishing, is a system designed to make the rich richer at the expense of everyone else. At its core, Wokeism is the belief that unless you are a wealthy, heterosexual, Christian white man, your unhappiness is someone else's fault. Your inability to find fulfillment and purpose in this life is a consequence not of poor choices, bad habits, or a lack of drive. Your sense of frustration and despair is the result of living in a racist, exploitative system. *You are a victim.*

The real goal of the left never changes. They want to seize, secure, and maintain the commanding heights of political power. To reach this "holy grail" of total control, the progressive left seduces the American people into a mindset of learned helplessness, dependency, grievance, and fear. The left mocks individual effort, ambition, and self-discipline as a sucker's game. To the poor, the disappointed, and the struggling, Wokeism offers a narrative that allows unhappy people to avoid any personal responsibility for their failures. Over and over again, the left inculcates the notion that the last, best, and only hope we have for fulfillment and prosperity will come from a powerful, activist government.

It doesn't take much to get people to feel like victims. It's a natural human impulse to imagine that every calamity, every misfortune, and every disappointment that befalls us is unfair and unjust. When we didn't get that promotion, or when the cashier was rude to us, or when our kid didn't get into the college we wanted, we were victimized. When someone breaks up with us, or a spouse leaves us, they are always the ones at fault. My younger colleagues tell me that on social media, it's become common to "diagnose" every single ex-boyfriend or girlfriend as a "clinical narcissist" while claiming oneself to be an "empath" whose only fault is "caring too much." To put it mildly, that attitude is a recipe for loneliness and misery.

The appeal of victimhood is very old. More than four hundred years ago, William Shakespeare's King Lear lamented that he was "more sinned against than sinning." If you've read or seen the play, you know that's not true; Lear was very much the architect of all his misfortunes. Many of us are like Lear, and the Bard knew it. While we might admit that sometimes we've made mistakes, we still insist that the pain and disappointment we experience is primarily someone else's fault. Wokeism takes that ancient impulse to blame others, and identifies the culprit as racism, sexism, capitalism. It also identifies the solution: give the government enough power, and it will right the wrongs that have hurt you.

In a February 2020 speech in the House of Representatives, New York Congresswoman Alexandria Ocasio-Cortez delivered another of her many viral speeches. On this occasion, AOC denounced what she called "boot-strapping," a reference to the old expression made famous by Horatio Alger about the possibility of pulling oneself up by one's bootstraps. The young congresswoman wasn't just pointing out the obvious impossibility of physi-cally pulling oneself up by a bootstrap; she made it clear she was denounc-ing the idea behind the metaphor. No one, she argued, can rise through their own hard work. It's all a lie, AOC said; "the whole thing is a joke."[35]

I laughed when I heard the congresswoman's angry speech. I wondered aloud if AOC herself was aware that in any number of ways, she is the proverbial poster child for American possibility. Her father died when she was young. Her mother worked as a school bus driver and a house cleaner. AOC herself was—famously—a bartender and a waitress after graduating college. I obviously don't share AOC's politics, but I admire her tremendous work ethic. She put in the sweat and the effort, and it has paid off for her handsomely. Over the years, I've known many left-wing activists like AOC. They have pulled themselves up by their own bootstraps, and they work tirelessly for the causes they believe in. These progressives preach victim-hood, even while their private behavior shows dedication and responsibility. *Their actions show a faith in the system that their words deny.*

I know why AOC and others like her don't encourage their followers to do as they have done. Their real goal is power, and the kind of power the left seeks requires dependency. It requires grievance. It requires a sense of having been cheated and robbed by an unfair system. It requires a belief that the government can and will do for you what you can't or won't do for yourself. They frame their own success stories as "lucky exceptions" rather than rules. They insist that what they earned through merit and virtue was instead bestowed by rare and random chance. It's cynical, hypocritical, and infuriating—but it works to win over a gullible audience.

The good news is that human beings are not just slaves to the "victim impulse." We do have an innate urge to blame others for our misfortunes, it's true. Yet we have another great force at work in our lives: the natural human desire to learn, to grow, and to achieve. Each of us is born with a curiosity about the world, and a hunger to find a purpose. We are born with basic drives for food, shelter, and sex—but by virtue of being human, we also have an ingrained longing for fulfillment and achievement. We dream dreams for ourselves and those we love, imagining a better and more fulfilling life.

Whether you're on a basketball court on Chicago's South Side or in a dusty field in South Sudan, you'll see and hear children declaring their dreams aloud. "I'm LeBron!" shouts one kid as he drives to the hoop; "Kobe!" yells another triumphantly as he sinks a shot from a distance. "I'm Messi," announces a little boy as he kicks a ball through the red dust of an African village. When children do this, they're doing more than playing a game. They are dreaming dreams for themselves, daring to imagine a bright and brilliant future.

When your daughter pretends she's Taylor Swift or your son pretends he's Tom Brady, I'm fairly certain you don't mock them. You don't say, "Don't be ridiculous. You'll never be famous and successful like that." You encourage your child to follow his or her dreams, knowing that their aspirations will shift as they grow up—but also knowing that hard work will help them achieve a new or different goal. The left, on the other hand, is like the adult who ridicules a child's fantasies. The contemporary left sneers at ambition, discourages the pursuit of excellence, and reminds the child—and later the adult—that happiness and fulfillment can only be provided by the state.

The left takes the dreaming child aside and says, "You aren't going to reach those particular dreams. But we have something we think is *almost* as good: You can play a part in righting the wrongs of the past. You can make the world a fairer place. You just need to learn a little about what *we* mean by 'fair.'"

Any discussion of fairness points to a basic truth about how the contemporary progressive left assembles coalitions. They don't rely on grievance and victimization alone. They also cultivate guilt and anxiety among prosperous, mostly white suburbanites.

Put simply, there aren't enough people who believe themselves to be victims to sustain an electoral coalition. Grievance and entitlement alone cannot turn the handles of the Vise. The contemporary progressive coalition is made up of those who are reminded constantly they are victims—*and* those who are reminded with equal frequency that they have a moral obligation to rescue the oppressed. On college campuses across this country, white middle- and upper-class students are told that they are the beneficiaries of unmerited privilege. They are told that their ancestors were bigots who created generational wealth through savage exploitation. They are told that while they can never understand the world as well as a Black person, if they work very hard at renouncing their white privilege, they can perhaps redeem themselves.

The progressive left is also overwhelmingly secular; they don't often look to the church to find forgiveness for their sins. Though it's beyond the scope of this book, sociologists know that more frequent church attendance almost perfectly correlates with more conservative political views. With a few notable exceptions, the progressive left is unchurched, and so Wokeism functions not just as a political ideology but also as a religion. Religion promises comfort for the aggrieved and the wounded—and it also offers a path to forgiveness for the sinner. Woke ideology teaches the white middle-class that as beneficiaries of that unmerited privilege, they are tainted by the sins of their ancestors.

Fortunately for the guilt-ridden, Wokeism offers a path to redemption and fulfillment. You walk that path by demonstrating allegiance to the agenda of the woke left through your votes, your financial support, and ritualistic displays of white guilt. If you do well enough, you may earn the ultimate reward: to be declared an ally. Wokeism, like many fundamentalist religions, offers a strict moral binary: if you are straight, white, and male, you are either a hopelessly irredeemable bigot or you are on a kind of permanent probation. Your privilege makes it impossible for you to truly understand what the oppressed experience. You cannot be allowed to lead a movement. But if you defer often enough, and express your solidarity loudly and constantly, the woke left will call you an "ally." In the moral hierarchy of Wokeism, few titles are more sought after or more prized.

If we want to transform the culture—and retake the commanding heights for the cause of liberty—we need to be serious about the appeal of Wokeism. That means being honest not only about Wokeism's appeal but about the way it offers its followers something approaching real fulfillment. If we don't see just how seductive the ideology is, we will consistently misunderstand how to defeat it.

It is no accident that a key tenet of the woke movement is an anti-Christian and anti-family animus. They understand that it is through faith in God, not government, that human fulfillment reaches its full potential. They understand that Christianity, and the broader Judeo-Christian moral code, is liberty's secret weapon against the woke culture that ultimately destroys the soul.

The good news is that more Americans are entering faith journeys. Belief is growing, and these trends are barriers to the left's ascendence. A recent study showed that 66 percent of adult Americans have renewed their commitment to belief in Jesus, a 12 percent increase since 2021.[36]

Further, young men, mostly Gen Z, are now more religious than young women.[37] It is no coincidence that men are turning to faith when the woke left is constantly telling them they are toxic oppressors of everyone else. There is no place for them in the grievance coalition. Women, on the other hand, find much comfort and often heroine status. As noted, the victim mindset is very real and appealing. It is my belief these trends bear out the truth that faith is one of our most powerful antidotes to the woke mindset and governing philosophy.

While the reasons for these encouraging trends are complex, it is my belief that the emptiness of the woke mindset, rooted in intolerance, coercion, and submission, is finally revealing itself to those who the left has been seducing for all too long. While I am no theologian, the core of Christianity is forgiveness, acceptance, love, kindness, and generosity. How can that not prevail over the divisiveness and intolerance rooted in Wokeism?

The more the left attacks faith and family, the more vigorously, the more overtly we must fight back. They know that faith and family are the secret weapons to defeating their aims. We must understand that as well and deploy that strength accordingly. We must stand proud of our beliefs every chance we get and resist those attempting to silence us.

Sometimes, my colleagues on the right will see something on television or read something in the paper or social media, and they'll throw up their hands in frustration. "How can people believe this stuff? Are they stupid?" I have spent most of my adult life listening to progressives sneer at conservatives, accusing us of being ignorant, malicious, or intolerant bible thumpers. More than twenty years ago, the historian Thomas Carr Frank published what became a bestseller: *What's the Matter with Kansas? How Conservatives Won the Heart of America.* Writing for an affluent liberal audience, Frank made the case that conservative voters had been hoodwinked into voting against their own best interests. His recommendation to the left was to tone down their disdain for the easily deceived rubes. The book masqueraded as a plea for understanding, but it was shot through with paternalism and mockery. Contempt is the default mode for the left. We on the right cannot make that same mistake.

It is part of the human condition to long for more than what you have. It is part of the human condition to wonder why others have things you lack. It is part of the human condition to feel unfulfilled—unless you take action to provide that fulfillment. To the poor and many minority groups, the progressive left has instant appeal because it provides an easy-to-understand narrative about why they are so unhappy. *You have no agency. You are adrift in life, and the rapacious capitalists and white supremacists, blindly loyal to self-interest and the toxic ideology of individual liberty, have caused you and your ancestors terrible pain. But that pain can be assuaged. We can help you! We—using the power of the government—can right what is wrong. Using the state for its true purpose, we can properly allocate opportunity and resources to give you the justice and fulfillment you crave.*

To white liberals, the progressive left says: *You are unhappy. Deep down, you know the discontent you feel is because of guilt. Your ancestors robbed and stole and enslaved others to give you what you have now. Join us, support our agenda, and lend your money and your voice to our cause. In return, you will atone for the sins of your forebears. You will be righteous and superior. You will be freed from that awful nagging guilt, and you will play a part in creating a more just and kind world. If you do this, you will surely find real fulfillment!*

Perhaps you're rolling your eyes. That's fine, but I'm not writing just to poke fun at the fundamentalism of the woke left. I don't oppose Wokeism and the progressive agenda because I find these ideas strange or distasteful or fanatical, though they are all of those things. I oppose them on principle. I believe in the consent of the governed and that the people are sovereign. The left wants people to submit to what starts out as a nudge, but which soon becomes coercion—and all too often, force. The left is about coercion and submission; I am about persuasion and consent.

But I also oppose the left's ideas because they don't work. There is no utility to them. They don't deliver on their promises. They do not offer a road map out of either Black poverty or white guilt. These ideas don't work because they are premised on a series of lies. The truth is that government cannot fix our problems. The truth is that the left has no blueprint for either prosperity or liberty. And the truth is that no political movement, no matter how all-consuming and passionate, can lead its followers to the fulfillment they crave.

Since the New Deal of Franklin Roosevelt, the left has succeeded in steadily expanding a culture of dependency. Democrat presidents beloved of the left—FDR, Lyndon Johnson, Barack Obama and Joe Biden—created massive new government spending programs designed to lift people out of poverty. Many Republican presidents did the same thing, unable to resist the inexorable pressures of the Progressive Political Vise. Over the decades, we have spent trillions on policies and entitlements ostensibly intended to give poor and needy Americans not just food and medical care, but dignity, purpose, and fulfillment. The spending on most of these programs is unsustainable, but my objection to them is not merely economic. I object to these programs because they invariably fail to deliver the fulfillment they promise. Those failures never lead to a reconsideration of the premise of the program—rather, the left insists that success will only come when still more money is spent. They blame insufficient financial investment for the inability of these government-run programs to deliver on their promise. The reality is that these programs cannot deliver on their promise because they are based on the wrong premise.

I did not always agree with Mitt Romney, the Republican nominee for president in 2012. I winced when news broke of a speech he'd given to a group of wealthy conservative donors. It became known as the infamous "47 percent speech," and many argue that it ended Romney's rise in the polls and ensured Barack Obama's re-election.

> There are 47 percent of the people who will vote for the president (Obama) no matter what. All right, there are 47 percent who are with him, who are dependent upon government, who believe that they are victims, who believe that government has a responsibility to care for them, who believe that they are entitled to health care, to food, to housing, to you name it . . . These are people who pay no income tax. Forty-seven percent of Americans pay no income tax. So, our message of low taxes doesn't connect. And he'll be out there talking about tax cuts for the rich. I mean that's what they sell every four years. And so, my job is not to worry about those people—I'll never convince them that they should take personal responsibility and care for their lives. What I have to do is convince the 5 to 10 percent in the center that are independents that are thoughtful . . .[38]

The emphasis is mine. Governor (and later Senator) Romney was right that a huge percentage of Americans pay no income tax. As another retired senator, Phil Gramm, has shown in his recent book, *The Myth of American Inequality*, the media and the progressive left work overtime to conceal a fundamental truth: the poorest 20 percent in this country—tens of millions of our fellow Americans—receive the majority of their income in the form of government transfer payments. When we account for those transfer payments, the lowest quintile (that bottom 20 percent) makes nearly the same amount as the middle quintile. It's just that those in the middle are actually working for what they bring home, while those below them reap the benefits with little to no work.

Mitt Romney was more or less right on the facts, but utterly wrong in his lament that he could never convince "those people" to "take personal responsibility and care for their lives." Mitt did not understand the power of the Political Vise. Respectfully, I'd also argue he didn't understand his role as Convincer in Chief. In this particular instance, the Republican nominee made the grave mistake of giving up on that 47 percent. He accepted the premise that the 47 percent had willingly chosen either victimhood or guilt and had no other impulse or instinct to which to appeal.

If I could have jumped in during that donor dinner, I would have said something different:

> The people you are talking about are one of the main reasons I am running for president. The people who are looking to government for their food, their shelter, their clothing, their housing, their transportation, and their healthcare have been seduced into a dependency class. And when a political party uses its power to create a system that encourages capable people to become welfare dependent because it turns them into reliable Democrat voters, we must call that what it is—it is immoral and evil.
>
> It is also evil to turn one group of citizens into indentured servants to fund the lives of others who are perfectly capable of

working. But far worse, it is an assault against each person you are seducing into government dependency. Within each of them, with better opportunities, with a quality education, with helpful job training, with real compassion and caring, within each of them lives a very personal American Dream. That dream—a longing for something better for themselves and their families—has been numbed by dependency. That dream is dormant, but it is not dead.

I am running to awaken the dreams of the 47 percent. I am running to show them that aspiration, not victimhood, is the key to fulfillment and flourishing. And let me be clear: I am not doing this just because I want to inspire the 47 percent. I am running because our bright American future depends on that 47 percent breaking the chains of dependency. If we are to have the most dynamic, thriving economy possible, we need everyone to dream dreams and do the hard and hopeful work of turning those dreams into reality. That's why I am running. I am not running *despite* the 47 percent. I am running *for* them—and for all of us.

Don't worry, I'm not announcing my run for president. I do work very hard, however, to influence those who are running for high office—and those working to elect good people to those offices. I want to convey the message that we cannot abandon those people who have lost all hope of fulfillment except for what the state can provide. We may be able to win elections without the votes of the dependent, the aggrieved, and the guilt-ridden—but without transforming their hearts and minds, we cannot become again the nation we were meant to be.

Defeating Wokeism isn't just about getting one more vote than the progressive left candidate. It's about winning back their voters by awakening aspiration, ambition, hope, and faith. It's about sharing the message that human fulfillment isn't only about economic prosperity. Human fulfillment is not the magic consequence of social equity. Authentic human fulfillment manifests in infinite ways. The left may shriek about their love of diversity. The truth is that reverence for diversity means acknowledging that we each find fulfillment in different ways and by pursuing different paths. The most compassionate government isn't the one guaranteeing equality of outcome. The most compassionate government is the one that gets out of the way. The most compassionate government understands its role is to create circumstances that allow creativity, imagination, and ambition to flourish and thus create infinite opportunities for all people. The most compassionate government allows each individual to use their own unique gifts to pursue their own chosen outcome—and find their own fulfillment.

There's an old joke from the Soviet Union that illustrates this principle:

> It is 1917. Lenin is barnstorming Russia, sharing the promise of Communism to curious crowds. "When the Revolution comes," he tells a group of peasants, "we shall all eat strawberries and cream!"
>
> The crowd cheers. One brave peasant tentatively raises his hand. "But Comrade Lenin, I'm allergic to strawberries."
>
> There is a terrible silence. Lenin's thugs close in on the hapless peasant. Just before the poor fellow is dragged away, he hears Lenin say in a cold voice, "Come the Revolution, comrade, even you will eat strawberries and cream."

The woke, progressive left may or may not admit to revering Lenin. This story is almost certainly apocryphal. Regardless, it illustrates the fundamental flaw in the left's vision of human fulfillment. Their understanding is too narrow, too uniform, too impoverished.

I found my "strawberries and cream" playing touch football in the park every Saturday morning for decades. I found deep fulfillment running, catching, and throwing alongside many different men from so many different walks of life. I don't expect everyone to share my passions or interests. (I recommend against it: I'm a Detroit Tigers fan, and that's a recipe for near-perpetual disappointment—until recently!) My commitment to the cause of liberty isn't rooted in a sense that everyone should be like me. My commitment to political, economic, and religious freedom is rooted in my great gratitude for having found a path to deep and lasting fulfillment. I want to do all I can to remove the barriers that stop others from pursuing that same fulfillment.

The fight against the progressive left is a fight for the right of Americans to aspire, to dream, and to flourish. Those are lofty words. They require a tangible plan of action, and it is to the details of that plan—the plan to retake the screws of the Vise—that I'll turn to in the next two chapters.

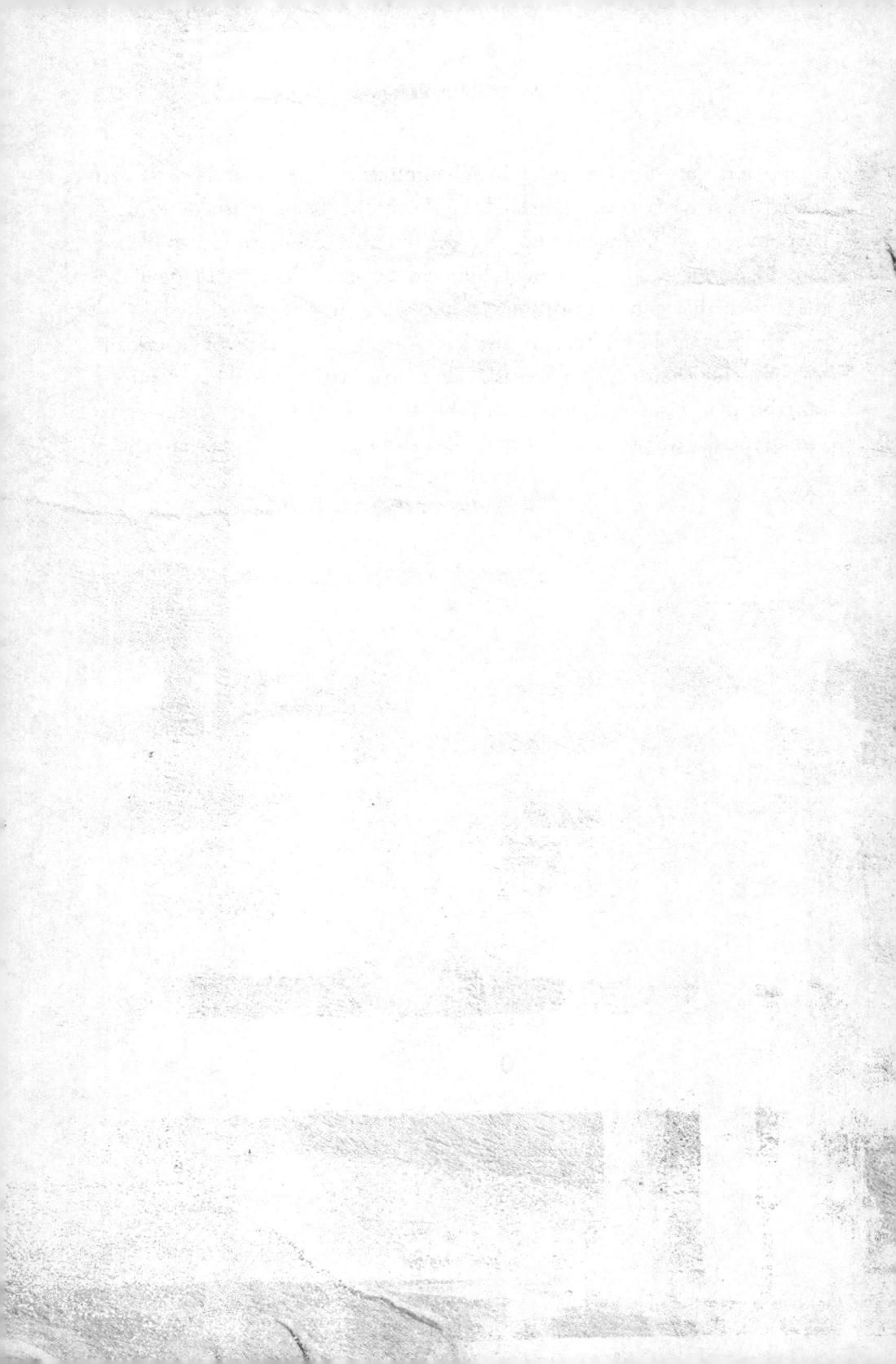

Chapter 13

THE INFLUENCERS, PART TWO: CHOOSING BETTER ELITES

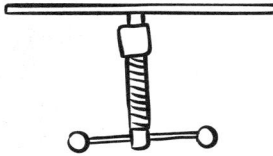

More than once in this book, I've called on my fellow citizens to join me in taking back the "commanding heights" of American culture. The words conjure a compelling image, but you might be surprised to know who said it first: Vladimir Lenin. In a 1922 speech, Lenin surprised his fellow Bolshevik leaders by announcing that he was relaxing controls over Soviet agriculture. He reassured them that the Communists would continue to control heavy industry, including the factories and the railroads. This would allow the Party to continue to control the "commanding heights" of the economy—and thus, control the nation.

I am obviously not a Communist, nor a particular admirer of the monstrous Vladimir Lenin! Like every American of my generation, I grew up in a world where the United States and the Soviet Union were locked in an existential battle. The struggle was between two radically different ideologies, two different economic systems, and two different visions of human fulfillment. The United States won that fight; the Marxist ideology that undergirded Soviet society was repudiated. Where it still endures, in

191

places like Cuba, North Korea, Venezuela, China, and elements of the American progressive movement, it brings nothing but misery and despair.

Considering all that, why quote Lenin? I assure you it has nothing to do with sympathy for a terrible dictator or admiration for the inhuman ideology he embraced. For all his monstrousness, however, Lenin's phrase is still useful. He used it to describe the Bolshevik strategy for retaining control of every aspect of Russian life. I use it to set out a goal and to remind my fellow Americans of the scope and scale of the challenge that lies before us. Those of us who love liberty can once again take control of the culture, but to do that, we must retake the summit from the forces of authoritarian statism. To hold the heights will mean a chance to restore American promise and potential—not for the sake of telling our fellow citizens how to live their lives but to return to them the freedom that was and is their birthright.

Remember, when we say, "take control," we mean once again building an American consensus on who we are as a people. That consensus rests on liberty, persuasion, and consent, not coercion and submission at the hands of the state.

That sounds stirring enough. But you're right to ask the obvious question: *How the hell are we supposed to do that?* In the previous chapters, I've made the case that the left controls those heights. Heights is plural, and the flag of the left seems to fly from them all. They control Hollywood and popular entertainment. They have a stranglehold on K-12 education. They run university campuses in almost every state in this nation. They have seized many corporate boardrooms, and they control corporate advertising and human resources. They run the health-care industrial complex, and (to mix metaphors slightly) have at least established beachheads in the military and the intelligence services. They have the entire apparatus of the Deep State at their disposal. Of course, President Trump and his team are doing all they can to take on these forces, but the battle will not be won in one term. We need to build a movement that lasts long after Trump leaves office.

The truth is that to no small degree, the left *is* the Deep State.

Yet there is good news. The good news is that the American people can still control our destiny as a nation. We can make the twenty-first century more glorious than the twentieth. We can reverse the decline, and we can ensure that our grandchildren can grow up in a nation where they can still dream dreams and pursue their goals. It won't be easy, but you already knew that. You know the obstacles we face. It is tempting to despair, to believe that our numbers are too few and the forces marshaled against us are too great. How do we take back a culture so thoroughly dominated by one side? How do we take back a government staffed with millions of loyal apparatchiks?

In recent years, many liberty-minded people have spoken wistfully of a national divorce. Perhaps red states could go one way and blue states another. Perhaps we can have a great re-shuffling, and people can move to more politically congenial communities. To some extent, that's already happened organically. I've noted before that when the pandemic lockdowns happened, many Americans voted with their feet. Restrictive lockdown states like Minnesota, New York, Illinois, and California saw tens of thousands leave. States that stayed open and chose a more pragmatic course—like Florida, Texas, Georgia, and Tennessee—saw a net inflow. Red state governors like Greg Abbott, Brian Kemp, Kristi Noem, Doug Burgum, Kay Ivey, Kim Reynolds, and (above all) Ron DeSantis have worked hard to create strong climates for investment, parental rights, and individual liberties. I'm a big fan of some of these leaders, Governor DeSantis and Reynolds in particular, and I hope that their number increases.

I understand the temptation of a national divorce. Surely, it is easier to use the Political Vise as it was originally intended in a state dominated by conservative voters. The theory of the Political Vise obviously applies at every level of government. With so many setbacks for the liberty movement at the federal level, it is reassuring to be able to shift our focus to racking up big wins for freedom in places like Florida, Iowa, Montana, and North Dakota. Look, I re-launched an organization called *Illinois* Policy! I have spent most of my life in advocacy based in Chicago, battling in the very heartland of the liberal Democratic machine. I know better than most how important it is to focus on state-level work. But that doesn't mean I'm ready to accept a national divorce.

Part of my opposition to national divorce is practical. Fracturing into two nations is simply untenable economically, politically, and geographically. The attempted secession of the Confederacy was, at the risk of understatement, a bad idea. Yet even if the North had allowed the South to depart in peace, it is not at all clear that the Confederacy would have survived and thrived on its own for long. Both what remained of the United States and the nascent Confederate States would have been weaker as a consequence of their separation.

Another reason a national divorce among the states is a bad idea is because almost all of America is red. We don't have a blue state problem, we have a blue *cities* problem. In nearly every case, when you look at the red/blue map of America by county, we are a red country. It is the dominance of the progressives in big blue cities that turns Arizona, Georgia, Michigan, Minnesota, Nevada, and Pennsylvania into purple or blue states. A key strategy for restoring American consensus is for our movement to make inroads in these blue cities. Blue cities are dominated by Blacks, Hispanics, and affluent, virtue-signaling whites who vote overwhelmingly for Democrats. But there are conservatives in urban areas who have been ignored, as well as independents and persuadable Democratic voters that can be moved by the truth we know—our policy ideas are better for them. We need to make that effort at persuasion, not to win a majority but to move enough voters so that the political power of these "blue islands" will be diminished and a pro-American voting coalition can win in unexpected places.

A much bigger part of my opposition to national divorce is that I remain an optimist about the future of the union. Economic decline and moral decay are not foregone conclusions. They are what has happened as a result of the pressure exerted by the Progressive Political Vise, and they are what will continue to happen if we do not get our own hands on those screws.

But there's a difference between a sober assessment and a surrender. There's a difference between giving up and continuing to fight. With respect to those who continue to advocate for a national divorce, I'm ready to continue to fight.

Wresting back control of the Political Vise won't be easy, but it is achievable. Our primary challenge is whether we can marshal the strategy and harness the resources to prevail in this fight against the Radical Left. At a high level, that means that, as in any fight, we must understand the other side's strengths and weaknesses as well as our own. This understanding of assets and liabilities is what will inform us about the strategy we must adopt. The left has exploited their opportunities very well, but they have taken many risks as well. We have the chance to take advantage of the vulnerabilities created by those risks. Above all else, we must incorporate human nature into our thinking and planning.

We are fighting for the soul of what it means to be America and American in the twenty-first century. As I have explained, the authoritarians have an emotionally attractive appeal that caters to one aspect of the human experience—that of victimhood and grievance. The woke left is exquisitely skilled at manufacturing and exploiting resentment. We cannot beat them at that game. There are many on the right who want to capitalize on the justified grievances of "our" voters, and I understand the strategy. Yet as we've seen in recent years, there are limits to the effectiveness of weaponizing resentment. We must appeal not to the rage, but to the hope. We must appeal not to the desire to destroy, but the desire to build. We can tap into anger when needed, but to win the real victory, we must be a movement about hope, about aspiration, and about American flourishing.

If these sound like glittering generalities, bear with me. It's important to have an overview of who we are and our long-term goals. At the same time, as many great leaders have pointed out time and again, "hope is not a strategy." We do need concrete, actionable plans. We need not only to inspire people to seek a way forward, but to map out the journey ahead. The good news is that there are specific things we can do, individually and collectively, to push the liberty movement forward, to get the Political Vise back into the hands of the people, and to seize back the commanding heights. The first step? *Changing the elites, who are—of course—influencers.*

As a singular adjective, "elite" is a compliment. We use it to describe someone who is the very best at what they do, like a great athlete. As a plural noun, "elites" is often a derisive slur. In each of his three runs for the presidency, Donald Trump has railed against the corruption, incompetence, and cynicism of our political and cultural elites. Much of Trump's success lay in correctly identifying these enemies of liberty. The promise to "drain the swamp" was, in part, a promise to wrest the screws of power away from political, corporate, media, and cultural elites whose contempt for the American people had become so obvious.

I'll have more to say about Donald Trump in a moment. But I want to clarify a common misconception about "elites" and their role in American life. If you trace back the etymology of the word, "elite" comes from the Latin verb *eligere*, which means "to choose." Words like "election" and "elected" (but not "electricity") come from that same root. What this very brief language lesson conveys is that our elites were meant to be those we chose to lead us. The fact that our elites today come from a self-perpetuating class far removed from the concerns of ordinary Americans is infuriating. It is also a reminder that the problem isn't that we have leaders and influencers in the first place. The problem is the moral character and the self-serving agendas of those elites. The problem is that they chose themselves and then imposed themselves.

It is not wrong to want to be led by elites. If I need to have surgery, I want the doctor who cuts me open to be an elite physician. I want my doctor to have been chosen by the hospital for his or her skills. When my doctor first applied to medical school, I want him or her to have been chosen for their excellence and abilities. When I choose a lawyer, or an accountant, or—for that matter—a quarterback for my fantasy football league—I am choosing someone whom I believe to have elite skills in their profession. It doesn't mean I am signing my power over to them. It doesn't mean that I am relinquishing my autonomy. It means I recognize that to live in human society, we need to have a division of labor. That society functions best when we can choose the most skilled, talented, and reliable to help us do what we cannot do on our own.

The woke left likes to make the case that our Founding Fathers were wealthy, powerful enslavers born into privilege. In other words, they argue that the Founders were able to do what they did only as a function of their riches. This is not the book to delve into the social backgrounds of the men who founded our nation, but it bears noting that only a few of the Revolutionary generation were born to great wealth. George Washington and Thomas Jefferson did grow up in considerable comfort by the standards of the time, but John Adams, Benjamin Franklin, Alexander Hamilton, and arguably a majority of the remaining Founders grew up in much simpler circumstances. Franklin's father was a shoemaker! What made them "elite" was not what they inherited in terms of land or slaves or gold. What made them elite was their education, their intelligence, their extraordinary courage, and their vision for this brand-new nation.

Our next great task as Americans is to choose new elites. We must choose men and women who revere our founding principles and who have the courage to fight for them. We must choose elites who possess the imagination to approach this fight with brand-new strategies and innovative tactics. And in a world where the progressive left holds so many corporations and legacy institutions captive, we need elites who can raise the resources to make it possible to win this fight.

Elites are not incompatible with democracy. Elites are necessary even in a constitutional republic. They are one of the sides of the Traditional Political Vise and have been since this nation's inception. The elites of the past understood that just as elected officials gained their power from the consent of the governed, public figures became influential through their capacity to motivate, to inspire, and to offer a compelling vision for the American future. The traditional elites understood that the preservation and subsequent growth of a free society rested not on the genius of the few but the convictions of the many. To the extent that the traditional elites played an outsized role in our national life, it was generally with a sense of deep reverence for our institutions. Just as players on a football team might elect as captain someone with a particular gift for inspiration, Americans can and must return to a system of choosing elites for the leadership skills they offer and their commitment to America's founding principles.

Today's failing elites do not wish to inspire. They wish to distract, redirect, mislead, and control. They have a very specific agenda that I've laid out in the preceding chapters. In recent years, the elites have become afraid of the people; they are frightened of an engaged populace. In all the silos and summits of American life—from the news media, to government, to universities, to corporate boardrooms, to entertainment—the elites can sense a growing rebellion. They can see the seeds of rebellion starting to sprout. This rebellion isn't about overthrowing the American system. It's about restoring it. That restoration of the American ideal will mean a calamitous loss of power for these new (and unchosen) elites. This is why they work overtime to control and suppress information. This is why they are so desperate to stamp out dissent.

In some instances, these frightened elites cling to power by firing, silencing, and canceling their critics. To keep the masses at heel, they warn constantly of an existential peril that is always just about to overtake our government. They peddle hysteria about everything from global warming to civil liberties. We are always one election away from "losing democracy as we know it." The hyperbole is absurd, though sometimes effective. What it really indicates is that the elites are scared. And they should be.

What have our incumbent elites brought us? Failure, dissension, division, and decline. Out-of-control spending has led to out-of-control debt. Entitlements are bankrupting the country, with the elites refusing to lead a serious discussion on how to fix it. Educational performance in our elementary schools is plummeting, especially since the elite-mandated pandemic lockdowns. Our universities are laboratories for performative outrage and grotesque anti-Semitism rather than sanctuaries for mastering critical thinking or understanding the gifts of the Western canon. Our health-care system, laboring under the unaffordable dictates of Obamacare, is more about charts and records than actual patient care. Our military—the institution that provides for our national security and is the guarantor of our freedoms—focused on providing gender reassignment surgeries more than standing up to the rapidly growing Chinese threat. The disconnect between the elites and the people has never been greater, and their fear of being replaced is both justified and well-earned.

The good news is that we can replace them. We can look at this litany of failures and say, "Enough." The beauty of the American system is that even now, the mechanism still exists to hold accountable those who have betrayed us. Outrage alone, however justified, cannot move the mechanism by itself. Anger alone does not power the Vise. We need new elites—literally meaning, of course, new leaders whom we choose—to impose that accountability. And this means finishing what Donald Trump started.

Earlier in this book, I discussed what we can learn from Donald Trump in terms of movement-building. What is very certain with Trump returned to the White House for a second term is that he will continue to be a potent and disruptive force in American life for the foreseeable future. The lessons of his extraordinary rise over the past decade reflect every aspect of the Political Vise and its power. Conservatives must leverage the corporate media while building their own. Conservatives must communicate directly with the American people and rally them to the movement to take back the commanding heights of American culture. As Trump has demonstrated with his cabinet and staff appointments, we must replace the failing influencers and elites and replace them with those loyal to the Constitution and the American people.

Because Donald Trump has been the central figure in American public life for a decade, it's all too easy to misunderstand and misinterpret his legacy, which is still being written. Whatever else may be said of him, Trump has been able to harness that righteous anger at failed elites more successfully than any other leader in recent American memory. Tens of millions of Americans were fed up with a government that no longer seemed to work and a system that seemed calcified, inhuman, and incompetent. Trump tapped into that resentment and harnessed an anger that had been bubbling up for years. The Tea Party movement existed before his rise to power, but it had no leaders capable of uniting and focusing all of that righteous rage. Trump had the skill to gather in an army of the justifiably discontented and unite them around his political campaign. Most importantly, he didn't just harness the anger; he offered hope and aspiration as the destination—"Make America Great Again." It speaks volumes that the left has tried to turn that into a pejorative.

One of the most potent memes of the 2016 campaign—and of the entire MAGA movement—features a photograph of a stern-looking Trump staring into the camera. The accompanying caption, which would soon find its way onto posters, coffee mugs and T-shirts, read "They're not after me. They're after you. I'm just in the way." It sounded like a "log line" for an action TV series, but it proved to be a galvanizing political message. It was a message with three sentences and three pronouns: you, me, and they. The genius of the meme was that no one had to ask who Trump meant by "they." It wasn't just the Democrats, or university professors, or nanny-state bureaucrats. The "they" were the entrenched elites whose regulations, agendas, and prejudices squeezed hundreds of millions of ordinary Americans in the Progressive Political Vise. It was so obvious it didn't need further explanation.

Over the past ten years, Donald Trump has been subjected to a dizzying, unrelenting, and unprecedented series of attacks. The elites have unleashed "lawfare" on Trump, using the power of the institutions they control (starting with the media and including both federal and state courts) to try to discredit and destroy this one man. Trump's own instinctive combativeness only lent credence to the campaign against him. The tragedy is that in the early years, Trump's own bombastic lack of self-control lent an air of legitimacy to these deeply illegitimate and unconstitutional efforts to derail his movement. We can be grateful for the unprecedented challenge he posed to the elites. While his indiscipline frequently undercut his effectiveness in his first term, we can see the transformation of his approach in his second term. He has learned that the power and durability of his message must take precedence, not his own personal grievance campaign. In 2024 he won re-election, in part, by channeling his combativeness and his willingness to say what had always gone unsaid into a more disciplined and focused campaign that proved record-breaking and victorious.

Whatever happens in his second term, Donald Trump has demonstrated that it was possible to take on the elites—and, in a very real way, replace them. His victories at the ballot box in 2016 and again in 2024 are the most consequential wins for liberty in the last fifty years. Those weren't just because of this one man or his specific policies. It was because he demonstrated that the elites were vulnerable. "Elite" means chosen—and the people chose differently than everyone anticipated. We can and must do that again and again.

Earlier, I mentioned four of our Founders: Washington, Adams, Franklin, Hamilton. They are famous enough that their surnames alone bring to mind faces on currency, countless public statues and streets, and stories we grew up hearing. Here are four of their contemporaries: Thomas Hutchinson, Thomas Brown, Joseph Bryant, and Boston King. Do they sound familiar? Are you drawing a blank? (Don't worry, there's no test.) These latter four men were among the elites of Colonial America, powerful and well-connected. They have all but vanished from history because they each took the side of the British Crown in the Revolution. They chose loyalty to George III over their fellow Americans—and their fellow Americans chose to reject them. The American people picked the Founders to lead them and consigned previous elites like Brown and Hutchinson to obscurity, shame, and the occasional footnote.

We can and must do the same.

The recent pandemic provided an outstanding example of what this "replacement of the elites" can look like. Even many of Donald Trump's most devoted supporters concede that his initial reaction to COVID-19 left much to be desired. To a disastrous extent, Trump allowed Dr. Anthony Fauci—and his coterie of alarmists—to become the public face of the federal government's reaction. As Fauci, Dr. Deborah Birx, and others proposed ever more extreme and draconian responses to the crisis, Trump erred in allowing these "experts" to dominate the stage. Aided by a compliant media and the hesitation of the Trump administration, these elite influencers put the American people—and the economy—in the Vise. You no doubt remember those surreal days in the spring of 2020! What I remember best is realizing how badly we were all getting crushed in the Progressive Political Vise.

As the weeks passed, the worshipful deference initially shown to Dr. Fauci and the "experts" began to fade. It was clear that other countries, such as Sweden, weren't locking down as we had done—and their results were no worse. As more and more Americans began to lament that the human toll of the lockdowns was worse than the disease itself, the elites began to respond as they always do. They began to crush dissenters, deriding anyone who dared question the party line as hellbent on "trying to kill grandma." Americans pushed back.

It took too long to change the narrative. When the narrative shift finally arrived, it did so at the hands of alternative elites. Republican governors like Ron DeSantis in Florida, Greg Abbott in Texas, and Kristi Noem in South Dakota reopened their states—and their schools. The national press, Dr. Fauci's handmaidens, breathlessly anticipated mass death. The wave of deaths did not materialize. Democratic governors who had embraced stringent lockdowns—like Gavin Newsom in California, the soon-to-be-disgraced Anthony Cuomo in New York, and Gretchen Whitmer in Michigan—held out. As their businesses closed, their children languished in loneliness, and their citizens literally began to leave, the lockdown leaders remained defiant. Eventually, however, they too had to reopen. The pressure generated by the common-sense governors who rejected the elite consensus eventually became too much for even the COVID fanatics—like Newsom and Cuomo—to resist.

As I write this, there are still voices in the media and in medicine peddling alarmism about COVID, or some imminent future pandemic. These voices have not been silenced, but they have been marginalized. Few listen to them. How did the lockdown elites go from near-absolute power to almost total irrelevance? They were pushed aside by the alternative elites, and by the people. The overthrow of Dr. Fauci and his enablers is a case study in how we reclaim the power of the Political Vise.

We must understand that this overthrow by those bold governors took courage. With the passage of time, we may not remember just how vilified these leaders were. We may not remember that they were vindicated when total disaster did not appear. They stood strong and pursued the course of human freedom of action rather than controlled submission. We should keep this story alive, as we need to be heartened by their courage.

The pandemic was a defining experience of our age. We will not be able to take back the commanding heights merely by taking advantage of a singular historical event. Though conservatives too do well to live by Rahm Emanuel's maxim about never letting a crisis go to waste, we cannot wait for crises to generate opportunity. This work of elevating new elites must continue in "ordinary times" as well as in emergencies. One excellent example of someone doing just that is Vivek Ramaswamy.

In May 2023, while still a longshot candidate for the Republican presidential nomination, Ramaswamy wrote an op-ed for the *Wall Street Journal,* taking the Federal Reserve to task for its failure to adhere to its singular job: maintain a stable dollar. Ramaswamy argued effectively that when the Fed focuses on a stable dollar, prosperity follows. But when the Fed chooses to respond to political influence, and focuses on employment and inflation, bubbles are created. Uncertainty grows, and economic contagions (of the kind we've seen many times in our history) emerge. The op-ed was very well-received, and the editors of the *Journal* added a glowing endorsement of Vivek's thesis.

Vivek is now a candidate for governor of Ohio. I suspect he will be very competitive and likely win. During the few months he actively pursued the presidential nomination, millions responded to his articulate, passionate, wry case for restoring American principles. Vivek Ramaswamy represents a new kind of elite, not merely because he is wealthy but because he has a vision that resonates and inspires. What will make him (and others like him) truly influential isn't a self-made fortune. For someone like Vivek to turn the screws of the Political Vise, he will need to be an "elite" in the true and literal sense of the word: He will need to be *chosen* by the American public. The evidence is that he's well on his way. We will need more like him.

It is easy to be cynical about our chances of seizing back those commanding heights. Too many people think we have missed our opportunity to reform and reclaim the American experiment. Too many are resigned to the growing authoritarianism of the left. Too many want to just appease and capitulate in the hope of being left alone. They hope that if they stay quiet enough, the Progressive Political Vise won't crush them. They are wrong. Cynicism and fatalism are dubious luxuries we cannot afford.

Donald Trump will leave office in January 2029 (I do own a hat that says Trump 2028, but the dictatorship so feared will not come to pass by the political right). We can be grateful for his example even as we look for younger, disciplined leaders of the liberty movement. We can be grateful for the Ramaswamys, the Elon Musks, the Joe Rogans, the J. D. Vances, and the DeSantises without waiting for the *Wall Street Journal* editorial page (or the discerning voters of Florida) to offer up a new and inspiring leader. It is up to each of us to look at every aspiring candidate for any office—from school board to the Senate—and ask if they are going to go along with the failed elite consensus, or if they are going to fight for the Constitution and liberty. To take back this country, we need new leaders, leaders who are both reverent about the republic and the freedoms of those they wish to serve. We each have our part to play in the reclaiming of the nation, and one key element is taking responsibility for elevating and empowering the right people to inspire and lead us. Remember the basic image of the three-sided Vise. We the People are one vital side. The elite influencers are another. What we have forgotten is that we have the capacity to choose these men and women. We must exercise that power again.

Every day in your life, make your choices about who to follow based upon their loyalty to empowering people instead of empowering government. Do they revere the Constitution or do they want to gut it? Do you stand with those who are aligned with your values when they come under attack, or do you sit silently? Did you have a sign in your yard during the 2024 election, or were you too intimidated to put the sign out and risk your reputation among your neighbors?

To pick better elites, it begins with you. You must put your sign out, figuratively and literally. Today people like Vivek Ramaswamy, Elon Musk, David Sacks, Marc Andreessen, Bill Maher (on free speech), Mollie Hemingway, Michael Shellenberger, Glenn Greenwald, Matt Taibbi, Abigail Shrier, Bari Weiss, Kim Strassel, Megyn Kelly, and so many others have stood up to be counted. You can "choose" them by subscribing (paying them money!), consuming, and sharing their work.

But even that is not enough—you can do more. We each can. We must consciously stop patronizing those aligned with the progressive left. While fully eliminating every dollar will not be possible, a thoughtful approach can put a dent in their monetization strategies. As practitioners, we should use them. As consumers, shunning them is a good start, both in terms of consumption and payment. Further, I suggest shaming those who rely on the *New York Times*, *Washington Post*, broadcast news, and all the rest. I like to ask where one gets their information. If they cite these sources, I laugh out loud. "You have to be kidding me—you know those are propaganda outlets that don't tell the truth, right?"

Further, when your local elections take place, ask the candidates for their governing philosophy (empowering people versus empowering government). Ask them about the *hard* questions—gender transitioning for children, the Second Amendment, freedom of speech versus regulating hate speech, border security, attitudes about crime, educational choice, etc. You will quickly find out if a candidate should be chosen by you.

Of course, picking better elites alone will not ensure victory. We need the right strategy, sufficiently funded to compete and win. Let's take a look in the next chapter at how we can do just that.

Chapter 14

A GRAND STRATEGY FOR RETAKING THE COMMANDING HEIGHTS

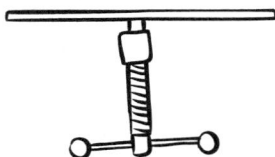

American greatness is not a birthright. Every generation must earn it. We earn it by understanding where we are and where we want to go and by developing the right strategy to achieve that destiny.

We know what our **vision** is—to once again have an American consensus that reveres our founding principles and our Constitution, capitalism and our free enterprise system.

We know what our **mission** is—to build an American movement that competes and wins control of the handles of the Political Vise so we can bring that vision to life. The MAGA movement is the foundation from which this post-Trump movement can grow.

The next question is, what is our **grand strategy** to achieve that mission and thus move toward that vision?

Before we dive into that, let's make sure we are all on the same page about what I mean by grand strategy. The word *strategy* means a "plan of action." Sounds simple enough, but this is the most important part of any great undertaking, and it is usually anything but simple.

Creating an overarching "grand" strategy to achieve an audacious mission forces you to develop a plan of action that provides your team with the best possible likelihood of success. That means facing the truth of the battle and the reality of the enemy you face.

Such plans revolve around:

- Understanding the world in which your undertaking operates
- Knowing your opponent's strengths and weaknesses and what their grand strategy is
- Understanding your strengths and weaknesses and fashioning your grand strategy, and thus allocation of resources, to counter their strengths while maximizing yours

The key idea here is that your overarching strategic imperatives drive your allocation of resources. My basic premise in this book is that the freedom movement has not yet effectively allocated its resources to the battle we face in the media, in engaging the American people, in building liberty-loyal influencers (elites), and in electing and holding politicians accountable. I will address that more specifically below.

What's the first step to overcoming a problem? Admitting the problem is real. They teach that in Alcoholics Anonymous, and in every other program designed to help people overcome addictions. It's as true in politics as it is in recovery. If we want to retake those commanding heights, we have to start by understanding why and how we lost them. In the preceding chapters, I've told that story, explaining the rise of the left and the various ways they took the heights—and seized control of the Political Vise. I've explained how the left invests in capacities that allow them to turn the screws of the Progressive Political Vise and how they deploy Wokeism and grievance to maintain and expand their control.

The truth is that "admitting the problem" goes beyond acknowledging the ascendancy of the left. It also involves admitting the enduring weaknesses of the right.

In December 2023, my friend and colleague Sergio Serrato shared a memo with me. The subject title: "The Progressive Ecosystem of Influence." In this memo, Sergio shared some details about Civis Analytics, a data technology platform. Just one year before he sent me this memo, Sergio had stepped down as Civis's head of product. He was intimately familiar with how Civis (and other similar platforms, such as Data for Progress) analyze, curate, and utilize data on behalf of the Democratic Party and other left-wing organizations. (The full memo is in Appendix B to this book.) It was sobering to understand the sheer sophistication of the left's operation. There is no way to sugarcoat the reality that the left's capacity to harness data for polling, message testing, digital ad targeting, fundraising, direct mail, get-out-the-vote operations, and much more is simply light-years ahead of our own. To use just one obvious metaphor, it's as if we on the right are getting around in a sturdy old 1963 Ford pickup, while the left is driving a 2025 Tesla Cybertruck.

The authoritarian left has a clear vision, a defined mission, and a grand strategy with which they intend to seize and hold the commanding heights of the American cultural narrative and thus the political power that flows from it. It is that vision, mission, coherent strategy, and their massive financial investments in that strategy, that allows the left to determine electoral outcomes despite the relative unpopularity of their views.

Sergio offered one example. In 2021, Republicans won several key elections in Virginia, including the governorship. Widespread anger over the draconian COVID lockdowns led to a repudiation of Democrat policies. It was a historically bad election for the teachers' unions, which had grown increasingly powerful in Virginia. Alarmed, Data for Progress and other similar groups spent millions analyzing the habits, convictions, and anxieties of Virginia voters. The goal was to win them back—or to be more honest about it, to nudge those voters toward a different choice. By the time the 2023 Virginia midterms (they are off cycle) rolled around, the left had designed a campaign focusing on a handful of issues (abortion rights chief among them). As a result, the Democrats won nearly every close race in

Virginia. Polling showed the voters hadn't changed their minds about fundamental issues. But the Democrats had proven far more effective at targeting a message, and as a result, hundreds of thousands of Virginians voted against their own liberty interests.

As Mollie Hemingway explained in her superb recent book, the Democrats are leaps and bounds ahead of the Republicans in terms of understanding how to win political campaigns. (Let me again endorse Mollie's book, *Rigged: How the Media, Big Tech, and the Democrats Seized Our Elections*, for a clear and compelling summary of how the left pulled off their 2020 victory.) For example, while things have improved immensely, Republicans still have an instinctive dislike for universal mail-in voting and distrust ballot-harvesting; the more conservative the voter, the more likely he or she is to want to vote in person. It is absolutely true, as Mollie explains, that ballot-harvesting and early voting are invitations to corruption and malfeasance. On the other hand, if the left is using these tools and techniques to win elections, it is absolute madness for conservatives to decline to do the same. And yet, in state after state in 2020, Republican officials obstinately refused to use the tools at their disposal. One of the reasons Trump won in 2024 was that Republicans had come around to embracing these election tools, but still too many resist competing by the rules of the game.

There is nothing admirable about being so principled that you end up fighting with one hand tied behind your back. Put simply, the left is ruthless and sophisticated. We can complain about it, or we can take decisive action. As I see it, we have neither an excuse nor a choice to do anything other than to cultivate that ruthlessness in ourselves—and to invest in matching the left's technological prowess. Until we are willing to do that, we will continue to lose when we should be winning. To return to the twelve-step analogy, we will stay stuck in the problem.

In the last chapter, I argued that we needed to cultivate a new generation of elites. The good news is that with Trump's victory for a second term, an entire cadre of new leaders is emerging, including his cabinet, his senior staff, legislators, business leaders, and others. In states all around the country, from the strong pandemic governors to new emerging local leaders, the public is hearing from liberty-loyal voices more than ever before. I recently listened to a George Mason University professor, Bryan Caplan, make a compelling case against DEI, rightly comparing it to the worst aspects of McCarthyism. He is a new elite leader with courage, standing up for what is right.

Even more interesting are the evolutions of Mark Zuckerberg, Jeff Bezos, Bill Maher, and others. Some have questioned the motivations of Zuckerberg and Bezos, and others have noted that Maher is still a loyal progressive, but their change in attitude and openness to engaging Trump and support for free speech are huge wins for the cause of liberty.

The shift has begun. We need to build on that foundation and spread new leaders in every institution possible. We need leaders everywhere who understand the existential threat our republic faces. We need leaders who are committed to the cause of liberty, not just as a lofty ideal but as an attainable goal. With respect to resources and building capacities, we need leaders who are willing to deploy their resources to fund a coherent vision, an attainable mission, and an overarching strategy. The stakes couldn't be higher: If these new elites are willing to make this commitment, then our republic will be saved. If that investment isn't made, the elites of the progressive left will steadily gain more control. Sooner or later—and frankly, probably sooner—the left will extinguish the extraordinary American experiment in liberty.

We cannot allow that to happen. And yet, through strategic ineffectiveness that might as well be inaction, that is exactly what we have been permitting.

This may strike you as harsh. There are any number of very wealthy donors on the right who have been heroically investing for many years. I know many of them, and I cannot express my respect and gratitude enough. These leaders are many wonderful men and women who have created foundations and political action committees, hosted fundraisers, and worked tirelessly for the cause of liberty. I am overwhelmed by their generosity, their leadership, and their commitment.

We do have areas that can improve, of course. If we are to get stronger as a movement, we must face the truth that many of the liberty movement's most generous donors have not been well-served. It is not just that the left outraises and outspends us—it is that the left has proved a far shrewder steward of its resources, pouring hundreds of millions into cutting-edge technologies and building leveraged capacities while our side consistently lags behind.

Here's the maddening thing: The left *wins* when they shouldn't. The right *loses* when we shouldn't. They snatch victory from the jaws of defeat, and we . . . to change the metaphor, we fumble the ball time and again. Most frustratingly of all, we don't learn the right lessons from failure. When a SpaceX rocket explodes moments after liftoff, Elon Musk doesn't wail, gnash his teeth, or fire all his engineers. He does what great innovators and leaders have always done: welcome the opportunity to learn from failure. Failure often teaches more than success. We teach that timeless truth to rocket scientists, and we teach it in business schools. We don't embrace it on the American right. (Space X and Musk handle failure with humor as well. When a Starship exploded during a test flight, the Space X statement was: "As if the flight test was not exciting enough, Starship experienced a rapid unscheduled disassembly before stage separation.")

The left learns from failure very effectively. The adjustments they made in Virginia between the 2021 and 2023 elections bear out that willingness to learn. We on the right don't need to share the left's convictions to admire their strategic ability to pivot. Too often, we meet electoral setbacks with recriminations and blame. Some of that is tied to the unique personality of Donald Trump, but this culture of bickering and finger-pointing on the right did not begin with him. In my own career in Illinois politics, I've encountered that backbiting. I don't take it personally (or at least, I try not to do so). I do lament it, not just because it's unproductive and hurtful, but because it puts us at a competitive disadvantage in the existential fight for the soul of America. If we're going to retake the commanding heights, we must learn the real lessons past failures teach.

One of the reasons the United States has a great safety record in commercial aviation is because of a change in the approach after deadly air disasters. The post-accident investigations shifted from a focus on assigning blame to a focus on diagnosis of what actually happened mechanically as well as the piloting. Pilots became more willing to open up and share everything they knew. Over time, lessons were learned and those lessons were applied to all future aspects of aviation. Crashes plummeted and lives were saved. This is the approach the right needs to take on all that we do to advance liberty from elections to policy battles in legislatures to propaganda battles in culture.

Perhaps the most important lesson we must learn as part of this is how to more effectively allocate capital. As noted earlier, establishing a clear set of strategic imperatives (our grand strategy) drives the proper allocation of capital. In business, that's a chief task for boards of directors in their governance roles—and for CEOs in their executive capacity. For our country, effectively allocating capital in media, in the American people, in building liberty-loyal influencers, and in picking and holding accountable the right politicians is what turns the screws of the Political Vise. Those investments, joined with well-honed operational execution, ensure the health of our nation. The right leader understands that and allocates both money and talent to key goals, projects, and initiatives. The right leaders understand that allocating resources is *the* vital component of any bold strategy. It is the only way to achieve the vision and mission of any organization, company, or movement.

The good news is that the cause of liberty has those resources. We have our philanthropists, entrepreneurs, private equity investors, venture capital leaders, and angel funders. What we too often lack is the strategic overview to direct those resources effectively. We lack sufficient cutting-edge marketing capacity. We lack sufficient ability to exploit data on the scope and scale of the left. We lack sufficient capacity not because of lack of will but because we have yet to focus like the proverbial laser on functionality and outcome. Perhaps most importantly, we lack sufficient capacity because we are too focused on not ceding more ground rather than retaking those heights by going on offense relentlessly.

One of my favorite real-world examples of "retaking the heights" comes from recent American history and the decisions of one of our greatest presidents. Not long ago, I read *The Grand Strategy That Won the Cold War: Architecture of Triumph*, a comprehensive analysis of how Ronald Reagan brought down the Soviet Union and ended the Cold War. It was particularly enjoyable both because I remember that era well, and because the lessons the story conveys are timely and useful for the liberty movement. The basic thesis of *The Grand Strategy* is that since the end of the Second World War, the United States had pursued a policy of "containment" against Soviet aggression. Indeed, George Kennan, the diplomat who coined the term "containment" in 1947, continued to advise the same approach for decades. Democrat and Republican presidents alike sought Kennan's counsel and followed his approach. The goal was to ensure peace by keeping the status quo. The two sides fought hot proxy wars and engaged in cold propaganda conflicts, and tensions rose and fell, but remarkably little changed from the Truman administration to that of Jimmy Carter.

Ronald Reagan believed we could do better. He had a clear *vision* of a world not dominated by Communist aggression. He made it his *mission* to not merely contain the Soviet Union, but to bring it to its knees—all without a cataclysmic Third World War. As *The Grand Strategy* explains in compelling detail, Reagan patiently and effectively executed that vision and mission. The Reagan administration cut off Soviet access to Western hard currency by every means possible (a strategic imperative!). We pursued a massive military buildup, relying on the technology advancements that come naturally to capitalism, but not to central planning (another strategic imperative!). As the Soviets fell further behind, Reagan focused on growing the domestic economy to fund the huge buildup (and again!). All the while, he confronted the Soviets, publicly and repeatedly, on moral terms (and again!). President Reagan called the USSR an "evil empire," scandalizing the American left with his willingness to speak so boldly to a nuclear rival. Reagan knew what he was doing: To execute a grand strategy, you must bring pressure to bear on every front.[39]

In the authoritarian left, we face an adversary every bit as ruthless and committed to victory as the Soviets. The USSR wanted global domination; the American left wants to dominate permanently the commanding heights of our society. They possess not only ruthlessness and sophistication, but they also have the hubris to be certain of their eventual victory. In 1956, Soviet leader Nikita Khrushchev told a group of Western diplomats, "Whether you like it or not, history is on our side. We will bury you!" Today, the progressive left says the same thing, with the same swagger and confidence. We have given them too few reasons to believe otherwise. We need our Reagan moment. (Though this too is beyond the scope of the book, I note that the American left has made common cause with China, Iran, Russia, and—especially since October 7, 2023—Islamic terrorists. The enemy is both within and without, and increasingly, their sympathies align, and their efforts are coordinated.)

We will retake the commanding heights through vision, mission, and, as I see it, four key grand-strategy imperatives. This is not a detailed manual, but it provides the essential overarching summary of the plan.

- **Vision**: Defeat progressive authoritarianism and restore the cultural consensus on the virtue of America's founding principles. Rebuild understanding of and reverence for capitalism and free enterprise, and by doing so secure American security and prosperity for the twenty-first century.
- **Mission:** To build an American movement that competes and wins control of the levers of the Political Vise so we can bring that vision to life. We do so by building the content and distribution capacity to engage—and ultimately, transform—the culture. Policy and politics are downstream from culture. We can and must go upstream to take the headwaters.

To achieve that mission (bear with me—we'll get to those grand-strategy imperatives in due course), we must reshape the Political Vise to become the Liberty Political Vise.

The Liberty Political Vise

Output: Material economic growth providing abundant opportunities for all people; consensus on America's virtue in a civil environment of robust debate within the constitutional framework.

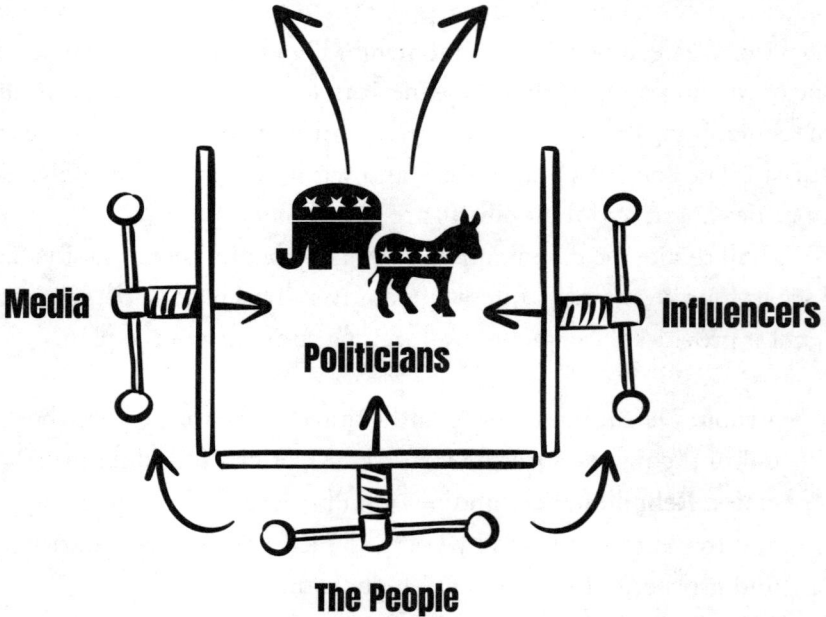

Media   Politicians   Influencers

The People

While choosing better media and influencers, the people hold politicians accountable and make decisions based upon three criteria:
1. Personal Aspiration
2. Personal Opportunity
3. Personal Fulfillment

The most powerful side of the Vise is the bottom side. It directly impacts politicians but also has high sway over the other two subsets of the people, media, and influencers. We the People, as noted in the chapter on choosing better influencers, control what media and which influencers we choose to put in control of the commanding heights. We must choose more wisely.

■ ■ ■

Before laying out the grand-strategy imperatives to reshape the Vise in this manner and achieve the mission, let's once again review the landscape in which we operate. You are now familiar with the three sides of the Vise and how they interact in various configurations. It is important to also understand the arenas in which we compete.

Our investors are already spending materially in elections, policy, and issue advocacy. I believe that spending can be vastly improved with better use of twenty-first century marketing tools in data and analytics.

Where we are not investing sufficiently is upstream of elections. Elections are won and lost upstream—meaning much earlier on the calendar, months and years before the actual votes are cast. When you are upstream, you are investing in the cultural arena—in entertainment, in news, in corporate communications and more.

Let's visit one example from my own work that illustrates why we must invest upstream in culture. In 2020 the Democrats put a measure on the ballot that would change Illinois's constitutionally protected flat income tax to a progressive tax. Nearly everyone thought it would pass easily. Democrat Governor J. B. Pritzker put about $55 million into the campaign. Ken Griffin, then an Illinois resident and founder of Citadel Capital, stepped up and also put in about the same amount of money in opposition to Pritzker and in support of the no vote. Other donors of note also put in millions. The television battle between the two sides was epic.

Polling showed we would lose. But we had some cards to play. Illinois Policy (a 501c4) had for years been building an "owned audience" in Illinois. We had been putting out content through various social media channels inviting people to join our cause. By 2020 we had about 1.5 million people in this audience. Six million votes would be cast and three million or so would be required for us to win. We had *half that number* in our owned audience. They had voluntarily given us their first name, last name, zip code, and email address. We were also able to obtain a high percentage of cell phone numbers as well.

We began communicating with them, and with all their social media friends—millions more, all the way upstream back in 2016, 2017, 2018, and 2019. By the time we got to 2020, we had the largest megaphone in the state. We had pre-seeded "no" votes among this audience long before the election. We then deployed this audience through social media channels to influence others not in our owned audience.

While the air war was raging with over $100 million in spending on mostly television, we were spending about $3 million to facilitate deep engagement among millions of Illinois voters among friends and acquaintances. And we were testing messages to find out which ones worked best to convert yes voters into no voters.

We discovered many messages that worked well and began using those. Others spending money alongside us also began using these messages. In March 2020 it looked like we would lose by as much as twenty points. By the close of the election, we had a six-point victory and defeated the progressive tax in one of the bluest states in America.

We won because of the courage of investors like Dick Uihlein, Ken Griffin, and so many others. We had sufficient resources. But we also won because our strategy was to get upstream in culture long before the election and gain audience, test messages, and then persuade with the best messages when the time became ripe. Finally, we also won because a unified coalition functioned well with many independent people and groups coming together in the common cause of defeating the progressive tax amendment.

With that in mind, the following are the four grand-strategy imperatives.

- **Grand-Strategy Imperative I:** Create material inroads with Blacks, Latinos, single women, younger voters, Asians and LGBTQ+. We can and will destroy the left's Blue Wall coalition and their "Blue Cities" dependence. Yes, there is a culture war—and yes, we can win it with a message of liberty.
- **Grand-Strategy Imperative II:** Content—On a selective basis, build sustainable assets in film, television, podcasting, news and entertainment.
- **Grand-Strategy Imperative III:** Distribution—Build the world's largest "data collection funnel" to fuel state-of-the-art, one-to-one direct marketing campaigns that reach and scale audiences—independent of woke tech companies and corporate media.
- **Grand-Strategy Imperative IV:** Build a command-and-control "brain trust" to go *on offense* in culture, policy, and politics. Create both synergy and a multiplier effect through better planning and cooperation among all the aligned capacities who together share the vision and mission outlined here. (To be clear, I don't mean a centralized command and control of all things on the right. Rather, I mean a tight-knit command and control of selected, strategic *offensive* campaigns of high value. One example would be a campaign to build consensus that the income tax is a form of slavery and thus the Sixteenth Amendment must be repealed. The details of that idea are for another day!)

I emphasized going *on offense* for a very simple reason: We hardly ever do it. We on the liberty side practice defensive containment at best. Historically we have been on defense on abortion; on the border crisis; on critical race theory; DEI, and free speech. We are defensive about election integrity;

January 6; the Hamas/Israel war; the transing of our children; the expansion of the welfare state, and the increasingly deplorable state of our military readiness. We have been on defense about free enterprise and capitalism itself. We are like the United States from the inception of the Cold War until Ronald Reagan came to power: doing our best to maintain the status quo against an ever-more aggressive foe.

Notice I say "have been" on defense. Donald Trump has flipped the script and gone on offense far more effectively than any other Republican politician in modern times. In the past, he too often confused going on offense with simply being brash and offending people. But even Donald Trump learns and adapts. His tone in the 2024 cycle and since has been much, much better overall, and that certainly is one reason he forged a broader and deeper coalition in his victory. This has carried over into his second term, which is one reason it is going at warp speed.

In the face of unrelenting attacks, I don't blame President Trump for getting defensive and even offending. No public figure in living memory has been so bitterly and relentlessly attacked. At the same time, the example of Trump's first term points to a harsh reality: If even the most pugnacious Republican of our era ended up on defense, our movement is in crisis. More recently, Trump won in 2024 and is making progress in his second term because he is relentlessly on offense and has the Democrats on defense. It is wonderful to see.

You may read those four grand-strategy imperatives and say, "Sounds great, but how?" The idea of winning back material numbers of minority voters, not to mention LGBTQ+ Americans, sounds audacious—but also unreasonably ambitious. It is lofty, yes—but the commanding heights themselves are lofty. The simple truth is that as long as we see these strategic imperatives as unattainable, we will continue not to attain them, and the more ground we will cede to the progressive left. The first step Ronald Reagan took to bringing down the Soviet Union wasn't a massive military buildup. The first step was rejecting the pre-existing terms of our relationship with the Soviets. He refused to buy into the myth that the Cold War had to go on indefinitely. He decided the United States could defeat Communism, not merely contain it. And all the triumph that followed was the result of his belief and his decision.

In other words, the grand strategy will only work if you first embrace the vision and the mission.

The liberty movement must have a centralized command (created by volunteers, not coercion!) and control operation for our targeted campaigns that can plan and launch *offensive* initiatives and projects that put the left on defense on cultural, economic, and social issues. We have the moral high ground and we must use it. Further, the right has the talent to do this, but that talent (our most gifted and insightful leaders) is scattered, affiliated with various philanthropic groups, think tanks, and election teams that coordinate too rarely. The second task—after the initial buy-in to the vision and mission—is to end the siloing of our best and brightest minds. There must be a place where our elites and practitioners come together, and where a modern "skunkworks" team can take advantage of the emerging trends and technologies.

As I've argued before, there will always be elites. The question is not whether we can create a world without them—given human nature, that's not likely. The question is which elites emerge to control institutions. Are they elites with fealty to our founding principles and respect for the American people? Or are they elites, as we have today, with contempt for the founding—and for the people? Today's governing elites want to govern for the American people, not be governed by them. Today's elites want to use authoritarianism and collectivism to control the population and press them towards their desired end.

The elites we need will oust these contemptuous controllers of our institutions and replace them with leaders who respect both our founding principles and the American people. They will devolve power back to the people rather than aggregate power into the state apparatus.

They will do what our own founding elite did 250 years ago; our forebears shifted the power concentrated in the British crown to a decentralized union of colonies. The Founders' wisdom still holds today, and we can and must do as they did if we are to secure America's twenty-first-century destiny as the most free and prosperous nation on earth.

Now, having read this you might be filled with some skepticism—this is too big to do, they have too many advantages, the vision and mission are gargantuan! I understand that, but here is what too many people don't see: We are already making progress in every one of these areas. One of the strengths of our governing philosophy founded in liberty, free will, and self-governance is that individual people take initiative to solve big problems. They then partner with others to add capacity and talent, and progress is made. We are making progress right now on all of these strategic imperatives; it just may not be obvious yet.

Today, all across the country, we have people investing in culture as never before. From Wonder Project, Angel Studios, and Acceleration Studios in film and television, to liberty-loyal podcasters like Joe Rogan, Megyn Kelly, Mark Halperin, and many others, to authentic news platforms like the *Federalist*, *Just the News*, *The Center Square*, *RealClear Politics*, and so many more, options with fact-based news (with transparent points of view) continue to build audience.

On the distribution side, we have many growing centers of investment in data collection, analysis, and deployment. We have ongoing message testing on how to reach those who are disaffected by the dystopian left's conception of America. And we are winning converts.

It is important to remember all those slices of the pie graph we covered in chapter 5. We don't build a majoritarian consensus all at once. We build it one slice at a time, little by little. We build it by taking what has always been a core American value—the big tent—and inviting in disparate people based upon common beliefs. The foundation of our common beliefs is the nature of the American miracle itself that encouraged so many to come here to pursue their version of the American Dream.

This vision is a big one, but think about all the past visions that, at their conception, were daunting and seemingly impossible. The very founding of this country is perhaps the most obvious. Only about one-third of the colonists bought into the vision. One-third remained loyal to the British crown and one-third were ambivalent. The tenacity of the Founders and those that joined the cause is what carried the day.

The abolitionist movement is another great example. Slavery was embedded in our founding and in Southern culture. It took decades, it took a relentless willingness to face the moral truth of slavery's evil, and it took the Civil War to eliminate it. We take the Civil War for granted, but remember that Lincoln and his allies had to build, little by little, slice by slice, a majoritarian consensus in the North to sustain the material and manpower requirements to win.

The temperance movement was also impressive in its ability to change a fundamental aspect of our society. Beginning in the early nineteenth century and reaching its peak in the early 1900s, the temperance movement managed to build a social-reform campaign nationwide that changed how Americans thought about alcohol consumption. The temperance leaders convinced Americans that poverty, crime, and family disruptions were all too often caused by the excessive use of alcohol. They succeeded in passing the Eighteenth Amendment, which was ratified by the states in 1919 and went into effect in January 1920.

It unleashed a crime wave of violence, bootlegging, speakeasies, and gang wars unlike anything we had ever experienced as a nation. It was finally repealed in 1933. Both the adoption of and the repeal of the Eighteenth Amendment illustrate the power of We the People when fully engaged in the Political Vise's power structure.

In the twentieth century the civil rights movement, the gay rights movement, the war against drunk driving, and the ongoing battle over life are all examples of cultural wars where the odds looked long in the beginning but the right vision, mission, and strategy, with sustained investment to build the core capacities required, prevailed. Our liberty movement battle is daunting, but it is winnable if we are willing to invest and fight. Best of all, we have the moral high ground on our side.

Our moral high ground is built on the premise of the American miracle. The American miracle is that no matter who you are, no matter where you come from, no matter Black, brown, or white, no matter your sexuality, no matter whether you are rich or poor, in America, with good effort, personal responsibility, and a desire to make tomorrow better than what you have today, this is the one place on earth where your dreams can come true. And as I have said before, the dream matters, for it is our fuel that drives our ambition, but the journey itself is worthy and wonderful.

It is by inviting everyone in who believes in this miracle that we regain the American consensus as expressed in our shared vision.

I noted at the beginning of this chapter that American greatness is not a birthright. Every generation must earn it. It is time for our elites, those blessed with the capacity to make a difference, to come together to do the earning for this generation. It is, as Ronald Reagan said, a time for choosing.

I invite you to join me in choosing to believe our greatest days still lie ahead. Join me in building this movement!

Conclusion

WHY THE VISE MATTERS

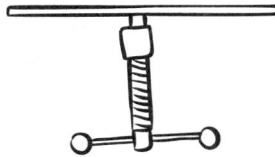

It bears repeating: American greatness is not a birthright; every generation must earn it.

In Chapter 2 I told the story of Mark Janus, a regular guy working for the State of Illinois who did not want his government union taking his money—and spending it on political speech with which he disagreed. Mark went to the United States Supreme Court and won. That 2018 ruling freed over five million government workers to take back their free speech rights.

Mark is one of many reasons this fight matters. It matters for our country writ large, of course, but it matters for individual people as well, people like Claudia Perez and her 1.1 million friends.

In 2015 Claudia was a sixty-two-year-old Mexican immigrant. She came to the United States in 1995 seeking a better life. She believed in the American Dream. She put her daughter through college and employed as many as twelve people in her food-cart business. She started her days at 2:30 a.m. and finished most at 10 p.m.

"We came to make our own jobs, from what we know how to do in Mexico. To demonstrate to people that we can get ahead, not to take away jobs, not to steal, no," Claudia told us. "We come to work honestly."

That is all America can ask for, right? Not so in Chicago. Chicago was one of the few major cities in the world that banned street food vendors, including food carts. For many years, the city, in its efforts to protect brick-and-mortar restaurants (influencers), made food carts illegal. Illinois Policy set out to change that.

But first we had to meet our hero, Claudia. Claudia had read a column on criminal justice reform written by one of our writers (media!). She contacted the author and our team then reached out to her. Claudia introduced us to a whole new world we had not previously understood.

"Every day, every year, summer, winter. These people don't stop," said Mario Gonzalez, flanked by hundreds of pallets of imported foods, stacked as high as the warehouse ceiling.

He was the assistant manager at La Hacienda, a grocery wholesaler on Chicago's southwest side. "[Food-cart street vendors] aren't a majority of our business, but I'll say this: We open at 5 a.m. every day . . . they're here before that, waiting. It makes me feel good that we can serve them."

Two salespeople for La Hacienda sang similar praises in a nearby parking lot. Sylvia Kestler mentioned how the food-cart vendors often help poor people with food and money even though they know they have no intention of paying them back. Andrea Caballero says she remembers speaking to them since she was little.

Food-cart street vendors command respect in communities across Chicago—from those selling chicharrones and shaved ice in Little Village and Pilsen to the tamaleras in Albany Park.

Back in 2015, Chicago's City Hall gave them no respect.

In Chicago, no prepared food could be sold from a cart. Only whole, uncut fruit and frozen desserts are permitted. Try and serve others well by preparing delicious, traditional tamales, and law enforcement may come after you.

Claudia's most popular item was her tamales. She operated in Chicago's Little Village neighborhood. She told us that one morning, a police officer confronted her. "Throw away all this trash," the officer said. "It's worthless. It's garbage."

Her food, lovingly, painstakingly made, was intended for hungry construction workers in Little Village. Instead, her tamales were thrown onto Chicago concrete sidewalks. Claudia cried. But she didn't give up. "I'll go ahead, I'll fight, as many others have done."

Thankfully, not all the police are this mean-spirited.

Food-cart operators face other risks as well, made worse by too little policing rather than too much. They operate in communities that present serious safety risks. Claudia was robbed while pushing her cart before dawn in Little Village. Two men grabbed her, threw her in their truck, took her to a nearby bank, and demanded she withdraw money. Claudia lost $4,000, a large chunk of her savings.

"Of course, I'm scared. But God willing, I will stay safe," she says.

Then Chicago Mayor Rahm Emanuel had been promoting mobile vending as a solution to the city's food deserts—areas where people lack access to fresh, nutritious food—but he withheld praise for the delicious food offered by hundreds of Chicagoans already operating in those areas.

To illustrate how disconnected politicians can be from the people, their presumed constituents, Emanuel held a press conference on July 10, 2015, to herald the launch of a city-funded "produce bus" project called Fresh Moves. This was the second attempt of the program. The buses posted more than $200,000 in losses from 2011 through 2012, according to the *Chicago Tribune.*

Whether it is ironic or tragic (or moronic) for a bankrupt city to put its boot on the necks of hard-working immigrants ready to serve the underserved, all while wasting taxpayer dollars on a program already proven to fail, is up to you to decide. As anyone who's walked down 26th Street on a summer day can tell you, there's no shortage of Chicagoans trying to feed their communities—the city only needed to unleash them.

Keeping in mind that politicians make decisions based upon political imperatives, the Illinois Policy Institute expanded its work to pressure all three sides of the Vise.

The video and content team from Illinois Policy spent early mornings in the Little Village neighborhood of Chicago with the Street Vendors Association, meeting and interviewing local street vendors. From those interviews we created a short documentary called *Una Mujer y Su Carrito* (*A Woman and Her Cart*), which chronicled Claudia's daily routine. For years Claudia worked in the shadow of the law to make a living and support her family.

The video was released in February 2015. The team leveraged Facebook's video capability to target Latinos age twenty-five and older, ranging from Spanish-dominant to English-dominant. The video was viewed more than 1.1 million times; nearly three-quarters of these views were organic, meaning viewers came across the video and watched on their own.

Claudia's story was powerful and compelling. Claudia later told us that people from as far away as St. Louis had traveled to Chicago to buy her tamales. She makes damn good tamales, but it was her story that drew people to her and helped change the law.

The goal was to create a movement, to form a parade centered on people with Claudia as the centerpiece. We included an online petition when someone viewed the video. The petition supported Claudia and the effort to legalize food carts. It featured an illustration by cartoonist Eric Allie that portrayed Claudia Perez caught between Chicago cronies (lobbyists for brick-and-mortar restaurants) and police enforcement.

Almost 7,000 people signed the food-cart petition: 75 percent of signatures came from Democrats and Independents. Nearly 60 percent of all petition signatures came from Latinos. We the People in action, applying pressure.

Most importantly, the video introduced Claudia to the Chicago media and finally put a very human, sympathetic face on a grassroots movement that was continuing to grow.

Media outlet Chicagoist, a well-known website popular among Chicago Millennials, ran an article, "Why Doesn't Chicago Have Its Own Food Carts?" promoting Claudia's video in March 2015.

Additional media weighed in. NPR and its local Chicago affiliate, WBEZ, ran stories on the movement to legalize food carts shortly thereafter. Claudia's story also gained attention among Spanish-language media, including Latino USA and Univision.

The efforts, not surprisingly, caught the attention of several influential aldermen and even Mayor Rahm Emanuel, who finally came out in support of food-cart legalization. The people joined the parade. The media covered it, and the politicians, wisely, took notice.

When a growing parade forms, well covered by the media, legislation tends to move quickly. With a vote scheduled in September, our media team generated nearly fifty earned media appearances in the month leading up to the vote. We secured placements with all the major Chicago television stations, including NBC Chicago, ABC 7 Chicago, CBS 2 Chicago, Fox Chicago, and WGN-TV. The team also placed stories with the top Spanish-language media outlets such as Univision, Telemundo, and *Hoy*.

We knew that impressive as this pressure was, it still was not enough. We had to make this issue matter to the politicians in a language they could understand. Remember, it is always about the money.

Research from the Institute showed that legalization would be a boon for both entrepreneurs and city coffers. According to Institute analysis of survey data from nearly 200 of the estimated 1,500 food-cart street vendors across Chicago, food carts generated an estimated $35.2 million in annual sales, $16.7 million in annual income, 2,100 jobs, and as many as 50,000 meals served per day. The income from food-cart street vending supported over 5,000 people in the vendors' families.

The survey data also gave insight on broader trends among Chicago's food-cart community.

The average food-cart street vendor in Chicago was a Hispanic, middle-aged woman from Little Village or Pilsen. She supported three dependents with her earnings, which came from serving dozens of customers daily. She often risked ticketing for selling food (nearly 40% of vendors surveyed told researchers they had been ticketed at least once).

The illegal status of the food-cart trade was the biggest impediment to growth. And that, of course, is what brick-and-mortar restaurants wanted to stop—competition.

Comparing Chicago's food-cart street vendor population to cities with more welcoming legal climates, the Institute was able to estimate the potential impact of food-cart legalization.

Los Angeles enforced its ban on food carts only when someone made a complaint. LA's huge land area allows vendors to operate relatively unencumbered and has about 25.8 food carts per 10,000 residents. That number is just 5.5 in Chicago. If legalization yielded a food-cart industry approaching the size of Los Angeles's, Chicago would gain:

- 6,400 new jobs
- $127 million in new retail sales
- $60 million in additional income
- $8.5 million in city and county sales-tax collections
- 180,000 additional meals served each day

Benchmarking growth in Chicago food-cart street vending to other major cities reveals potential effects of legalization

Annual economic impact of legalizing Chicago food-cart street vending under various scenarios for growth

	Growth scenario			
	Base + 15% increased sales	Base + 15% doubled (NYC, Portland)	Base +15% tripled (Washington, D.C.)	Base +15% quadrupled (Los Angeles)
# of food carts	1,500	3,000	4,500	6,000
Total employees (including self)	2,145	4,290	6,435	8,580
Food carts per 10,000 residents	5.5	11.0	16.6	22.1
Annual revenue	$40,527,150	$81,054,300	$121,581,450	$162,108,600
Annual expenses	$21,289,950	$42,579,900	$63,869,350	$85,159,800
Annual profit	$19,237,200	$38,474,400	$57,711,800	$76,948,800
Meals	57,500	115,000	172,500	230,000
City and county sales-tax revenue	$2,127,675	$4,255,351	$6,383,026	$8,510,703
State sales-tax revenue	$2,026,358	$4,052,715	$6,079,073	$8,105,430
State income tax and personal property replacement tax revenue	$770,651	$1,541,303	$2,311,954	$3,082,606

Note: Figures calculated using the 2015 combined sales-tax rate of 10.25 percent.

Source: Illinois Policy Institute analysis based on food-cart street vendor survey data, Asociación de Vendedores Ambulantes, Energy Vision, The Portland Mercury, The Washington Post, Los Angeles Bureau of Street Services, U.S. Census Bureau   @illinoispolic

For the Chicago City Council, always seeking more revenue, the millions of potential tax dollars flowing into city coffers was enticing. The jobs growth, the improvement in people's lives, lifting the boot off people's necks—what mattered most to us—was just a side bonus to the politicians.

We had media pressure, and we had influencer pressure as we worked directly with members of the city council, along with the Street Vendors Association. We had a compelling, genuine hero in Claudia—and now we had the money too. *The Vise squeezed harder.*

The Political Vise began to turn because legalizing hundreds of legitimate, minority-owned businesses and reaping the associated tax revenue would be a win-win for politicians. We used every tool and tactic, always staying aware of the power of the Vise, to bring this campaign to a successful conclusion.

On September 24, 2015, victory. The Chicago City Council voted unanimously to lift the ban on food carts in Chicago. What once could not even get a hearing or sponsor and was impossible became law. Food-cart vendors can now sell delicious food in neighborhoods across the city without fear of heavy fines and police harassment.

In the years since, the City of Chicago, not surprisingly, has done a poor job of actually implementing the ordinance. It has too many restrictions and imposes too many costs. But it is a start. The work continues because American Dreams—for Claudia and others—are still alive.

Serving others, with pride in work well done, lifts the human spirit. You can see that spirit soar in Claudia's own words about making the tamales, or as she says it, the Oaxaqueno:

"I make the dough, very well mixed. I heat the lard—very hot. Then I add the dough until it is cooked very well—thick—well cooked. Then I make the sauce, with chile "morita" with tomato, garlic, and pepper. Then I cut the banana leaf and put it on the pieces of aluminum foil, then put the dough on the leaf, then the meat, then the sauce. They taste delicious."

Pride in work makes the spirit soar. That is why this matters.

It matters too because the free-enterprise system is the greatest force for good ever created in the human sphere. Capitalism, vilified by so many, is actually the kindest, most caring service enterprise ever created. When you serve others well in our system, you are rewarded. When you serve others poorly, you are punished. Capitalism is based in persuasion and consent while socialism is based in coercion and submission. It should be an easy choice between the system that honors human potential and the system that chokes it. Sadly, it is not.

The American miracle is that no matter who you are, no matter where you come from, no matter rich or poor, Black, brown or white, no matter what makes you unique and special, our American principles and values mean that you can pursue your version of the American Dream with success.

The most important part of those American Dreams is not the destination, though that matters greatly, but rather the journey itself. That is where human fulfillment and flourishing are found. All of that is at risk, for there are forces in play that want to change our principles and values to make the state supreme, to coerce you to submit to the values and ideals of the radicalized left. They believe they know best how you—and all of us—should live our lives.

We cannot allow them to win. We must come together as "We the People" to use the power of the Liberty Political Vise to strengthen our republic and earn our twenty-first-century greatness as a nation and as a people. Mark, Claudia, and every American alive today and in the coming generations are counting on us. Can we count on you?

■ ■ ■

To get involved at whatever level your life makes possible, go to **ThePoliticalVise.com**. It is easier than you think!

APPENDIX A

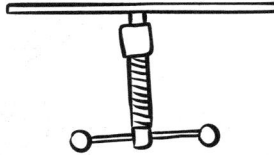

The Traditional Political Vise
1789–1987

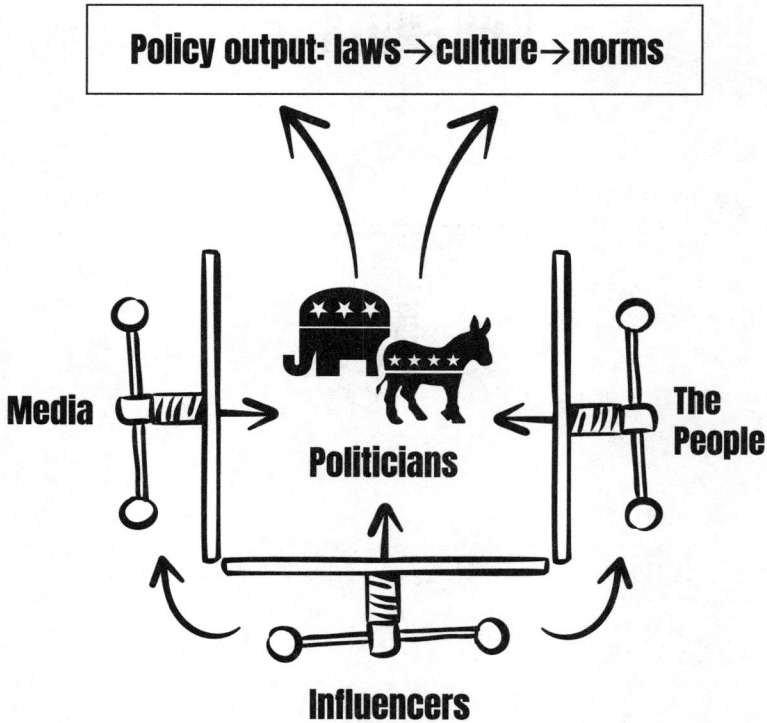

Politicians are compelled to make decisions based upon three criteria:
1. Political Expediency
2. Political Fear
3. Political Principle

The Progressive Political Vise
1987–Present

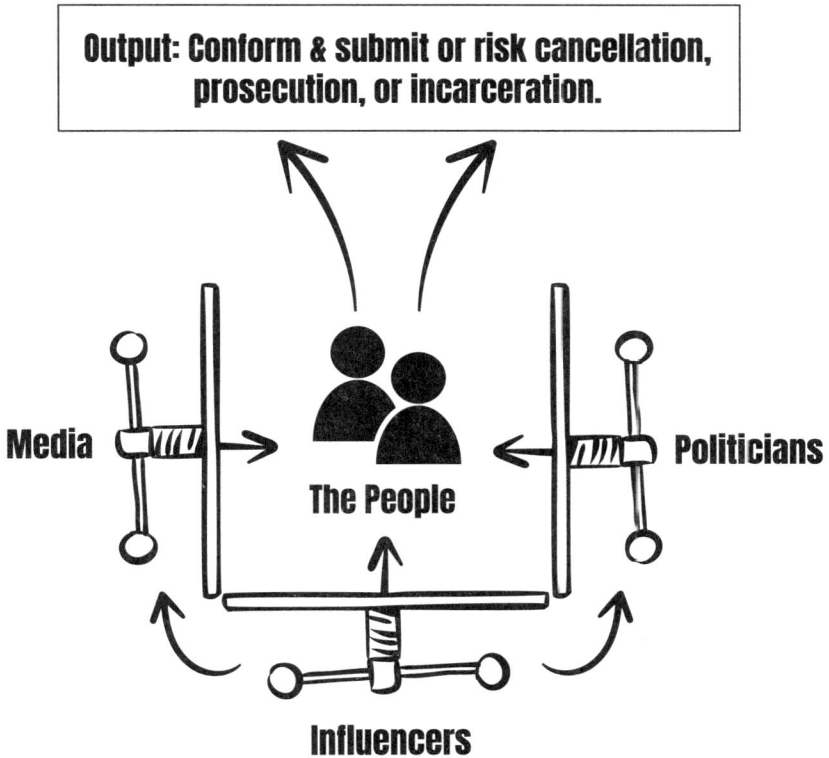

Output: Conform & submit or risk cancellation, prosecution, or incarceration.

Media → **The People** ← Politicians

Influencers

People are compelled to make decisions based upon three criteria:
1. Personal Expediency
2. Personal Fear
3. Personal Principle

The Liberty Political Vise
2016–Present

Output: Material economic growth providing abundant opportunities for all people; consensus on America's virtue in a civil environment of robust debate within the constitutional framework.

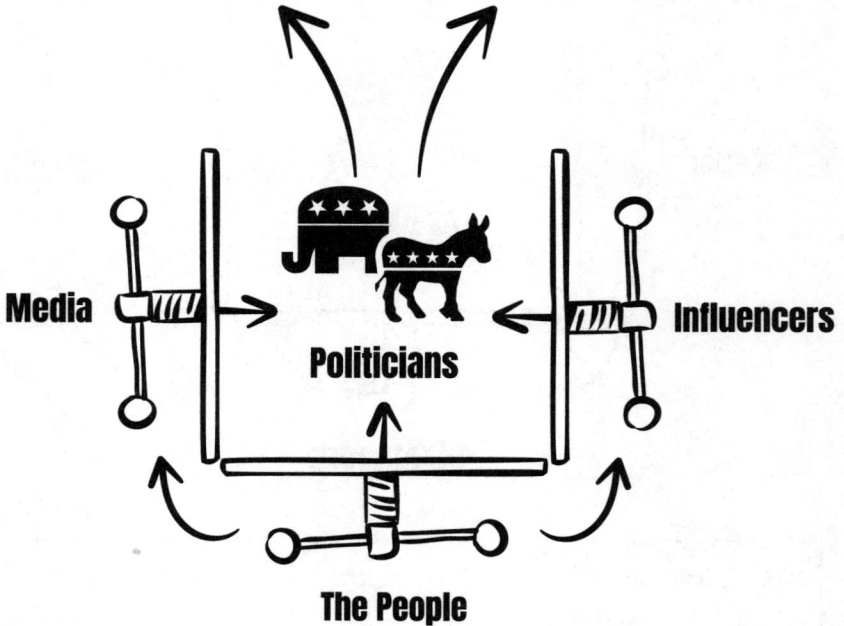

Media

Politicians

Influencers

The People

While choosing better media and influencers, the people hold politicians accountable and make decisions based upon three criteria:
1. Personal Aspiration
2. Personal Opportunity
3. Personal Fulfillment

APPENDIX B

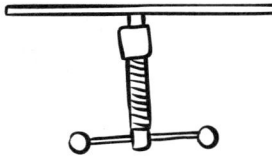

To: John Tillman
From: Sergio Serrato
Date: 12/22/23
Re: The Progressive Ecosystem of Influence

From Q4 2019 to Q4 2022 I was the head of product at Civis Analytics. Civis Analytics is a data technology platform that at the time had over one hundred data scientists on staff composing the consulting arm of Civis. These data professionals have highly technical client counterparts on the Democratic campaign and policy advocacy nonprofit organizations. These people are operators of the data that powers an apparatus used by the progressives to influence the media, the voting public, and politicians to push evermore left. The most prominent of these operations is Data for Progress, and is a model of what the right of center is missing. This memo outlines Civis, the progressive ecosystem of influence, and review of Data for Progress.

Civis Analytics: 2020-2022—Progressive Data War Room

- Civis Analytics clients spanned the Biden For President, National Education Association, Planned Parenthood, Priorities PAC, Bully Pulpit Interactive, Senate Majority PAC, and the Movement Cooperative. During the Democratic Primary in 2019-2020 they powered the analytics teams for Elizabeth Warren, Pete Buttigieg, and Kamala Harris.
- Civis' customers are part of the communications and marketing network focused on engaging and motivating action in support of the advancement of progressive policy objectives. Civis provides technology that enables the data and models for polling, message testing, digital ad targeting, fundraising, direct mail, and get out the vote by mail and ballot curing operations.
- Altogether, the progressive data professionals staff campaigns during presidential and midterms and off season work at nonprofits that focus on outreach to interest groups or around specific causes and use the battle tested message testing tools developed during the 2020 election craft winning messages in favor of progressive policy goals, like promoting the elimination of cash bail or the weaponization of abortion to activate swing and lower-propensity voters.

Progressive Policy Wins from Civis Data

- The Bail Project has proven unusually successful at reaching voters across political lines. Using Civis Analytics' Creative Focus online testing tool to gauge the persuasiveness of its bail reform messages, The Bail Project determined that economic-themed messaging was most successful at increasing support for legislation ending cash bail, while messages spotlighting the moral toll of the cash bail system proved most effective for driving donations to its cause—insights suggesting the organization should disambiguate these messages for maximum impact. The elimination of cash bail has been deployed in Chicago, and other major American cities with predictably terrible results for public safety.

- In the wake of Democratic losses in Virginia in 2021, Civis Analytics conducted research on the strength of CRT vs Covid-19 messaging to understand what motivated swing voters, with some additional research on abortion which became salient in 2022 midterms post-Roe SCOTUS ruling. Those results powered Democratic messaging strategies in 2022, and in 2023 with positive outcomes for Democrats.

Data for Progress: A Policy Narrative War Room

- Civis Analytics is one organization but there are others that do similar work at helping push forward progressive policy and media narratives. Data for Progress, Blue Labs, Blue Rose Research, GrowProgress, and PrioritiesUSA PAC all have former Civis Analytics employees on staff but a model for a war room should be Data for Progress.
- Data For Progress serves as a "one-stop shop" for left-wing policy development, polling, and using media to gain public recognition for progressive goals.
  - ▸ Data for Progress works with progressive movement organizations to provide data and polling that empower progressive activists.
  - ▸ Data for Progress polling has been used by journalists from the New York Times, Washington Post, and hundreds of other trusted news organizations.
  - ▸ The American Rescue Plan was one of the most significant pieces of legislation this century—and the White

House utilized Data for Progress polling to push legislators to vote for it. In a February 2021 call with House
Democrats, President Biden cited Data for Progress polling showing bipartisan support for the American Rescue
Plan to help build momentum around the bill in Congress. As Politico wrote, that call between the president
and House Democrats demonstrated Data for Progress'
growing impact on national politics.

▶ Data for Progress has used their best-in-class polling to
show leaders in Washington and across the nation that
ambitious climate policy isn't just the right thing to
do—it's also overwhelmingly popular. Their polling has
helped the progressive movement lead a paradigm shift
in climate policy, changing the conversation toward green
jobs and climate justice. They've influenced through their
polling the Biden Administration by crafting narratives
that voters across party lines support green jobs and
"clean energy investment," and have helped "climate
champions" across the country win crucial local elections
through their Green New Deal Slate.

ACKNOWLEDGMENTS

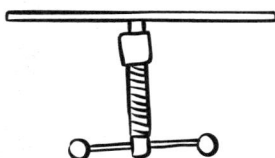

This journey I have been on for more than twenty years in politics, public policy, and issue advocacy has been deeply enriched by so many people who have shown me kindness all along the way. While I can't mention every single person, a few must be included here.

I am so grateful for the day the incomparable Kristina Rasmussen said yes to my long, relentless recruiting of her in 2008 and 2009. She was the key partner in building what became the Illinois Policy Institute and all that has flowed from that since. Kristina is a great liberty warrior and a treasured friend.

A special thanks to one of the most courageous and kind people I know, Paul Jacob. When I was a naïve newcomer to this world, Paul was patient, generous, and always willing to educate me on my vast areas of ignorance. Paul was also threatened with jail time in Oklahoma during one of our initiative campaigns—he faced that very real threat with courage and grace.

Ryan Green, a visionary marketer who understood the power of the data and digital world long before others, always said yes to my insane ideas that had never been tried before.

In more recent years, I've been blessed to work with the unicorn that is Austin Berg, one of the most versatile talents in writing, speaking, thinking, and strategizing. Austin came to us as an intern and now is among the most impactful people in the cause of liberty in Illinois and across the country.

To Tracie Sharp, Joe Lehman, Jon Caldara, and all the Armadillos, to Kim Dennis, Lawson Bader, Christine Czernejewski, to JP, Audra, Rick, and so many others, I am so grateful for your friendship and support over so many years. Each of you in your own way helped me navigate my failures and helped me reset and move forward toward the goal.

To Matt Paprocki and everyone, past and present, at Illinois Policy—you are among the most effective and happy warriors in the cause of liberty and have always been amazing friends and colleagues. Thank you.

Howie Rich and Eric O'Keefe—I cannot thank you enough for giving me my start when I was so obviously unqualified. Thanks for (as the late, great Bob Costello suggested) "taking a chance" on me.

Perhaps no one has a harder job than the indefatigable Jordan Schneider, my longtime executive assistant and director of executive and board management. Those titles do not do justice to all you do to keep me on track, to keep me focused, to keep me producing, to keep me humble, and to perk me up when I need it most. You are a Godsend, and I am so very grateful.

Finally, to all the members of the board of Illinois Policy over these years—you have allowed me the great privilege to be an entrepreneurial risk-taker in an arena that usually shuns such efforts. Thank you for your stewardship, your passion for the cause, and your wise counsel throughout the years.

NOTES

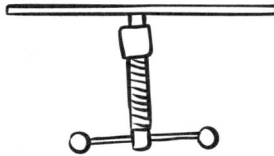

1   Matthew Dallek, "What Happened When LBJ Announced He Wouldn't Run,"
    History.com, March 30, 2018, https://www.history.com/articles/
    lbj-exit-1968-presidential-race.

2   Molly Ball, "The Secret History of the Shadow Campaign That Saved the 2020
    Election," *TIME*, February 4, 2021, https://time.com/5936036/
    secret-2020-election-campaign.

3   Cheyenne Roundtree, "Chart shows how Trump FINALLY changed his tune on
    coronavirus - after denying it while cases skyrocketed," *Daily Mail*, March 19, 2020,
    https://www.dailymail.co.uk/news/article-8132265/Chart-shows-Trump-finally-
    changed-tune-response-coronavirus.html.

4   Holman W. Jenkins Jr., "The Lockdowns Were the Black Swan," *Wall Street
    Journal*, April 24, 2020, https://www.wsj.com/articles/the-lockdowns-were-the-
    black-swan-11587765416?gaa_at=eafs&gaa_n=ASWzDAhh4tDNMYehDW3Fz_
    F23ayl-BMoxUAzqTEpu8BC_T7ah1tW1n992nCyA1uM7JE%3D&gaa_
    ts=68bb56d9&gaa_sig=EZ1ePMIfpHMxVZFMs_BevAS6pX3QPYFJvFE-O45RY
    w6s_9MqrRnN6jZZ7E10y_xljQRJIsy1CatiCY-zAP1Mfw%3D%3D.

5   Michael Grunwald, "Have We Learned Nothing?", *Politico Magazine*, March 25,
    2020, https://www.politico.com/news/magazine/2020/03/25/
    coronavirus-economy-stimulus-house-democrats-148512.

6   Chris Churchill, "Almost Everyone Loves Andrew Cuomo (For Now)." *Times-
    Union*, April 3, 2020, https://www.timesunion.com/news/article/Churchill-New-
    York-s-love-affair-with-Andrew-15172400.php.

7   Adolph S. Ochs, "Business Announcement," *New York Times*, August 19, 1896, https://embed.documentcloud.org/documents/2271357-business-announcement/.

8   Sean Illing, "How Trump Should Change the Way Journalists Understand 'Objectivity,'" *Vox*, August 4, 2020, https://www.vox.com/policy-and-politics/2020/8/4/21306919/donald-trump-media-ethics-tom-rosenstiel.

9   Tom Cotton, "Send in the Troops." *New York Times*, June 3, 2020, https://www.nytimes.com/2020/06/03/opinion/tom-cotton-protests-military.html.

10   Emma Jo Morris and Gabrielle Fonrouge, "Smoking-Gun Email Reveals How Hunter Biden Introduced Ukrainian Businessman to VP Dad," *New York Post*, October 14, 2020, https://nypost.com/2020/10/14/email-reveals-how-hunter-biden-introduced-ukrainian-biz-man-to-dad/.

11   *New York Post*, editorial, October 12, 2021, https://nypost.com/2021/10/12/one-year-later-the-posts-hunter-biden-reporting-is-vindicated-but-still-buried/.

12   Amanda Seitz and Nomaan Merchant, "DHS Disinformation Board's Work, Plans Remain a Mystery," AP, May 5, 2022, https://apnews.com/article/russia-ukraine-europe-united-states-freedom-of-speech-alejandro-mayorkas-69f658351103d4d049083ad20a713e2a.

13   Office of the Attorney General, State of Missouri, May 5, 2022, https://archive.ph/20220506044151/https://ago.mo.gov/home/news/2022/05/05/missouri-louisiana-ags-file-suit-against-president-biden-top-admin-officials-for-allegedly-colluding-with-social-media-giants-to-censor-and-suppress-free-speech.

14   Mollie Hemingway, *Rigged: How the Media, Big Tech, and the Democrats Seized Our Elections* (Regnery, 2021), 331.

15   John J. Miller, "The Worst Republican Governor in America," *National Review*, December 18, 2017, https://www.nationalreview.com/magazine/2017/12/18/bruce-rauner-illinois-worst-republican-governor-america/.

16   Despite all the challenges with former Governor Rauner, I deeply respect his commitment to helping poor children in Illinois' urban centers get a better education. I also respect his commitment to entrepreneurs and those who create businesses. We had our disagreements. But he tried. Too many don't.

17   NCC Staff, "On This Day: Senate rejects Robert Bork for the Supreme Court, National Constitution Center, October 23, 2023, https://constitutioncenter.org/blog/on-this-day-senate-rejects-robert-bork-for-the-supreme-court.

18   Rich Miller, "Illinois Policy Institute at odds with stay-at-home orders," *Illinois Times*, April 16, 2020, https://www.illinoistimes.com/news-opinion/illinois-policy-institute-at-odds-with-stay-at-home-orders-12059570/.

19   "REPORT: Scholars Punished for Their Speech Skyrocketed over Last Three Years," FIRE, April 20, 2023, https://www.thefire.org/news/.report-scholars-punished-their-speech-skyrocketed-over-last-three-years

20   Rachel Weiner and Karina Elwood, "Loudoun Schools' Bias-Reporting System Might Violate Free Speech, Court Says," *Washington Post*, April 14, 2023, https://www.washingtonpost.com/education/2023/04/14/loudoun-school-bias-appeal/.

21   EPA, "ICYMI: EPA Press Office Fact Checks Washington Post Coverage of Waste & Abuse of Taxpayer Dollars," news release, March 7, 2025, https://www.epa.gov/newsreleases/icymi-epa-press-office-fact-checks-washington-post-coverage-waste-abuse-taxpayer.

22   Ursula Perano, "Republicans and Democrats in Congress Try to Be Friends Again—Sort of," *The Daily Beast*, December 12, 2022, https://www.thedailybeast.com/republicans-and-democrats-in-congress-try-to-be-friends-againsort-of.

23   Fred Lucas, "Will Judge in Sussmann Case Consider Recusal After Wife Represented Lisa Page?" Fox News, September 23, 2021, https://www.foxnews.com/us/judge-sussman-case-recusal-wife-lisa-page-lucas.

24   "Public Sector Unions Summary," OpenSecrets, accessed June 12, 2025, https://www.opensecrets.org/industries//totals?cycle=2020&ind=p04.

25   "Illinois Household Income," Department of Numbers, accessed June 12, 2025, https://www.deptofnumbers.com/income/illinois/.

26   Tyler O'Neal, "Who's Funding the 'Burn a Tesla, Save Democracy' Protests?" *Daily Signal*, April 2, 2025, https://www.dailysignal.com/2025/04/02/.whos-funding-burn-tesla-save-democracy-protests-george-soros-woketopus/

27   Ken Silverstein, "How Washington's Elite Mourned One of Their Own," *The Intercept*, January 30, 2015, https://theintercept.com/2015/01/30/washington-mourned-tommy-boggs-friend-worst-people-world/.

28   Abe Greenwald, "The Wrong People Are Doing the Right Thing," *Commentary*, June 7, 2012, https://www.commentary.org/abe-greenwald/the-wrong-people-are-doing-the-right-thing-obama-milton-friedman.

29   Richard H. Thaler and Cass R. Sunstein, *Nudge: Improving Decisions About Health, Wealth, and Happiness* (Yale University Press, 2008).

30   Elizabeth Kolbert, "What Was I Thinking?" *New Yorker*, February 17, 2008, https://www.newyorker.com/magazine/2008/02/25/what-was-i-thinking-reason-irrationality.

31   Francis Menton, "There Are Two Fundamentally Irreconcilable Constitutional Visions," Manhattan Contrarian, July 1, 2022, https://www.manhattancontrarian.com/blog/2022-7-1-there-are-two-fundamentally-irreconcilable-constitutional-visions.

32   Jimmy Carter, "Restoration of Citizenship Rights to Jefferson F. Davis Statement on Signing S. J. Res. 16 into Law," October 17, 1978, The American Presidency Project, https://www.presidency.ucsb.edu/node/244072.

33   "Mayor Emanuel Blasts Illinois Policy Institute Cartoon As 'Racist'," CBS News, August 17, 2017, https://www.cbsnews.com/chicago/news/mayor-emanuel-racist-cartoon-education/.

34   Jeffrey Jones, "LGBTQ+ Identification in U.S. Now at 7.6%," Gallup News, March 13, 2024, https://news.gallup.com/poll/611864/lgbtq-identification.aspx.

35   Theron Mohamed, "'It's a Physical Impossibility to Lift Yourself up by a Bootstrap': Alexandria Ocasio-Cortez Argues Everyone Needs Help to Succeed," *Business Insider*, February 7, 2020, https://www.businessinsider.com/aoc-ocasio-cortez-blasts-bootstrapping-argues-everyone-needs-help-succeed-2020-2.

36   "New Research: Belief in Jesus Rises, Fueled by Younger Adults," Barna Group, April 7, 2025, https://www.barna.com/research/belief-in-jesus-rises/.

37   Ruth Graham, "In a First Among Christians, Young Men Are More Religious Than Young Women," *New York Times*, updated September 25, 2024, https://www.nytimes.com/2024/09/23/us/young-men-religion-gen-z.html.

38 "Full Transcript of the Mitt Romney Secret Video." *Mother Jones*, September 19, 2012, https://www.motherjones.com/politics/2012/09/full-transcript-mitt-romney-secret-video/.

39 Douglas E. Streusand, Norman A. Bailey, and Francis H. Marlo (eds.), *The Grand Strategy That Won the Cold War: Architecture of Triumph* (Lexington Books, 2016).

ABOUT THE AUTHOR

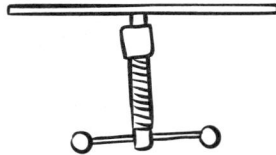

John Tillman is CEO of the American Culture Project and one of the nation's most prominent leaders in the free-market public-policy arena. He is best known for building the Illinois Policy Institute (IPI), which he currently chairs, into one of the most influential state-based think tanks in the country while he was CEO from 2007 to 2021.

While leading IPI, he cofounded and served as chairman of the Liberty Justice Center, which won the precedent-setting *Janus v. AFSCME* case before the US Supreme Court in 2018. IPI was also a key part of the coalition that defeated Governor J. B. Pritzker's progressive income tax in 2020. He has founded and chairs numerous other enterprises within the liberty space, including the Franklin News Foundation—which has news bureaus in every state and Washington, DC, and whose wire service, The Center Square, has a daily readership of 2.2 million—and digital marketing agency Iron Light.

You can learn more about John's work at
TheCommandingHeights.com